RAW | MARTIN CROWE

RAW | MARTIN CROWE

National Library of New Zealand Cataloguing-in-Publication Data

Crowe, Martin.
Raw / Martin Crowe.
ISBN 978-0-9864615-6-9
1. Crowe, Martin. 2. Cricket players—New Zealand—Biography.
3. Cricket. I. Title.
796.358092—dc 23

© 2013 Martin Crowe
© Design and format – Trio Books Limited

Published in 2013 by Trio Books Limited, PO Box 17021, Wellington, New Zealand.
www.triobooks.co.nz

Designed by Sally McIntosh, Auckland.
Printed by PrintStop, Wellington.

All rights reserved. No part of this publication may be reproduced or transmitted, except for review purposes, without the permission of the publisher.

This book is dedicated to Lorraine and Emma.
Love is Living.

CONTENTS

Acknowledgements 9

Foreword by Grant Fox 11

PART ONE: FEAR AND LOATHING

Introduction 15

Prologue 25

1. Retirement Blues: Depression 30
2. Maximus: Creating the Future 36
3. Executive Life: Exciting Times 40
4. Caught and Bowled 66: My Amazing Dad 46
5. Mud in the Eye: Indignation 49
6. Fatherhood: Emmy Lou 53
7. Grave Digging: Sky Watching 58
8. Hair Raising Oddities: Truth be Told 68
9. Skylarking: Paying the Price 72
10. Guardian Angel: Lorraine 78
11. Shifting Goalposts: Rugby Channel 85
12. Mid-life Madness: One Last Time 89
13. Turning Five O: Redundancy 93
14. In a Heartbeat: Cancer Diagnosis 101
15. Nasty Snakes: Open Wounds 110
16. Letting Go: Let the Restoration Begin 121

PART TWO: FOR THE LOVE OF THE GAME

Introduction 127

1. New Zealand's Dilemma: Taylor or McCullum 128
2. The Influential Leader: Stephen Fleming 140
3. Reminiscing: The 80s Mafia 145
4. Timing is the Thing: Twenty20 Hype 161
5. IPL Launched: Royal Challengers Saga 165
6. Technology Wars: Decision Review System 171
7. The Game has Changed: Money, Men and Methods 185
8 Spirit of Cricket: Cowdrey and Murali 194
9. Best Movers and Shakers: My Top 100
   Exceptional Test Cricketers of All Time 204
10. The Dream Test: At Lord's 242
11. National Pride: Each Country's Greatest Team 265
12. A Century-Maker's Bible: How to Bat Six Hours in a Test 281
13. One Final Word: Gratitude 303

ACKNOWLEDGEMENTS

This was not an easy assignment, so I am extremely grateful to a number of people.

First to Joseph Romanos, for having the courage to join me, guide me and ultimately publish the book. His unauthorised book of me back in 1995 was more of an accurate story of my life than my own autobiography at the same time. He could see what I couldn't. I wanted to work with him and it's been a privilege. I think he is a fine writer and publisher, a good man, a trusted friend.

I must thank Keith Quinn for encouraging me to write and to work with Joseph. Keith has become the father figure I lost and as always, made our relationship special and gave me genuine hope.

Journalist Gael Woods and Roger Moses, a good, keen cricket man and these days the headmaster at Wellington College, read my manuscript and offered helpful observations. Sally McIntosh designed the book with her usual expertise.

My thanks also to Fairfax New Zealand for kindly allowing me use of its photo file, to Andrew Harvey Photography for the front cover photo and to Neil Mackenzie for his *Dancing with the Stars* photo.

Grant Fox, who I sat next to on our first day at Auckland Grammar, has given me constant support and advice and has written a foreword that touched me deeply.

To all my other great friends who have kept in touch constantly over the past few months – Mark Greatbatch, Steve Wilkins, Rodger Curtice, Ross Taylor, David Morris, Ash Fogel, Richard Reid, Dan Kemp, Tim Roxborogh, China Gillman, David Howman, Steve Brebner and many more, including cricket mates from all over the globe – thank you.

To my family – Audrey, Deb, Jeff and Lara, their sons Oscar and Henry, my niece Sherry and her family, and my adorable Emma Louise – you are all amazing and have made all the difference. Also to Lorraine's family – children Hilton and Jasmine, mother Glad and stepdad Noel, sisters Sue, Jen and Carolyn and families – heartfelt thanks.

Finally, to my beautiful Lorraine, who rightly wondered at times if the writing was draining me and doing my head in. It sometimes did and she was there to pick me up. But mostly she encouraged me to do what I needed to do and she knew writing was an important outlet, a chance to shed the emotions and move on. She saw the difference when certain chapters, the raw ones, were finished. I bet she was relieved. She saw the joy when I wrote about cricketers I admired. Lorraine provided the all-important balance I required throughout the project.

Without Lorraine I wouldn't probably be here to tell my story.

Lorraine, I love you with all my heart.

FOREWORD

I greatly admire my good mate Marty Crowe for having the courage to write this book.

These past few months, since his diagnosis with cancer, have not been easy for Marty. I've spoken to him at some length and understand the process of self-evaluation that he has undergone since receiving his shocking news.

It hasn't been a total surprise to me that he would go down that road. Marty has never quite walked an orthodox path. The New Zealand way is generally to keep things fairly bottled up, not show too much emotion. That has not been Marty's way. He tends to live his life very openly, to question and evaluate.

I have known Marty can be rather emotional, and he has often spoken about the emotional side of top sport. But then again when you get sports geniuses, which I believe Martin was, they are often slightly different. To me though, he's always just been my mate, who I've known since we were kids.

It has been quite revealing to me to talk to Marty recently about how he has looked back on his life as an adult, with the various complications along the way. You'll see what I mean when you read this book, because it is brutally honest and upfront. Knowing Marty, I would have expected nothing less.

As I leaf through the pages of this book, all sorts of images come flooding back to me. I met Marty at the beginning of 1976, when we were in the same third form class at Auckland Grammar. We quickly found we had a common interest in sport and became really good friends early on. It's stayed that way ever since.

Neither of us was especially interested in the academic side of school, but we found plenty in those years to keep ourselves entertained and amused. I was convinced early on that Marty was going to be a cricket star, and his subsequent career for New Zealand more than bore that out.

I played some cricket, too, but rugby was my No 1 game. Marty didn't play winter sport until the sixth form. It wasn't because he lacked ability – anything he played, he played well, whether it was golf, tennis, squash or cricket.

In the sixth form he decided to play soccer and he immediately went into the Auckland Grammar soccer First XI. In the seventh form he turned to rugby and went straight into the First XV, as a winger. He was a big fellow for a schoolboy winger and mustered impressive pace, too, so he scored more than his share of tries.

We were always fiercely competitive. I remember one bet we had, with the confidence of youth, at the end of our seventh form year. He was the cricketer and I was the rugby player and we had a bet as to who would play more tests for New Zealand. We were both probably arrogant, brash schoolboys, but when you're that age, you don't see why you can't go out there and conquer the world. Well, I gave it my best shot, but he won that one pretty well. I eventually had one of my All Black jerseys signed and framed and presented it to him, because he won the bet. Not too long after, Marty reciprocated. I have a print at home of the Lord's pavilion, given to me by Marty. With it came a note: "Foxy, we both won. Hogan." That print is one of my most prized possessions.

We were competitive in other ways. I'd go over to stay at the Crowe house in Titirangi and soon we'd be picking teams from among the world's best cricketers and playing life-and-death games in the hall with a table tennis ball and a miniature cricket bat.

At Auckland Grammar, the unusual cricket matches continued with a tennis ball and a cricket stump in the prefects' common room, which was sometimes left the worse for wear.

Or we might be out on the paddock having a goal-kicking competition or using the slips cradle for a catching contest.

We weren't always rivals – each year we played together in the school tennis championship doubles and we did quite well, too, making junior and senior finals, even though neither of us was really a tennis player.

I have many memories of Marty from those years. One time I nearly chopped off his finger when I was wielding a chainsaw while we were pruning a shelter belt at my parents' kiwifruit orchard in Te Puke. During our seventh form year, Marty was largely responsible for maintaining the school cricket pitches, and he would call on me when it was time to roll them because, having grown up on a farm, I was more comfortable backing the big roller.

We've stayed close since, and I know of some of the struggles he's had at times, being the youngest in a team of achievers, living his life in the public gaze. I can certainly identify with some of those situations, though I was at an advantage in that I played rugby, which was more of a team game in the normal sense of the word. Cricket is really more a sport where 11 players perform individually to the best of their ability under the umbrella of a team. I imagine being a batsman out there in the middle during a big test match is a fairly lonely business.

I have been fortunate with my own family, with Adele and our two children. We've had a very strong and committed relationship that has provided me with great stability. I'm pleased that Marty has now found that sort of relationship, with unconditional love from Lorraine and Emma.

I'm sure they will play a big part in helping him heal and stay healthy and find true contentment.

I wish Marty the very best with this book. It can't have been easy to write some of the chapters but, as always, he has faced up to the truth bravely.

Grant Fox
APRIL 2013

PART ONE: FEAR AND LOATHING

Introduction

Fear. That is the emotion I have fought all my life.
Fear of rejection.
Fear of unworthiness.
Fear of humiliation.
Fear of failure.
Fear of not moving forward.

I wasn't born with this fear; it was something that I developed very young. I couldn't escape it growing up, and in the end it has dominated my life.

My greatest fear, that of death and leaving abandoned those I love, called me out in the form of lymphoma. My cancer diagnosis in October 2012 gave me the greatest wake-up call and the strongest message. I looked in the mirror and told myself: "Face the truth Marty. It's time; it's not too late."

It was at the age of eight, after a bit of teasing and taunting between my older brother Jeff and I turned nasty, that I first experienced a truly negative destructive emotion like fear. Jeff and I were play-fighting, as is normal for brothers competing for attention. No-one meant any harm, but the incident that ended with me snapping into an angry rage, left me shaking. Isolated, it meant nothing. But I soon developed the feeling of "not being good enough". I felt small and unworthy. It was wrong, of course, but I was a boy, the youngest by far, and I didn't know better. I know that now.

My parents gave me everything a boy could want – nurturing, support and opportunity, but unfortunately this feeling – "Am I good enough?" – kept growing as I entered the adult world way beyond my years, away from Mum and Dad, away from my safe place.

I was 14 when my world went in a direction that I had little control over, especially being so young. It was the moment when I was selected in the 1976 Auckland Rothmans Under-23 team. Inevitably, I was completely out of my depth and in personal turmoil. It was an odd decision by selectors, who thought a 14-year-old would be able to cope.

I was a good cricketer for my age, but somehow I found my way into the Auckland Grammar School First XI fairly quickly, which proved a bit daunting, with big 17 and 18-year-olds hovering around me. Many thought I would grow up quickly. I did physically, but emotionally it went the other way.

All of a sudden, and out of the blue, I was flown to Dunedin with young men seven or eight years older and was billeted by a 19-year-old Otago University student during the under-23 tournament. This random guy, my billet, took me to the pub because he had no food in the house. He bought me a jug of beer and told me to drink up, then gave me another and another.

The next morning, the opening day of the tournament, I awoke to a loud knock on the door. As I heard the knock, I looked around to find myself half out of bed, covered in vomit. There was vomit everywhere. I was in bad, bad shape with a massive hangover, my first ever, and I was shaking to the core.

I staggered to the door to see a very large figure, my Auckland captain, Greg Jones, looking at me. "You know what time it is?" "No sir," I replied. "It's 10 past 10 and we start in 20 minutes!" He looked at me and the house we were in and summed it up immediately. "Grab all your gear. You're not staying here any more." I burst into tears and felt worthless. I didn't play that day, naturally, and was re-billeted with an elderly couple.

But some damage was already done. I achieved nothing in the few games I played. For the first time in my life I felt complete humiliation. I really struggled with being so young in the team. It felt like being the youngest back at home.

The next year the Auckland selectors, despite my complete lack of form for the Grammar First XI, decided this time to select me in the Auckland senior team to travel to Christchurch to play in the Shell Trophy final against Canterbury. Their team included New Zealand's greatest, Richard Hadlee. I was always designated with 12th man duties, but if anyone had gone down overnight I was in to play.

For goodness sake, I was only 15! It kept on happening, with inclusion in the New Zealand Brabin (under-20) team and the New Zealand Secondary Schools team at 15.

I was in a state of shock the whole time. I was totally and utterly out of my comfort zone and completely at sea with the reality of the situation. Again, I was easily the youngest, in some cases half the age of those around me. In my fragile state, I felt the slight teasing and taunting, and it wounded me further.

I was selected to play for the Auckland team at 17, straight out of sixth form. I had enjoyed a good New Zealand Secondary Schools trip to Australia, but when I got the call while at the beach a few weeks later, it felt like, "Here we go again". I started with a fifty, and then held my own for two years with steady but not startling performances.

I was quickly pulled into line and mentored by the senior players in the Auckland team. Captain John Wiltshire was superb, as were John Reid, Peter Webb, Gary Troup, John McIntyre and Austin Parsons. They taught me good hard lessons about accepting failure, how to treat others, being consistent day in and day out. They were great – no teasing and harassing, just nice fatherly figures, helping out the "young fella".

Then just when I was getting a proper education on and off the field from these good men, I was inexplicably selected to play for New Zealand against Australia at 19. I had played only 18 first-class games and made my maiden first-class century on the day the New Zealand team was named. Most likely it was picked before I scored that hundred. That was the greatest shock of all.

It didn't take long before I realised it was all a mistake. We were in Dunedin for the second ODI, having won an exciting first-up game in front of a record crowd of 43,000 at Eden Park (owing to the frenzy following the underarm match). I wasn't required to bat in that first match, so I still hadn't confronted the jitters with bat in hand.

For the Dunedin match I was again nominated at the team meeting to bat at No 6. I was told to be myself and play my shots, to express my talent.

Batting at No 6 meant going in with the end of innings in mind, to go for boundaries or run hard and give the strike to Richard Hadlee and Lance Cairns. I was happy with that role and thought I might do okay. I was also there to bowl a few overs, as I had in the first ODI in Auckland, and to field my butt off. Yes, I thought, I could fit in as rookie one-day all-rounder.

Then 25 minutes before the start of play captain Geoff Howarth, having already tossed, entered the dressing room – there were two rooms in fact – and shouted at me to put on the pads. I was going to bat at No 3. I freaked out. John Reid had pulled out with a back complaint just before the toss. Australia had won the toss and put us in, as we would have done, given the very green nature of the pitch.

My first experience of batting for New Zealand was horrific. Australia's bomb squad – Dennis Lillee, Jeff Thomson and Terry Alderman or Len Pascoe – had the chance to intimidate in any way they chose. Somehow I got three runs before edging Alderman to slip. I was so freaked out by the pace, bounce and movement they got on that fiery pitch that I truly did not have a clue how to combat it. We lost easily.

Only days later in Wellington I walked out to face the second ball of the match. Wright was out first ball and again I was required to bat No 3, ahead of Howarth, Coney and Co. We were bowled out for 74, my effort worth seven, caught in the gully, again off Alderman.

At this point my confidence, self-esteem and faith in myself were zero, and my fear had risen to massive proportions. Not only was I out of my depth in the middle, but I was completely lost in the dressing room, especially in my relationship with Geoff Howarth, my first New Zealand captain. I couldn't work him out. He seemed either incredibly hardened, or sadly insecure. Whatever it was, it made me negative and very unsure.

Howarth would often say out loud: "Well, if the show pony is good enough to be selected he can go out and prove it." Why was Howarth like that? It all started to come flooding back, the teasing and taunting from those so much older in the same rooms, in the same teams as me. Despite wonderful care by Lance Cairns, John Wright, Bruce Edgar, Stephen Boock and Richard Hadlee, fine senior men who helped in so many ways, I just wanted to run away from it all. I just wanted Howarth to leave me alone.

Little did I know that a decade later he would return controversially as the coach of the team I was captaining. New Zealand Cricket took away my greatest ally in Wally Lees, my right-hand man during the 1992 World Cup campaign. They sacked him unceremoniously, replacing him with a man who had already tormented me in our first exchange. I lasted one more test as captain, before once more he did my head in. It was extraordinary how I could be so unlucky to start and finish my career with a man who didn't want to engage appropriately and at times behaved appallingly towards me.

It's hard to be critical of the New Zealand selectors, who were only trying to pick the best team possible, always with an eye to the future. But why send an immature kid out to face some of the hardest campaigners the sport has ever produced? And why did they continue to do it to others? Ken Rutherford got the worst end of the stick of anyone I know, having to open against the Windies in their snake pit, at the age of 19. Chris Cairns, also only 19, got rushed into the team in Australia, hurt his back and had his spirit dented. Adam Parore was a young 19 when he got picked to tour England in 1990. He didn't recover from it until 1997. All four of us failed horribly and took years to recover our confidence. Ultimately it left a scar for life.

How overwhelming it was for me to face Dennis Lillee and Jeff Thomson, with Rod Marsh behind the stumps, and the opposition led by Greg Chappell. These were names and reputations that made you shake just thinking about them, let alone literally brushing shoulders.

We lost that final ODI and the series and the focus turned to the tests. Surely I was to be cut loose and be given the benefit of going back to my province to continue my development at the proper level for a year or two more? No.

Bowled by Bruce Yardley for 9 in Christchurch. The end of a horror series for me. Graeme Wood (in helmet) and Greg Chappell watch me depart.

I was in the test team, batting at No 6. I had no idea what was required of me. The rest of that summer was a numbing, horrible, humiliating experience. Scores of 3, 7, 9, 2, 0 and 9 were all I could muster and I did well to make that many. Worse still was the damage done to my emotional state of mind. Once again, I was feeling humiliated, as I had in Dunedin at the age of 14.

When it was finally all over, I ran to my sister's home in the far north to hide. After a couple of days I ventured down to the local pub in Houhora and began to play a game of pool. Just as I began to shoot, a booming voice shot out from a corner of the bar. It was a local, Big Norm, who yelled: "Hey Crowe, hope you can play pool better than you can play cricket!" I dipped my head and acknowledged to him that I was better at pool.

A week or so later I was off to England and the anonymity of some league cricket in Yorkshire. There were no runs in the first few weeks but life came good again. The humiliation subsided and I started to enjoy what I loved to do – score runs freely.

Upon returning to New Zealand, I was rightly dropped from the national team. It was done in the most humiliating way. Jeff had returned to Auckland after five years in Adelaide and we lined up for Auckland against Otago in a one-dayer on the Outer Oval at Eden Park. A big crowd was in. Suddenly over the loud public address system the announcement of the New Zealand team to tour Australia in a few weeks' time was made. "Cairns, Chatfield, J Crowe, Edgar…" I was on the boundary on my own when whispers from the crowd came forth about my axing from the team. I could have dug a hole and buried myself. I was naturally pleased by Jeff's first selection, at 24. He was an outstanding player and thoroughly deserved it. But I felt humiliated in front of everyone that day.

Still, I was allowed to return to first-class cricket and regain my self-belief. It was nice to be back at my level learning my trade and I enjoyed a good season with the bat for Auckland, scoring a record tally of runs. But while I was enjoying playing with mates my age – Trevor Franklin, Paul Kelly and Mark Greatbatch – I was confronted by a new team-mate, John Bracewell. John had decided to leave the Deep South and relocate to Auckland. There was no doubt about his ability to play cricket and compete. To me, though, he had aggressive and bullying ways. It was his style, his way of dealing with his own pressures, but I struggled intensely with it all, and stupidly took it all personally, especially following the Howarth treatment. Almost everyone ignored his angst. Trevor and Mark stood up to him often, but I couldn't handle it. By the end of the season, I had decided to leave town and for the next summer Hawke's Bay was my new home and Central Districts my new team.

At the end of that season, 1982-83, the national selectors threw me back into the Howarth-led set-up. I earned a man of the match award in the Bushfire match in Sydney and that secured me a place in the touring squad to England for four tests and the World Cup.

I toured England without any success in the tests, though I did okay in the World Cup. The trend in tests continued in 1984 against England back in New Zealand, despite one isolated innings, a debut century at the age of 21 in Wellington.

At that stage I was, for some reason, batting ahead of Coney and brother Jeff, yet my average had only just reached double figures. I didn't get it. I shut up, put my head down and tried to ignore Howarth and his odd ways.

Then I suffered a major setback. On the tour of Sri Lanka after our summer of 1984, I got incredibly ill. I had broken my thumb on the first day of the second test and was in great pain. Not thinking, I ate the wrong food – two mussels off a plate on the table. I picked up a horrendous dose of salmonella, which lasted until late 1988.

That became a poignant moment in my life. My immune system took a hammering and it continued to struggle. In 1992 at the Hong Kong Sixes, I picked up the EB virus, or glandular fever. Almost every time I travelled and checked into a hotel, the following morning I would be down with some form of cold or flu or sore throat.

Straight after Sri Lanka, I joined Somerset County Cricket Club. I had recovered enough, but started poorly, then played well from June on and started to grow up and mature a bit as a player and person. I got lucky playing county cricket at 21. I formed a club for the uncapped players, all my age, and we got on great. I loved being around players of my own age. I felt I could be myself and I felt I was valued and had worth. The experience of batting almost every day in good conditions against all sorts of bowlers was priceless. I loved it all. I felt I was being myself again and I felt ready at that stage to show my international ability.

In my mind, the Pakistan tour of New Zealand in early 1985, when I was 22, following my full season with Somerset, was the real start of my international career, if not in the record books. There were no big scores, but I was consistent and competed hard.

From there my career improved and I made progress. Over the next decade, 1985-1994, I played 50 tests, scoring runs consistently at an average 56, including 16 hundreds and 13 fifties. Batting in the middle became my happy place. It was a decade to be proud of.

Despite that improvement and feeling of contentment in the middle, the same problem of fear – the fear of failing – continued to really bug me leading into a big match or series. There was severe nervousness and an anxiety that I felt before every innings. I began to experience blackouts, once in the middle of a team practice right in front of the media. I feared humiliation again. I feared failing again like before. FEAR. Because of that state of mind my game became methodical, technical and incredibly analytical. I lost that freedom of expression and that flair I carried as a kid. I was beside myself on a regular basis. I accumulated runs as opposed to dominating opposition.

So I began learning about mental strength and sports psychology to counter my fear. I learnt methods and techniques to remove a steady flow of negative thoughts and outcomes. I controlled the fear and anxiety, but it was incredibly draining. For weeks after a test match I was almost comatose – listless and exhausted. Mood swings were bad, relationships were strained. I tried to build bridges, patch up things, but my resentment was deep, really deep. Possibly an illness was being nurtured a long way back.

Fast forward to October 2012. Once I recovered from the devastating shock of knowing I had an incurable blood disease, I began to search for the deep truth as to why. Not: why me? Just: why? How and what was needed for it to go away and never return. First, I surrendered. I gave myself up to help. Through counselling and meditation, I discovered my fear was sitting there, strong and bold. I associated this fear with my ego voice; they were the same.

I began to face the ego and the fear. It was painful and disturbing. But I had to face it full on. As I did, my truth was revealed. There were flashbacks to the past and I saw clear images of what that 14-year-old boy was feeling. That boy was feeling lost. He was feeling alone in the adult world he was in. He was often feeling worthless.

By the time that boy hit the highest level, Geoff Howarth and John Bracewell triggered off unpleasant negative emotions – resentment, even hatred, and definitely insecurity. Those emotions never left; they became entrenched as if they were normal. Coaches, journalists and administrators weren't spared either. Anyone who criticised or questioned my motives or personality was the enemy. Yet they were just doing their job.

That innocent boy became a resentful man, a man who harboured grudges. He became the world record-holder for grievances. The longer life as a cricketer went on, the more expectations grew and the more opposition on and off the field mounted, the more that man lost touch. Not only with others around him, but with himself.

In a peculiar way, lymphoma has given me my life back, but with a caveat. If I mess up again, there is a gun to my head and I will die. Fear remains and I am scared, but I have found the problem and faced it squarely. In a sense it's a lucky break, to be given a second chance before it's too late. I have a lot to do to remove much of the fear and find some peace of mind.

The story I will tell is exactly what happened in my life and in my mind, at that time. But it is a mind that was not always clear. Only when the cricket ball was on its way did I feel some sense of clarity in my life, of being content. At times, I felt a heavenly bliss, such as when batting at Lord's. Only then did I feel worthy. In those pure moments I was living the dream.

When my daughter Emma was born, I began the seeds of recovery, of self-discovery through her unconditional love. When I fell in love with Lorraine, I found a pillar to lean against. She held me up and guided me through because of her unconditional love. My family have naturally been strong throughout, also offering their unconditional love.

Those three priorities are who I live for. Nothing else matters. Unconditional love is the way to healing my mind, body and soul.

This story is about a lost youth, a troubled man who stumbled his way through and ultimately made himself ill. In isolation, the various occurrences wouldn't normally be a problem, but in the context of the pattern of feeling worthless, each occurrence and each clash had an impact. It all grew into an uncontrolled emotional torment. The fear was in charge. As the experts tell me, my life as a "cricketer" for the past 35 years was one of a "shy performer reading the scripts written by others".

It was a revealing period of my life, full of brutal lessons, amazing highs and depressing lows, an abnormal life not handled that well at times, with a bitter-sweet end. I try not to hold grudges any more because I have learnt to let it go through therapy and even writing this book, but I do recognise what and who I prefer to stay away from. Mostly it's about how life should be lived, what is really important.

From here on, I can write my own script to live by, without fear. I am learning to love, to forgive, to be grateful and to be compassionate. It's time to live a loving, happy and peaceful life.

Prologue

Auckland. September 25, 1995. 1pm

I had turned 33 just three days earlier, and had arrived at Auckland Airport from Queenstown, to be met by a really good character, Tim Murdoch from WEA Records. He was much older than me, but we got on well and he had begun introducing me to the music industry. He picked me up and we went off to lunch, but on the way he decided he needed to pop in to Sky Television, the new Pay TV network that had been set up in Mt Wellington. Tim wanted a quick chat with Sky's chief executive, Nate Smith, about MTV and the like.

I had heard about Sky TV and that one of its founders was Terry Jarvis, a former New Zealand test opener, and a great bloke, too. Back in 1990 he had set up New Zealand's first pay TV network with wealthy entrepreneur Craig Heatley. Only a few years on, Smith, a New Yorker working for the giant American entertainment company Time Warner, had arrived on the scene with his sidekick accountant, the Arizonian John Fellet. They became the driving force of the groundbreaking new enterprise, so much so that Nate Smith had become a serious player in the networks war around town.

Tim introduced me to Nate as New Zealand's "Babe Ruth of Cricket". That quickly settled the conversation and Nate went into an enlightening chat about baseball, Babe Ruth, the virtues of American Television and what he was trying to achieve in little old New Zealand with Sky TV.

His underlying mantra was geared around the specific time frames for people to watch sport, "Live, Local, Exclusive".

I never forgot those three words, or that the first premise of making successful television and entertainment was time, that time duration was critical to the viewer and spectator. It sparked something deep within me, listening to him talk about making television for the fans. Then he turned to me and said: "Marty, can't you make that cricket game last three hours instead of 30? Geez, Marty, this cricket lark goes on way too long. What we need is a game starting at 7pm and finishing at 9.30pm, just like a good baseball game does. And why do you guys only get one innings? If my favourite player got out I would head home. Give him more innings like those tests you play."

I looked at him and then said in a determined tone: "Give me a week." Interestingly, earlier that year I had visited dozens of schools in the Wellington region promoting cricket, only for a lot of kids to tell me in their honest way that cricket was too boring, that they didn't like fielding and doing nothing, and much more. With this fresh in my mind and Nate's words ringing in my ears, I went to work creating an exciting new concept for a third-generation cricket format.

Jeff, my brother, grabbed the beers and I grabbed a large piece of paper to sketch on. We worked off the premise of three hours maximum and therefore 40 overs max. But we wanted to try to hold on to as many traditions as possible. So we settled for two innings for each team to allow for the important second chance that comes with first-class and test cricket, and so Nate could see his favourite player bat twice. Therefore 10 overs max per innings with all 10 wickets available per innings became the format. For the bowling we settled for four overs maximum for any bowler, to be bowled at any time during the 20 overs.

We changed the one-day 30-metre circle to a different shape, so a fielder outside the area could still be close enough to be a catcher. We decided that for such a short game we didn't need LBWs, but for the bowlers we gave them a fourth stump to aim at. We said no balls were to be discouraged, so offered a free hit after any overstepping, and wides were worth two runs, not one.

The final innovation was to allow any team to come from behind, so we positioned a zone in the outfield and if you hit through it or over it, you doubled your score. The maximum would be a 12! We decided that the best place was dead straight behind the bowler to reward the best shot in the game. So the Double-up Zone was born – 60 metres from the batsman on strike and 20 metres deep, 20 metres wide at the front and 40 metres wide at the back, creating a cool trapezium shape, with big high flagpoles at each corner.

We got a designer to draw up the ground and its new shapes with four stumps and typed the rules around the outside. We had a sharp-looking poster to sell our new game. As I looked around the poster the word that kept coming up time and again was simple, strong and powerful; it was the word Max. Cricket Max was the name. The game would be fast and furious, with action to burn. It would be played to the Max!

I presented our Cricket Max poster to Nate two weeks later, just before flying to India. His eyes lit up. Sky had no rights to any cricket, because TVNZ had held them for many a decade. The key to securing cricket for pay TV was to help reduce a pattern called "churn". That was when subscribers drove down to reception at Sky and handed back their decoders, no longer needing them once rugby had finished for the year. November was the worst month for the company and cricket was seen as the bridge to get Sky over this period, to get churn down.

Nate and I went over the design, the overall plan of using Max as a yardstick to seeing if cricket was the sport needed to shore up the complete sports year for Sky. After a productive chat, Nate said: "Go play well in India, and when you get back, let's get this baby rolling."

Mumbai. November 28, 1995. 6pm.

The New Zealand team filed into the hotel team room in Bombay (now Mumbai) and assumed seats, which were placed in a large semi-circle. In the front sat manager Gren Alabaster, coach Glenn Turner and captain Lee Germon. I sat down beside Chris Cairns, Mark Greatbatch, Dion Nash and the rest of the team.

We were meeting to prepare for the big decider against India the next day at Wankhede Stadium. In the last match, at Nagpur, we had played out of our skins to score 348, New Zealand's highest ever to that point, and smashed India by 100 runs to level the series 2-2. We were confident and feeling good.

Sadly for me, I limped out at Nagpur (stumped after scoring 63), but for a good period watched Nathan Astle score the first of his many ODI tons. I was playing well myself, having scored my fourth ODI ton during our first ODI victory of the series, in Jamshedpur. But the toll of that innings was apparent when my left thigh seized up again and I had to declare myself unfit for the decider, three days away.

Despite that setback, we felt we had the Indians on the run. To pull off a series win over India on their home tracks would be huge. There was a buzz in the group when Turner rose to speak.

"I have been involved with New Zealand teams since the 1960s and we have lost many matches that we shouldn't have. At the end of every tour we always lose because we can't wait to get home. After every good win we go and lose the next one. So I just hope you go out there tomorrow and don't lose by too much." Then he stopped. That was our team talk.

Well, you could've heard a pin drop. Jaws dropped all around the room. Every player was stuck in a stare at the person we had just heard speak. Our coach had spoken, but we were all trying to digest exactly what he had said. This was a former captain, one of our finest batsmen, scorer of 103 first-class hundreds, and he had just told us in no uncertain terms that we were going to lose, but that he hoped we didn't lose "by too much".

Then Glenn, with Gren and Lee in tow, walked out single file, past us all. "Holy shit," I muttered. Then Mark Greatbatch spoke. "Hey, hang on a minute!" And he got up and walked after Turner, but was held back by Cairns and Nash. Not looking back, the three wise men walked out and we were left in shock and anger. Mark sat down, clearly agitated: "Don't listen to that crap."

The shock ran deep. Turner and his mates sure ran a strange ship. In my whole life I have never heard anything like that which Turner delivered. What was he thinking? Reverse psychology?

I had worked under Turner when he was national coach from 1985-87 and found him brilliant but frustratingly odd. He provided me with the best advice for concentration and batting long periods and I was incredibly grateful. But he also orchestrated a declaration while I was 242 not out, just 45 minutes into day two of a Sheffield Shield tour match against South Australia in Adelaide. It was like he gave me a wonderful toy, and then snatched it away when I was in full flow. His theories were intelligent, but he never really rated his players to carry them out.

Turner had much to offer the game, as I mentioned in my autobiography, *Out on a Limb*. He ticked most boxes except man-management, much like me. So he needed a true foil in this important area to balance the atmosphere, but instead the management team he appointed created tension.

What was apparent to all of us in Mumbai that day was his fixation with a strange kind of management, a cold, unemotional fathering and talking down to his boys. We all wanted Turner to be our guide, to lead us to the Promised Land, but he seemed to prefer leading us into the quicksand first, to see what we were made of, before continuing. Or maybe he just wanted us all out and a fresh batch of rookies in.

There was no doubt he wanted me gone. I was keen to captain the test side again, for a year or so, to help us make progress, especially with the rebuild that was taking place. In a private chat in Queenstown during the winter before the tour, I had asked Glenn if I could captain the test side and Lee Germon could do the one-dayers. He preferred Lee Germon to do it all. Perhaps with my dodgy knee I was damaged goods, a nuisance.

I felt for those having to get up and play because his team talk was such a gut-kicker. The next day we were bowled out for 126 and India knocked them off in 32 overs. It wasn't just a severe loss; it was a complete capitulation of will and desire.

I never played for New Zealand again.

CHAPTER 1

Retirement Blues: Depression

Winter 1996

Upon returning from India, I realised fairly quickly that I needed to retire from playing and throw myself into my testimonial year, which included launching Cricket Max. On the very same date, January 17, that it was announced I was selected to start my first-class career as a naive 17-year-old at Eden Park against Canterbury, I announced my retirement from all cricket, again at Eden Park. This time there was no-one there except a TV One camera crew and *Holmes* show presenter Susan Wood. So after 16 years of first-class cricket, including 247 matches, and just 392 runs short of 20,000 runs, I was done. It was tempting to carry on and post the milestone, but enough was enough. My body was screaming at me.

My international days were definitely done following the debacle at Bombay. I had made three comebacks of sorts and one more was not an option. I picked January 17 and the venue and it felt right if not highly emotional. David Howman and his son, Tim, joined me for moral support as we did the interview at Eden Park and then went off to Radio Sport to spend an hour with Murray Deaker, who gave me an enthusiastic send-off. I heard nothing from New Zealand Cricket during the day and Glenn Turner commented on radio that I could "play a bit". I walked away from the game with mixed memories, but soon had focus for the next task.

Cricket Max was launched on Monday, February 5, 1996, a public holiday, at the club where it all began, Cornwall Cricket Club. It was a stunningly hot day and 8000 intrigued folk turned up for a free outing to witness the dawning of a new age.

The New Zealand World Cup team about to depart for India were playing the All Stars, including Richard Hadlee, Lance Cairns,

Dean Jones, David Hookes, Merv Hughes, Heath Streak, myself and a few other big names from the successful 1992 World Cup team. It was officially my testimonial match, but Roger Bhatnagar from Noel Leeming put up $10,000 for the winning team, so there was no mucking around. It ensured the match was played in a competitive spirit, which New Zealand won in the end.

It was a special but nervous day for me, my last hurrah with bat in hand. I was now unemployed and needed this new game to rock and roll.

Nate Smith, true to his word, got the baby rolling and all the TV crew were there for a full-on live broadcast. It was cricket as it had never been seen before – players in shorts, four stumps, strange markings, flagpoles and rules to intrigue. The day went swimmingly well and the crowd went away raving about the afternoon. Yes, the three-hour time frame it took to entertain everyone was spot on. The crowd were used to a one-dayer duration – eight hours – so now after only three hours they left wanting just a bit more. Their appetites had been whetted and hopefully they'd return.

Nate and Sky were pleased and we went into a review process not long after. It was fun being involved with clever folk who knew their business and wanted to take the gamble. Nate wanted a weekly league and he called for *Friday Night Cricket* to be staged as soon as possible. It followed the *Friday Night Football* slot that had recently been successfully launched on Sky.

We dropped the four stumps, as planned. It was only a one-off stunt based on an ad campaign to raise a stir. The ad agency ran a full-page promotion showing four large stumps and the words, "The King is dead, long live the King".

We dropped the inner square and returned to the 30-metre circle; we began to cull and simplify. Ultimately there remained only three innovations compared to a 50-over match: the Max Zone, the two innings each and the no ball rule. We thought that was enough for the conservative purists and plenty for the new young fan to enjoy. Best of all, we felt, was the duration of 40 overs in total, three hours and an exciting, fast-paced game.

Mostly, I wanted a game that was strategic and unpredictable, allowed teams to come from behind and held the viewers' interest from start to finish. In essence, the Max format was simply taking the first 10 overs and last 10 overs of a one-dayer – easily the two most entertaining periods of play.

My next job was to recruit the teams and convince New Zealand Cricket that this was the financial and commercial boon for which they and the players were looking.

However, I struck a problem I never envisaged, had never come across before and never wanted again: I became deeply depressed. Despite the buzz around the new Max format and the interest shown by Sky, my career of 16 years was over, at the relatively young age of 33. I couldn't shake the ending: my injuries and, overall, the state New Zealand's game was in. I had left it in a mess. Now I was a mess. The one thing I had a handle on was now over.

To add to the upheaval Simone and I were officially separated on January 28, 1996, and that had a massive effect as well. We were both devastated, but I needed to find my own happiness and stability before taking responsibility for another. I didn't know who the hell I was and the answer wasn't going to come overnight. I was in desperate trouble.

I moved out of Millbrook, which was sold along with the Piha Bach, and moved into a one-bedroom apartment in downtown Auckland. I couldn't get of bed. I was in a dark hole and I couldn't see a way out. For months I just lay there looking at the ceiling. I couldn't even decide what to wear some days. I rang those I trusted and slowly small things emerged. There were simple things like meeting up with friends, going to the gym, listening to music, reading books, eating good food and drinking less alcohol.

But then I faced a crisis point. Was I to go on prescribed antidepressant drugs to numb the depression, or somehow pull myself out of the darkness? In a snap move I flew to Queensland and booked into Camp Eden, a health clinic deep in the forest. I put myself in their hands, attending forums each morning with others to talk about issues we faced. I lost weight, trained hard and then did an amazing session called "rebirthing".

In a small hut sitting crossed-legged in front of an old woman with white hair, I started to perform a "connected breathing" exercise. Big deep breaths followed by another and another. This was supposed to go on for 45 minutes. After 20 minutes I was a wailing mess. Then from deep within, images and emotions from the distant past came forward as the connected breathing continued. In the blur of breath and emotion I saw my father, Dave. The image was of him in the distance, in another country, and then at home waving me off at the door saying, "I can't help you now". This went on for 10 minutes of strong powerful scenes of my dad and me apart.

I began crying and wailing from the pit of my stomach. The little old lady held my hand and said quietly to keep going. The message was that at the age of 14 I was missing my dad. He had unselfishly passed me on to supposedly better cricket men and encouraged me to go to other mentors to fulfil my potential. But I missed my dad. I missed his discipline and his fatherly wisdom. He had become my close mate, but most of all I had missed my dad's beautiful influence. I needed his strong guidance and care, but he didn't think he could give me what I needed.

The crying became horrible and I pleaded to stop. After 45 minutes we slowed down and stopped. I was exhausted. I looked at the old lady and I asked what happened. "You have missed your father since you were 14. It's had a massive impact on you. You want him back."

I returned to Auckland with some energy restored and felt ready to respond. I sold the apartment and moved to Western Springs, where I bought a lovely old villa, designed like an art gallery – high stud, white walls, wooden floors and space to burn. I bought some attractive art, built an Italian garden with a centre water fountain, bought lots of books and music and installed a pool table.

I rang Dad and told him I needed time with him. So every Tuesday he came over and we played pool, listened to Frank Sinatra and Bing Crosby, smoked cigars, ate steak, drank wine, and talked and talked. Mum was at bridge each Tuesday, so this became our night, just the two of us. It was the cure I needed.

He gave me the push to go back to Sky and begin the Max project. My dad and I were connected again. It wasn't his fault that we got disconnected, just a product of my cricket getting ahead of us. He wanted Deb (five years older), Jeff and me to achieve our dreams. Deb went to Perth at 16 and Jeff moved to Adelaide at 17, when I was 13. Dad himself went to work in Brisbane for a period. Without Dad around, I became a bit disconnected and lost as I dealt with an adult world when

Dad was always very proud to have had two sons who captained New Zealand.

it came to my cricket.

On those special Tuesday nights, Dad and I talked about everything. He told me of his upbringing and how Jack, his father, was at times incredibly tough when raising his four sons. Dad was the second oldest of the four, but they lost Charles, the youngest, when he was just 18 in a tragic diving accident.

Jack and Charles had gone diving for crayfish and Jack wrongly gave Charles his own diving belt. He was half Jack's weight, the belt was far too heavy and it took him to the bottom too quickly, killing him. Jack had to live with that nightmare and it became an unbearable burden to carry. Jack's agitation (and at times anger) was noticeable when we saw him. He couldn't forgive himself.

Dad, on the other hand, and probably as an opposite reaction to Jack's style, came out of his childhood with a very laid-back approach to life and people. He soon discovered that he loved selling and he became famous for remembering the name of every person he ever met. He had mastered the technique of recall. He was incredible.

Dad was a great guy, loved by all. He knew that I had not gained the same warmth through my life, due to my often aloof and focused approach to my passion of batting. He acknowledged that he wished he had been around more, taught me genuine humility and a little more discipline, and that winning and losing need to be treated the same. He acknowledged he saw a troubled son; lonely, lost and languishing in retirement.

So through these times we became inseparable. I loved this period of my life with Dad. It lifted me out of my dark hole and into the light. We had fun together driving the Max project, staging more games at Cornwall and around the country. We had a plan and it would launch me back into the workforce. Finding Dad again was a lifesaver.

CHAPTER 2

Maximus: Creating the Future

Spring 1996

Come spring, Nate Smith signed me up for a role in the Sky marketing department, and I joined a great crew, led by Rob Hellriegel. Rob set about giving Cricket Max a business plan and I set about convincing New Zealand Cricket and the major associations to embrace the new format.

The first selling to be done was naturally around the financial benefits New Zealand Cricket would gain from the project. At New Zealand Cricket I worked closely with chief executive Chris Doig and general manager John Reid, my former Auckland and New Zealand team-mate. We offered $300,000 a year to New Zealand Cricket – an unprecedented $50,000 was to go to each of the six major associations and that money was to go directly to the players.

This would be the first substantial payment to New Zealand players playing domestic cricket. By comparison, in 1987, when I led Central Districts to the Shell Trophy win over a long season, I, like the others, received a cheque for $261. That was our lot, apart from a daily meal allowance. Ten years later they would add a nought to that and double it, for only a quarter of the work.

We proposed playing a Friday night cricket league under lights. Trouble was there weren't enough grounds that had lights, so we were restricted to using only a few – Lancaster Park in Christchurch, Carisbrook in Dunedin, Cooks Gardens in Wanganui, McLean Park in Napier, and a redesigned Mt Smart Stadium in Auckland. Where there were no lights we played in the afternoons on the weekend, but we were keen to drive the Friday night slot.

We would play the league in the first part of the summer so as not to interfere with first-class cricket. New Zealand Cricket supported the idea and we launched our first domestic tournament in late 1996 at Hagley Oval, Christchurch, to test the waters. It went well enough for Friday Night Cricket to be launched properly.

In the Max final at Napier, Mark Greatbatch smashed Mark Priest for 34 in one over to take Central Districts to the first title. It was a blistering final, and set up Max for the next phase.

While we worked on New Zealand Cricket and the broadcasting side of things, the Sky legal team went about securing the patents and copyright for Cricket Max worldwide. We were confident that other networks and cricket boards would follow suit. We geared ourselves so that when they did, we had the rights.

The second season went superbly, with crowds of more than 5000 turning up to Mt Smart Stadium for the Auckland matches. It rocked along for eight consecutive Fridays and the players appeared to be embracing it.

My next stop was the ICC in London. Sky produced a brochure with all the facts and findings from the first two years and produced a video presentation to go with it. I was booked to present to the ICC top dogs in 1998 and see if we could get this baby rolling globally.

While we were doing all that, over the ditch Cricket Australia was designing its own third-generation game, Super 8s. This was a play on the Sixes format that had become popular in Hong Kong. The Australians ran a tournament in Darwin, so we approached them to combine forces.

The upshot was that 11-a-side was the way forward. We combined names and some of the formats, dominated by the Max format, and named it Super Max cricket. Allan Border for Australia and I headed to Lord's to launch the new third generation format.

The response was outstanding. So much so that the England and Wales Cricket Board asked for a special meeting and a chance to explore further. It had designs on such a time frame and now we had presented it with the solution. But the one major sticking point was the radical Max Zone. The ECB insisted it would never make it on to the Lord's Cricket Ground, but we decided to stick with the Max Zone, simply because it was the main patent we had locked in.

My concerns were obvious. If we kept the Max Zone, then the ECB would design a format similar and turn its back on ours. We decided to invite the ECB to send an England Max team to play the New Zealand Max team in a three-match series. That way we would get a true response to the way the English were thinking and what our next move needed to be.

The England Lions arrived and we put them through three games in three days in three cities. All matches were competitive, with England winning the first and New Zealand coming back to win the last two. We were confident Max was gaining momentum. Again, the players were positive and the fans were starting to enjoy the whole experience.

Overall, it had been an encouraging two years in the marketing of Max. Rob Hellriegel had been outstanding in his leadership and guidance. New Zealand Cricket and the major associations had given it a shot and gained some faith in the direction it was going. The ICC and its members had seen the potential, with England showing real interest.

For me, I had moved on from retirement into the business world. It wasn't easy going from the pitch to the office and a nine-to-five job, but when you are surrounded by positive, purposeful people it's a huge comfort and the lessons keep coming. I was on a massive learning curve, the biggest being in communication. Nate and Rob were a pleasure to work under.

I enjoyed the commentary too. We had flown Graham Hughes over from Australia to give Cricket Max some spice. Hughes was one of the best rugby league callers in the business. He knew his stuff, having enjoyed a fabulous playing career with Canterbury Bulldogs. Also, he had played first-class cricket for New South Wales, so he knew his cricket, too.

He taught me a lot. His ability to change his voice pitch to suit the moment was a massive strength. He thought about the fans and what they enjoyed, using the caller to make a bad game good, a good game great, and a great game an epic. I was learning from the best about everything to do with producing compelling, entertaining television. So after creating a format, I was quickly learning about how to tell the story of the game.

At one point Kevin Cameron, director of sport, asked me to present a cricket show, pre-recorded in the studio. I did so for 10 weeks and then he called me in to inform me that Ian Smith would become a fulltime presenter and I was earmarked as a fulltime producer. He had quickly identified our strengths and informed us of our pathways. I was quite relieved, because I did prefer the planning and producing side of television rather than being in front of the camera, where Smithy was such a natural.

Adding to the marketing education I was getting, life at Sky was full on, wonderful. I wasn't missing playing at all. Instead I was getting thirsty for more of what Sky was offering.

Little did I know what Sky had in store for me.

CHAPTER 3

Executive Life: Exciting Times

Winter 1999

For the first time Sky Television secured the rights to broadcast all international and domestic cricket in New Zealand. Out of the blue I was appointed executive producer for all the live cricket broadcasts. It was a huge opportunity and I was grateful to have a fulltime job working for such a great company. So I moved out of the bright and cheerful marketing room and downstairs into the dark, dreary dungeon of the sports department. Don't get me wrong, I was honoured to do so, but the people in the marketing team were such a delight, it was sad to leave.

My immediate boss was Kevin Cameron, director of sport. Below me in the producer's role was Kevin's son, James. They were both pleasant to work with, but it was never going to be easy working in the middle of such a strong family tie. This Cameron sandwich would provide me some with of my biggest challenges at Sky.

Kevin was a highly experienced producer and executive producer from his TVNZ days, where he oversaw many major events through the 1970s and 80s through to the 1990 Commonwealth Games. He was recruited to set up Sky Sport in 1991 and from there controlled every decision concerning securing rights to broadcasting sports events in New Zealand and around the world.

Kevin was a warm, friendly man on the surface, but a hard-working and highly protective man underneath. You could not get much out of him and I soon realised that I was supposed to get on and do my thing, because Kevin was doing his. That suited me fine, to a point. However, I was new to the game in television and needed feedback, as well as direction. Anyway, I was curious enough to ask many people about the right approach to this newly formed role, so there was plenty of information available. Plus, I had young James to tell me what to do. Talk about ambition! James had naturally set his father as his yardstick and was determined to follow in his footsteps.

Thrown in together, James and I were so raw that we just got stuck in and did our best in our new roles through 1999.

At one point James and I flew to Los Angeles with Graeme Hughes, who organised the trip, to try to meet with the most famous cricket producer of all, Channel 9's David Hill. David had started up Wide World of Sport for Nine and then World Series Cricket that followed. He was then head-hunted by Fox in Los Angeles to head its sports department. We waited in our hotel rooms and then got the call to go to see him.

Kevin Cameron largely left me to my own devices. *Photo, Fairfax*

He was unbelievable. He gave us three hours of his time, discussing the fundamentals of broadcasting live television and, in particular, cricket. It was the best three hours ever for what we needed.

David's mantra was to get the best cameras (the more the better), lenses and operators, then the best sound, including commentary, then graphics, and if possible add in the extras as he went along. The key, he said, was making sure the production continued to stay fresh and compelling for the viewer. He was big on commentary being a variety of voices and opinions, no in-house jokes, no dabbling in talk of sex, politics or race. He advised never to take it for granted that viewers knew all the rules of the game, and to keep them fully informed at all times.

David favoured using pauses and not stating the obvious, enhancing the picture rather than talking as if it were a radio broadcast. That was all solid advice. In the end, he said, "Every year change or improve what you are doing by at least 10 per cent. That way the viewer will always be

Chris Doig, left, and John Anderson – a great team. *Photo, Fairfax*

entertained." Just as Greg Chappell was during my cricket career, David Hill would become my mentor and yardstick in television.

By the turn of the century, life was flying along. Being an executive producer was challenging and rewarding. I felt alive again.

When I heard that Chris Doig was to take over running New Zealand Cricket in late 1995, I was relieved and delighted. New Zealand Cricket needed to evolve and the John Hood Report, which made key recommendations in how to modernise the administration of the game, provided it with the ideal foundation. The report recommended appointing Doig as the first board chief executive.

Backtrack to 1977, my fourth form year at Auckland Grammar and an English teacher named Chris Doig. To us young teenagers, Mr Doig was a larger-than-life sort of character with a loud, booming voice. He threw chalk with power and precision and commanded attention. Mr Doig was a big, strong presence.

A solid champion of New Zealand business and cricket, John Anderson, chairman of the National Bank, embraced the Hood Report and removed the amateur set-up for good, installing a New Zealand Cricket board and an administration that was entrepreneurial and forward thinking. Anderson found Doig, who after teaching became a world-class opera singer. So he knew the entertainment sector, besides loving sport and business in general. Doig was an ideal choice, an amazing appointment.

I admired the man. I enjoyed his mana and presence. He was a colossus for our game. He strode in with arms waving, voice booming, mind always alert and strong. What a change!

The first challenge was to consider coach Glenn Turner's situation against that of the players, in particular wayward young talent like Chris Cairns and Adam Parore, who had confronted Turner so brashly. They were the players who could fly the flag for the next decade. It was a tough call, but a necessary one for Doig and he decided to remove Turner.

His second decision was to recruit John Graham, former All Black captain and Auckland Grammar headmaster for 20 years, as New Zealand team manager. Chris knew all about John from his Grammar days. John was a very good leader, fair and honest. It was a master stroke to lure him to the cricket ranks.

Then the third call: Steve Rixon from Australia was named as coach. This was both bold and brilliant. Bringing a coach with no baggage or agenda was critical. Rixon brought energy, a work ethic and a hard-nosed Aussie never-give-in approach. He would guide a very young Stephen Fleming to great heights.

Fourth on the list: John Reid, former champion left-hand batsman, as general manager and Neil Maxwell from Australia, an up-and-coming marketer and also a useful cricketer in his day, as marketing manager.

Then an important fifth manoeuvre: Doig secured $1 million from Michael Watt, a New Zealander living in Britain and running CSI Octagon, a noted agency for TV and entertainment rights. Doig's plan was to use the money to create the equivalent of what Australia had done successfully with the Adelaide Cricket Academy.

He targeted Lincoln University as the location, so those attending the new High Performance Academy would have the chance for a proper education as well. It was all fantastic in theory. The bricks and mortar were built at Lincoln – a large tin shed to house three indoor nets and many offices for lectures and administration. It had enormous potential to put New Zealand cricket on the world stage.

I was so impressed when I saw it a few months after retiring that I rang the academy chief, Dayle Hadlee, and asked what opportunities existed. I saw it as another great part of the Doig master plan, and as I was retired, I was keen to contribute. Although I was rebuffed, it was worth asking.

Hadlee, a former headmaster himself, had recruited various schoolteachers from around New Zealand to come in and assist with the eight-month live-in that was planned for the 15 or so talented inductees to the first academy. It didn't involve anyone of recent international playing experience, just the old school tie with their level 3 coaching certificates.

He then recruited into the mix John Harmon, a professor in biomechanics from Australia. Harmon in turn brought in an instructor of biomechanics, Ashley Ross, who introduced the most destructive, stupid ideas about how to bat. In that one single appointment to Lincoln, New Zealand's chances of success at the top level plummeted.

In all the years I watched Chris Doig do his magic that was the one trick that didn't work. From a batting point of view it was a failure. Over the next decade every time skilled and talented batsmen spent any time in the Lincoln nets, they came out as cloned duds. It was sad to watch.

Doig created something special, but the execution by his charges let him down.

It was a real shame, watching keen young batsmen getting hoodwinked and sold a dummy. To cut a long, painful story short, Martin Snedden, the next chief executive of New Zealand Cricket, appointed another Australian, Ric Charlesworth, of hockey fame, and in 2007-08, he shut it all down.

In the meantime, back at the ranch and miles away from Lincoln, from 1999 onwards, New Zealand began playing a great brand of cricket and winning under John Graham, Steve Rixon and Stephen Fleming. They were a well-led, tough and talented bunch.

I was well retired by this time and into television broadcasting mode, so no longer had any direct dealings with the national side. I was an innocent bystander caring and interested in our fortunes on the world scene. I always wanted the best for our national team. Doig had turned the team around with astute leadership and decision-making. The scene was set for a golden run to match the 1980s.

What took place over the next 10 years can only be described as, pardon the cliché, a game of two halves. From 1998 to 2002, New Zealand soared and achieved much. It was a glorious rise. The following five years were among the worst in our cricket history, given the resources and support in place. It was an ugly fall.

With Stephen Fleming, Chris Cairns, Dion Nash, Roger Twose, Adam Parore, Nathan Astle, Mark Richardson and Daniel Vettori making up the bulk of the team, they were soon rising in the rankings and competing at the highest level. Their 2-1 series victory over England in 1999 was simply sensational. The following year in Kenya they lifted the Champions Trophy, New Zealand's first major tournament win.

In Australia in late 2001, helped by the discovery of Shane Bond, they pushed the No 1-ranked test team to the brink, with a worthy 0-0 series result. They were a close bunch, growing together, building confidence within and creating concern among the opposition. They became hard to beat. For me, they were a pleasure to broadcast. By the end of the 2001-02 season, the New Zealand team was in the top three in the world in both forms of the game.

Chris Doig had everything to do with that rise; he was the catalyst for change and executed things nearly perfectly. I thoroughly enjoyed my time dealing with Chris in my first years as an executive producer. I couldn't have wished for a better chief executive to deal with day in and day out. They were indeed happy times. Chris then moved on to work for the New Zealand Symphony Orchestra and became a sought-after consultant and director on many boards, including the New Zealand Rugby Union.

From ambitious schoolteacher and chalk thrower, to opera singer and booming voice, to New Zealand Cricket saviour, Chris Doig was a marvel who touched many.

Sadly, he died too young of cancer.

CHAPTER 4

Caught and Bowled 66: My Amazing Dad

Winter 2000

I had noticed Dad's voice start to lose its strength and asked him if he was okay. He said he was, but that his back was troubling him and that was a first. He got it checked out. Then he rang with the news. "The doctor says I have two weeks to live."

I put down the phone and drove over to see him. He was on his bed, defeated. He said: "I can't beat this. There are tumours in my spine and my liver, and my pancreas is gone, too. Two weeks." He was beaten.

What do you say to that? I hugged him and held him and told him it was okay to think he couldn't beat it. I just said to not fight anything, just be still. The next day we started to see if he wanted to get a special treatment of Vitamin B & C injected into him, to boost his immune system. He said he would, so I drove him each day for three days and then he said that he had had enough. He just wanted to rest, as he was in too much pain. He was soon on heavy morphine to ease it all. But he was counting down the days. It was surreal, horribly unfair.

Yet, deep down I knew that the time I had spent with him in the past five years was priceless – a blessing. I felt resigned. My best mate was about to die.

I rang my cousin Russell, who was shooting a movie with Meg Ryan. I told him about Dad. Uncle Dave was special to Russell, because he had been an inspiration to him through his teenage years. Russell wanted to do something special back. He asked me to book the Berkeley Cinema in Mission Bay on Saturday, May 6, for 6pm and to invite all the family and close friends to a sitting. So I did as he said.

Russell then flew from Ecuador direct to Auckland, 17 hours in a Lear jet, and drove straight to the theatre, where we sat waiting. Then up on the big screen, before anyone in the world had seen it publicly,

My cousin Russell (right), gave Dad a terrific send-off. We're pictured here at Russell's place in New South Wales, at the Dave Crowe Sports Field, so named as a lovely tribute by Russell to his uncle.

screened *Gladiator*. Russell had just received a copy of it and he wanted Dad to see it before it was too late.

Dad absolutely loved it. At the end of the movie he turned to Russell in the theatre, hugged him, and simply said: "You bloody ripper." We went home to my place and partied until 6am and then Russell flew all the way back to Ecuador. Russell's gesture was incredible, never to be forgotten by any of us.

Five days later Dad died. It was early morning on May 12, two weeks after his cancer was diagnosed. Russell had put the final smile on his face and the final sense of pride in his heart. Dad was a proud man as he left us.

The family came together and we celebrated his life at a funeral at Eden Park in front of 1000 people paying their respects. Up on the big scoreboard it read, "DW Crowe, caught and bowled 66".

Life would never be the same for any of us. It was my first real experience of death. Yes, my grandparents had all died, but that was it. My dad, that wonderful man, was dead.

They say that time can help to heal. I went to Britain and Europe for a break, but found myself in Florence wailing again – deep, painful sobbing and groaning at my loss, our loss. I felt I had lost him before, but now it was for good.

I returned home, sad. I sold that Western Springs house – the memories were too painful. I bought around the corner and tried to start again. But deep down the same feelings of despair came back again.

And with no warning at all my life was about to get even murkier. Shockingly so.

CHAPTER 5

Mud in the Eye: Indignation

Summer 2000

The first year of the new millennium had been dreadful. Losing Dad in May was a massive shock. I knew I needed to keep working, finding my answers and peace from deep within. That can be so hard when big chunks of your life go missing, or get questioned, or simply piss you off.

I was about to get really pissed off. The day was November 1, 2000. I was sitting in my Sky office at about 2pm when the phone rang and Andrew Dewhurst from Radio Sport was on the line. He spoke, I listened. He told me that all over the net there was news that an Indian bookie had named me as part of a group of international cricketers involved in another match-fixing saga.

Following on from the extraordinarily controversial Hansie Cronje match-fixing affair only months earlier, the news was explosive and unbelievably damaging. Andrew read the Indian police press release to me while I digested the nature of the accusations. Then he put me live on air.

MK Gupta, a Delhi bookie, had accused me of providing match information, not match-fixing. He stated in his testimony to Indian police that he had paid me $US20,000 to give weather and pitch information, that he had come to my house in Wellington and had lunch. He also stated I had been introduced to him in 1991 by Aravinda de Silva, the Sri Lankan batsman. It was all unadulterated lies.

At 7pm, I went live on the *Holmes* current affairs show to try to explain what on earth was going on. I denied any wrongdoing. All I could piece together as to why I was being accused was to say to Holmes that a man named Gupta had called me during the 1992 World Cup, claiming initially to be a journalist, and asking me to do a captain's column for a small fee. I had been doing a column for some years for *The Evening Post* and this World Cup column would be the much the same.

I explained that it was all very hazy because it was so long ago, but I guessed that on the third or fourth occasion Gupta called me, he had asked me to throw the round robin game against Pakistan in Christchurch. At the time I abused him and hung up, then told my room-mate, Mark Greatbatch, of the episode. We in turn told Wally Lees, who brushed it off, saying he had had a crank call as well. Back in 1992 stories about bookies approaching players were unheard of. They were regarded merely as stupid crank calls.

But by 2000, after hearing about Cronje, Azharuddin, Malik and others getting caught and banned, everyone had become acutely aware of the dangerous betting underworld and the dramatic effect it had had on cricket.

I was very worried and rang David Howman, my lawyer. He naturally advised me to remain calm and to avoid further comment. I then rang Chris Doig and asked what he had heard. He informed me that it was serious and that New Zealand Cricket, along with all other boards, would be conducting complete investigations into the allegations. I argued it was totally unjust that the Indian police and a known bookie could make such public accusations and get away with it. It was just plain rubbish, yet the boards were giving his stories some credence. Chris Doig said that following the Cronje cover-up New Zealand Cricket had no choice but to take such accusations seriously.

I sarcastically offered my thanks and a few expletives about what he was proposing. His final advice was that it wouldn't happen overnight and that I should stay patient. Gee, thanks again.

I was in shock and deeply hurt, knowing how this mud would stick the longer the saga dragged on. Yet I couldn't fight back, and had been told to keep quiet and do nothing. I felt like I was locked away doing a jail sentence. I had to wait for the process to unfold. The longer I waited and the investigations went on, the more the feeling from media and public was that where there was smoke there was fire. I waited for months for a chance to speak. In the meantime New Zealand Cricket set up its investigation team, led by Tim Gresson, a Timaru lawyer who had done legal work for the New Zealand Rugby Union over the years.

The wait was excruciating. Worse, it had a massive effect on my health. My anxiety rose as my sleeping patterns were affected. It was incomprehensible that a dodgy bookie somewhere in Delhi could throw mud in every direction and that people of importance – and New Zealand Cricket especially – might feel the bookie was telling the truth. New Zealand Cricket was following protocol following the Hansie Cronje match-fixing revelations, but it was a terrible time for me. To be told to shut up and wait for nine months seemed very unfair, and was potentially very damaging. Finally, nine months after the initial public release, my hearing was called for July 4, 2001, at the Northern Club in Auckland. Attending the hearing were Judge Ian Barker, Nicholas Davidson QC, Tim Gresson, a member of the ICC anti-corruption unit, David Howman and me.

I walked in with David Howman and sat down in front of Judge Barker. He handed me a letter and asked me to read it first. The letterhead was from the New Zealand Immigration Department. It clearly stated that after a thorough search by the department, at no stage had MK Gupta, the Indian bookie who had made the accusation of paying me $US20,000 in Wellington, ever entered New Zealand. He was not on New Zealand Customs or New Zealand Immigration records. In my hand was clear evidence that he was lying and that I was cleared of this absurdity.

I looked at Judge Barker in disgust. He said I was free to go. I said: "Hold on a minute! You've had me under investigation for nine months just to tell me this simple piece of information. Nine months! Are you kidding me! Surely it should have taken only nine days to get this." I was livid. I turned to Gresson and said: "Why so long?" He didn't answer, just a shrug of the shoulders.

I walked outside with David and unleashed my fury. Then after I calmed down David said to me that we should go back in and find out if there was anything else they would like to know from me, while I was still here. I just wanted to go to the pub and get wasted. For nine months my health had deteriorated, my moods had swung back and forth, and I had become depressed again.

Trying to do the right thing and follow David's advice, I walked back into the room. Nicholas Davidson asked if it was possible to go over what had happened during the World Cup in 1992, so I agreed to answer any questions. After 10 minutes of Gresson's questioning about trivial matches I had played leading up to the World Cup, Judge Barker asked him to sit down. Davidson took over and we went through the World Cup situation with the Gupta phone calls, step by step. We went through dealing with journalists in general and we went through whether I had any knowledge of match-fixing during my time as captain.

I answered every question honestly and they summarised by saying that they were sorry for the delay in the hearing and the inconvenience and pain I had endured as a result. I left with a sideways glance at Gresson, the man responsible on behalf of New Zealand Cricket for conducting a fair hearing. It's fair to say I was pretty ropeable with New Zealand Cricket, too.

My only consolation was that my father wasn't alive to have gone through the debacle.

Thankfully the mud thrown at me didn't stick. Other captains and players were investigated and also found innocent – Alec Stewart, Brian Lara, Arjuna Ranatunga, Aravinda de Silva – and Gupta crawled back into the gutter he'd come from.

One of the theories to emerge was that the Indian police had made Gupta single out a player from each country, preferably the captain of each team, to implicate all countries and not just India. They wanted it to look as though it was a global problem, not just India's.

CHAPTER 6

Fatherhood: Emmy Lou

Winter 2002

On a rainy Thursday in August 1980, the Auckland Grammar First XV abandoned outdoor training and headed to the indoor gym. The coach, Graham Henry, wanted a good warm-up and a few drills in preparation for our crucial clash with Kelston Boys High, on our patch, on Saturday. We were unbeaten with four games remaining. The title was ours if we got past Kelston on Saturday, and King's College, our long-standing rivals, the following week.

As we warmed up there was a bit of skylarking among the lads. Then in a flash, Kevin Thomas, the big lock forward, swung me over his shoulder and threw me to the floor. As my right knee hit the hard wooden floor I let out a deep groan.

I hobbled to the side of the gym to sit down and applied ice, hoping it was nothing, but believing the worst. On Saturday, the day of the Kelston game, I could hardly move. I arrived at the main field and declared myself a non-starter. Henry, keen for me to play, asked if I could give it a go. We were unbeaten all season, Kelston were the challengers and we had four crucial games left. I had scored 18 tries to date, was combining well and wanted to play. I agreed to try it, strapped up and hobbled out.

In the first 90 seconds of the match, Grant Fox, our captain and masterful first-five, went blindside and put me in the clear. As I caught the ball and went to accelerate into the corner for the try, my knee jerked in the mud and collapsed under me two metres from the goal-line.

I was carried off and never played again. It transpired that on the Thursday the posterior ligament had become torn away from the back of the knee joint. Now I had also torn my inside meniscus cartilage of the same knee. The prognosis was to rest and ensure the quads were strong enough to overcome any deficiency in the future. At the age of 17, I had suffered my first serious injury, my first major setback.

Throughout my Grammar years I had managed to ignore the call to play a winter contact sport. My standard answer was that I was a cricketer and didn't want to run the risk of injury. So by agreeing to play for the First XV, I had broken my own rule. That posterior ligament injury never went away, and it finished my cricket career at the age of 33.

By the age of 39 I could not walk properly. The knee was so bad that I had no choice but to book in for an osteotomy. During that procedure the surgeon cut my tibia in half just below the knee joint and moved the lower part across 10 degrees, then plated and bolted the tibia back together. This meant the loading would then be through the part of the knee, the right side, which had some remaining cartilage.

I chose Dr Garry Heynan to complete the operation. I had an epidural and early in the piece I woke up with a green sheet in front of me and the sound of a saw. Then I passed out again.

The operation was successful, but I had to endure two months of lying on my back and not moving, while the bones knitted back together. That was the plan and I was in no hurry to mess with it.

During this period, through an introduction from Danny Morrison's wife Kim, I met Huhaana Marshall, a director of a telephone IT company. We got on so well before the operation that Huhaana moved in to live with me and nurse me through the 10 weeks of rehab. During this time we discussed the dream of having a child. We were both 40 and alone, and the desire to have a child was strong. We made a big call. A year later, on April 15, 2003, Emma Louise came into our lives. It was the greatest feeling. The joy of seeing my own child, my first, was overwhelming. I felt as happy as I had ever been.

Sadly, my relationship with Huhaana didn't last. Again, maybe I rushed into such a lifelong commitment as having a child without really taking the time to truly establish a relationship with Huhaana. There was no fault on anyone's part, just the pressure of raising a child without really knowing each other. For me, it was familiar territory; I just didn't know who I was. I thought I had grown out of my insecurities and issues.

At 8.30pm on September 15, 2005, I left home, leaving Emma (aged two) fast asleep. As I walked away, I wept uncontrollably. That

Emma as a two-year-old. She has been one of the joys of my life.

was the darkest hour of my life. I went to share a flat with my great friend China Gillman, who was my PA at Sky for nearly 10 years. That was my home for the next six months while I finally got myself sorted. I then surrendered to professional help. I sought therapy and vowed to fix that on-going problem of mine – a disconnected spirit and soul overwhelmed by the ego and the emotional instability created from my unfinished teenage development.

What I needed was some consistent serious counselling about what had to be done so I could be a good father and a good partner to someone one day. Becoming a father became that catalyst for serious change and my need to work on my attitude and approach to life, people and myself. I worked with two fine counsellors, Peter Caughey and Susan Young, and we began to cut below the surface to find the problem and work on some answers.

I knuckled down and did the work, first to listen, then question, then change. I knew it would require a lot of work, given the deep-rooted issues. But also I believed that I would eventually bounce back and take

A happy day with Emma in difficult times, Christmas Day, 2012.

on the challenges with the right head space.

My first revelation was that I was a good person, but I had been taken away from a natural upbringing with my scripted journey through cricket. Now I could begin the long restoration down the right path.

Emma was my priority. I gave her and Huhaana the best support I could. What was most important to Huhaana and me was that we got on as well as possible to ensure Emma had a positive environment to thrive in. Hand on heart, we have achieved that superbly to this day. We are both incredibly grateful and lucky to have been given a daughter who fills us with love, joy and pride every day.

As Emma grew she showed a remarkable sense of calmness and assurance. Her appetite for life – family time, friendships, sports, arts, dance, and school – came to the fore, and she thrived on the happy environment around her.

With a broken home, the next best thing was to provide two caring parents working together, in two comfortable homes. Most importantly, Emma needed consistency and routine, creating a normality from which she could prosper and develop positively.

I became preoccupied with making sure she was okay, and that she and Huhaana were both coping and enjoying life. They moved to a place just around the corner, and that gave me the chance to pick up Emma each morning and take her to school, the best start to the day I could have, and I felt it was for Emma too.

We soon joined the Kohimarama Tennis Club and Emma quickly became attracted to the moving ball. The ability to move and hit was there. At school she loved her netball, and was good at moving, catching and passing, and efficient at shooting, too. Emma mainly loved the team spirit and the get-togethers. Huhaana and I watched every game together and that gave Emma a sense of overall togetherness.

By the age of 10, Emma had a grounding of love, affection, support and opportunity, as one would hope any child would have. Without question, the lifetime blessing for me was to remove all the bad stuff within me and feel nothing but unconditional love for another, as I did for Emma.

Emma was the very person who saved my soul and brought me back to life and to self-discovery. From there, I was able to feel I could move on to having a special relationship with someone for whom I could feel unconditional love.

CHAPTER 7

Grave Digging: Sky Watching

2003-2008

Becoming a father was unbelievably exciting and fulfilling. But working at Sky and producing the live coverage of the New Zealand team was becoming a grind. New Zealand as a cricket nation was about to head in the wrong direction. After a really good period, it started to point downwards. It started digging in the wrong places.

Success breeds success, but can lead to a certain power that can get out of kilter. This appeared to happen to Stephen Fleming in 2002. Steve Rixon was well gone and Denis Aberhart, a gentle background kind of fellow, had become coach and sidekick, very much a second fiddle to the ever-growing presence of Fleming.

Fleming was entering his prime as a player and, coupled with more than four years in charge, was getting a feel for what was required to win and prosper. His man-management skills were superb and his tactical ability was growing by the day. He was gaining worldwide respect.

However, instead of firing that knowledge and influence into producing more wins for New Zealand, Fleming got sidetracked. Two ambitious young men with no particular cricket ability, Rob Nichol (not to be confused with Rob Nicol, the test player) and Heath Mills, approached Fleming with a plan to set up a New Zealand Cricket Players Association in the summer of 2001-02, with the objective of demanding more pay and better conditions.

The battle plan had been designed by former Australian off-spinner Tim May, who now headed the international players arm, Federation of International Cricketers' Associations. May had set up the Australian Players Association and had successfully taken on the Australian Cricket Board to secure better pay and conditions for players.

Nichol and Mills became the players' union organisers, while

Fleming became a champion for the cause and alongside him were his strong lieutenants, Chris Cairns and Dion Nash. Craig McMillan was their natural enforcer. Their plan was similar to May's attack on the Australian Cricket Board – to secure a guarantee that up to 25 per cent of all generated income would go to the players. In Australia, May had drafted in the outstanding James Erskine, formerly of IMG, to do the negotiations. Erskine was a brilliant appointment to the players' cause and ultimately a fair deal was struck. Remember, though, the Australian team then were undisputed world champions and one of the greatest sides ever.

On the other hand, though New Zealand were competitive, they weren't in the same league as Australia, and nor did they have the same market size and support. Australia's national game was cricket, whereas New Zealand's without question was rugby.

While the New Zealand Cricket Players Association pitch to New Zealand Cricket was determined and bold, it transpired the players were too abrasive and gung-ho in their approach. They were within their rights to ask for a better deal and to ask strongly, but it all became too hard after a while.

In a calculated move over four long months, Stephen Fleming refused to communicate at all with New Zealand Cricket chief executive Martin Snedden. The stand-off was quite unbelievable when you think about it: the New Zealand captain refused to talk to the New Zealand Cricket chief executive! It was an attempt to shift the power, a power the players would come to call the "80s Mafia".

The players rightly felt that times were changing, and their views were reinforced when they looked across the Tasman at the goings-on in Australia. They saw the chance to create a fair playing field for the long-term. Correct again. However, not to have Fleming sit across a table from Snedden and work it through, but rather to send in Nichol and Mills, neither of whom was a James Erskine, proved to be a miscalculation with long-term ramifications.

The impasse lasted for six months up to the start of the 2002-03 season. The players went on strike for most of that time, refusing to practise, play or promote the game. Cricket Max was cancelled and never played again.

At one stage, Snedden was contemplating fielding an under-19 team to play India in the first test in December 2002, because nearly every first-class cricketer had been signed by the Cricket Players Association. Some young players were pressured into following the Cricket Players Association and ignoring New Zealand Cricket. It all got horribly nasty. Finally, it appeared Chris Cairns had enough and broke away. He approached Snedden, and a deal was finally done.

No-one really knows what was said, or not said, throughout the entire episode, but it left Snedden scarred and bruised. Not long after, he recruited his friend and former team-mate, John Bracewell, who was coaching Gloucester. Bracewell became the New Zealand team coach, starting in September 2003.

However, he wasn't just the coach. Bracewell also became the chairman of selectors, with power of veto. Fleming's rising power vanished. If any player power was to disrupt New Zealand Cricket again, then Bracewell was in a position to kill it. Bracewell had indeed come a long way. He had gone from digging graves in Dunedin as a student to becoming a power player in the halls of New Zealand Cricket in Christchurch.

It is unusual, in international cricket, for one person to have so much power. Certainly in rugby and soccer, the coach is also the chief selector, but in cricket the two roles have traditionally been split. There have been occasions, such as near the end of John Reid's long career, when the captain has also been a selector, but generally the roles of captain, selector and, in modern times, coach are much more defined.

Bracewell was always odds on to become the national team coach. After retiring as a player in 1990, he shaped his next career around becoming an international coach. He started with Auckland, coaching them for several years, and then ventured off for overseas experience. Knowing his determination from his playing days, I expected he would make a good fist of it.

For Gloucestershire he was certainly successful. The county had often seemed to under-perform, but under Bracewell, Gloucester became the best one-day team in England. He focused intensely on the nuances and details of the one-day game, the "one per cents" as he called it, and the trophies were duly delivered. Under Bracewell, the Bristol-based county won a handful of limited-over competitions and did so in a new and clever manner. There were no superstars, just athletic all-round talent that gelled under a Bracewell-designed blueprint of outstanding fielding, daring running between the wickets, specialist hitting and clever use of bowlers, who on paper seemed down on quality, but high on economy and consistency. Bracewell's way soon became much talked about.

Snedden, one would assume, was watching his mate from afar. His problem was that Gloucester had Bracewell locked into a long-term deal. I'm unsure if Snedden had plans to appoint Bracewell as chairman of selectors as well as coach. But as Bracewell was so successful doing both roles in county cricket (where the dual role was the norm), Snedden probably assumed Bracewell could do the same with the New Zealand team. The trend in England was based on the football manager model, the best example being Alex Ferguson at Manchester United. If there was ever a reason to give someone all the power, a first in New Zealand cricket, then the players' strike certainly was it.

Snedden, a lawyer before taking on cricket administration, managed to pull Bracewell out of his county contract and provide a ticket for him and his family to get home fast. Bracewell's appointment felt the right one and the good times looked set to continue for the New Zealand team.

I put our past history behind me and emailed Bracewell, offering my congratulations and support. I wrote that I had heard his coaching was very good, and that if he needed any assistance there were many of us who would be happy to help. All appeared friendly and positive from both sides.

There was no doubt he covered all aspects – batting, bowling and fielding – because he was accomplished in all three disciplines as a player. John was a resourceful cricketer with a strong determination. His off-spin was aggressive and attacking, his batting gritty and at times destructive, his fielding very assured. He could play, given the right conditions. Therefore he was a worthy member of any side. On the other hand, Bracewell as a man and a team-mate could be abrasive, confrontational, bullish and unsophisticated – a highly competitive fireball. He taunted and teased his team-mates like no-one else with whom I had played. So it was going to be interesting to see how much he had changed as a coach. No doubt there had been a natural mellowing as a man, along with a huge acquisition of knowledge as to what man-management required as a coach. Best of all, he had earned the position because of his undoubted success overseas.

The step up to international cricket was always going to be a tough initiation, but Bracewell was in it for the long-term, so early teething issues were not unexpected.

The team had just competed in the 2003 World Cup in South Africa. It had had the ability to go far in that tournament, but had again failed to nail down the finer details to ensure a consistent campaign. Withdrawing from the Kenya fixture didn't help, but it was felt that Bracewell was just the man to take New Zealand to greater heights in the next World Cup, in 2007.

Despite the appointment having a positive feel about it from fans and former players, the current players appeared a touch edgy about Bracewell's overall power. Fleming wasn't used to having a selector in the dressing room, let alone such a strong personality. Fleming, remember, was very much the leader and preferred it that way. The fallout with Snedden may have changed all that.

By late 2003 Bracewell was totally in charge of proceedings. The players, though happy with their new pay cheques, were not running the show as they had previously. This was a different ship to the one Fleming was steering just a year before.

How this was going to work with a successful bunch of strong-minded players was the big question. The lingering wounded feelings after the previous year's stand-off between New Zealand Cricket and the Cricket Players Association meant relationships had been affected and scarred. There was a strong possibility that a highly dramatic train smash might occur somewhere down the line.

From the outside, especially in my role as Sky's executive producer of cricket, I was beginning to get nervous. While I had total confidence that the team would play good one-day cricket, I had a sneaking suspicion that our test game might be more exposed if not enough attention was paid to it. My over-riding concern was that if we dropped our form as a test-playing nation, then not only would the world game start treating us less respectfully, but it would also start to affect our one-day game. I believed that playing the long form correctly had a stronger long-term effect on our play in limited overs formats, not the other way around. Bracewell's focus looked to be very short form-based.

In 2004, during the much-awaited tour of England, I saw from the commentary box the first signs of a team losing its way. New Zealand were in front in all three tests, only to lose them on the fourth and fifth days. They looked to have lost their will to claw and fight their way back. They looked resigned to defeat too quickly. Fleming, most of all, looked and captained without his normal energy and flair. It was as if he were treading water. This was not his team any more. It was John Bracewell's, the man sitting in the dressing room, laptop at the ready.

I have always believed that in cricket the captain has to be in charge. He is the person on the park. A coach can help prepare before a match, but once it starts he can have only limited influence. He has to be careful then not to trip up players, mess with their minds. A good coach, a successful one, will keep his distance and allow the players to dig deep within, rather than rely on outside help. There have been rare exceptions, such as when Bobby Simpson led Australia more as coach than the initially reluctant Allan Border as captain in the mid-1980s.

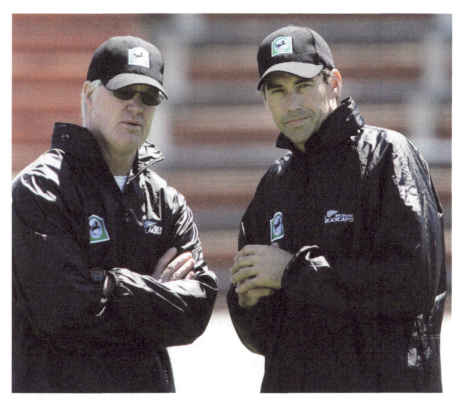

John Bracewell, left, and Stephen Fleming were thrown together as coach and captain and gradually their relationship disintegrated. *Photo, Fairfax*

But the reality was that since cricket began, the captain was always the leader and the coach, as Ian Chappell, the great Australian captain liked to state, got you to the ground and back. Times change, but as yet we haven't seen that change include the coach taking the field for hour after hour, day after day.

Yes, this was indeed a new era and style of leadership for New Zealand, and it didn't look promising as time went on. I preferred the previous regime and captain-coach combination with Fleming in control and Aberhart quietly in the background.

Doing things quietly was not Bracewell's way. He was in everyone's face, including the media. Some of the stuff he came out with was at times embarrassing. Certainly the Aussie media thought so. At Sky I began believing we shouldn't interview him, making the point that he needed to spend his core time coaching. Then I made a mistake and said to a journo that Sky would not interview him, preferring him to focus on his main role. That went to print and I looked stupid. My comment was an unnecessary idle threat. We continued to honour the duty of promoting the game, including hearing from Bracewell, but it showed the way it was affecting my thinking.

Meanwhile, I became concerned for individual players and the game overall.

As time went on the unease was visible in some of those players, though not collectively or publicly, because they needed to be seen to be conforming, especially after their Cricket Players Association battles. The public was very wary of the new attitude and didn't tolerate players making excuses any more. They were so well paid that the public wanted win after win.

The first man to speak was Nathan Astle. This laid-back but highly skilled player was no longer enjoying his cricket. He blamed it on Bracewell. He wanted the old ways back. It was not long before New Zealand's finest ODI batsman walked away disgruntled.

Then more came out – Lou Vincent, Andre Adams, Chris Cairns, Craig McMillan, Scott Styris. Then it was Stephen Fleming himself, when he found his captaincy questioned.

To be fair, other players talked affectionately about him. Mark Richardson, James Franklin, Jacob Oram, Brendon McCullum, Hamish Marshall, Daniel Vettori and most of the bowlers seemed happy with the Bracewell style. They liked his up-front, no bullshit routine. They liked his hands-on coaching, which was his key role. They were happy enough with the way he drove the one-day campaign.

I believe the potential was there for him to succeed, if he'd just stuck to coaching. But the need for overall say and to control player power was the tipping point. If he had put more emphasis on the test batting he would have been able to find some long-term performers for both forms. What the team didn't need was players like Fleming, Astle and Styris wandering away from the heat of the test match battle. It needed those experienced men to pass the baton to those coming through, to keep the team rolling along.

Martin Snedden had done a sterling job in all areas of his job. He had responded superbly to many crises and showed his mettle and composure on many occasions. It was no surprise when in late 2006 it was announced that he would head New Zealand's hosting of the 2011 Rugby World Cup. No-one would be more deserving or better equipped for such an important job. From my perspective, the only blot on Martin's copybook was that he entrusted too much power to Bracewell, instead of encouraging him to stick to his core role of coaching, the one he was good at.

An opportunity arose for New Zealand Cricket, under a newly appointed chief executive, to move away from Bracewell. In early 2007, the World Cup was being staged in the Caribbean and with the team making the semi-finals, there was a chance to encourage a new coach, given New Zealand's creditable showing at a world event. But Justin Vaughan, in his first month at the helm, reappointed Bracewell for two more years. It was a pity.

Test cricket is what all cricketers wish to be judged on. It is the game's premier format and what Bracewell should have been judged on first and foremost. Under Bracewell, New Zealand made one-day cricket their priority and built a pretty good one-day record. But let's face it, one-day cricket, apart from a World Cup every four years, is not the sharp end of the game. These days, especially with the advent of Twenty20, it is becoming irrelevant.

There can be no doubt that Bracewell largely maintained the form of the one-day side during his reign. In the 102 ODIs he coached and selected, the team registered 49 wins, 45 losses with eight abandoned.

That was a very good return. If he targeted the 2007 World Cup as his priority, then by reaching the semi-finals he came very close to achieving his goal. Yet still the over-riding feeling was that the team had gone backwards in terms of personnel and that the future looked shaky. Maybe it could be argued that New Zealand had come to the end of an era and needing rebuilding. But I felt it had all become too drastic, especially with the disenchantment felt by certain players.

In late 2003, Bracewell inherited the following squad of test players: Fleming, Cairns, Richardson, McMillan, Astle, Styris, Oram, McCullum, Vettori, Sinclair, Vincent, Hamish Marshall, Mills, Martin, Bond, Adams, Tuffey and Franklin. Sure they weren't all world-beaters, but they formed a talented group. There were four batsmen in the world's top 30 in test cricket (Richardson, Fleming, McMillan and Astle), and four in the top 30 bowlers (Tuffey, Cairns, Vettori and Bond). Not surprisingly, New Zealand climbed to a commendable world ranking of third in the test arena.

By late 2008, on the tour of Australia, only five survivors of that group of 18 remained in the test side, though others were still playing one-day cricket for New Zealand. There will always be players who retire, or seek greener fields elsewhere, but in that period several players terminated their careers earlier than they might have. Often they walked away from the New Zealand set-up disgruntled.

Bracewell's first tour away with the New Zealand team was to India in late 2003. His full test record as chairman of selectors and head coach was:

18 series, won 6, lost 9, drew 3.
43 matches, won 12, lost 20, drew 11.

If we exclude New Zealand's matches against Bangladesh (five wins from six matches) and Zimbabwe (two wins from two matches), who were not really of test quality, he won only two series out of 14 and five tests of 35.

By the end of his tenure, New Zealand had no test batsman in the top 30 and just three bowlers (Vettori, Martin and Oram).

It seemed clear that for the development of New Zealand as a test-playing nation, Bracewell needed to move on. But not according to Justin Vaughan.

Vaughan played for Auckland in the late 1980s and early 90s, captaining them in his latter years. He was a bits and pieces player, not good enough at batting or bowling but, as was the trend, able to sneak into sides on the basis of two strings to his bow. So he got a few chances, even opening the batting for New Zealand in the West Indies in 1996. He didn't last long and then headed into medicine, which was his professional field of expertise.

He also moved on to the board of Cricket Auckland, and from there to the New Zealand Cricket board. When Martin Snedden resigned as chief executive, board chairman John Anderson made an important decision. Anderson had been chairman for 13 years and had done a magnificent job resurrecting the game. He was probably the leading administrator in world cricket, such was his knowledge, influence and mana.

In one of his final moves as chairman he turned to Vaughan and asked him to take over from Snedden. So Vaughan became the next chief executive. On the surface it might have appeared as if New Zealand Cricket was getting another Martin Snedden-type figure as its chief executive, but that was far from the case.

In Adelaide in November 2008, New Zealand lost the test heavily and plummeted to eighth in the world, a new low. This proved to be Bracewell's last test.

From being third in the world in 2002, New Zealand had plunged to the depths. From being a side supremely led by Fleming, the team by late 2008 was prematurely in the hands of Vettori, and included a group of inexperienced youngsters struggling to make their way in the test arena.

The glorious rise of New Zealand Cricket from 1996, built by an opera singer, had become a substantial fall from grace by 2009, buried by a gravedigger.

Watching it all from the Sky commentary box was agonising and heartbreaking. Wrongly, I began to worry about the effect it would have on Sky, and on my role. Just as importantly, I was a former player seeing the game take a turn for the worse. I began to pull my hair out.

CHAPTER 8

Hair Raising Oddities: Truth be Told

Let it be said that by the turn of the century, at the age of 37, my hair was receding badly and, noting the shiny head of my brother Jeff, I knew I wasn't far away from official baldness. I didn't like the thought or the look of it, to be frank. The front bit of my hair was becoming a marooned island, slowly separating itself from the mainland. It looked like Stewart Island and the bottom of the South Island, with a strait of nothing in between! With my ego dented, I searched around for solutions. The most obvious one to me as a cricketer was Advanced Hair Studios, which had successfully recruited Greg Matthews and Graham Gooch to endorse its product and services. I met both of them, checked out their new hair and was mightily impressed.

Contrary to rumour, it's not surgical with plugs through the head to create a new and permanent look. Instead, it's a brilliantly synthesised second skin or membrane, which is non-surgically grafted to your head where required. Hair is added to the membrane that has been matched to perfection to that of your own in colour, density and direction.

It is checked monthly when it's time for a trim of your own hair. You head into its studios wherever you are in the world – it has more than 70 – and walk out feeling young again and fully armed! The thing I loved was that I didn't have to worry about it at all during the month, just make sure I kept it groomed accordingly.

There is no way I would ever undergo surgery to my head cosmetically, but this way I had the desired result and nothing to worry about. Of course, the only concern initially was the taunts that would naturally, and understandably, come my way. Overall though, the look was real and the good-natured barbs soon turned to positive compliments.

Advanced Hair has been hugely supportive since 2001 and I can only hope it will stick with me and my head for many more years.

* * * * * * *

During India's tour of New Zealand in 2003, I agreed to provide a column for a new website, Nirvana Cricket, originating out of India. The arrangement was fairly simple. I would be rung by an Indian editor, who would ghost-write my column. Then he would post it online after my approval via email. All went swimmingly well. The tour ended on a high positive for New Zealand and I was full of praise for our national team, who outplayed India, albeit in friendly hometown conditions.

As the New Zealand team headed off to South Africa to compete in the 2003 World Cup, I settled back into normal life, office work at Sky and enjoying home life after a busy schedule travelling all summer.

Then I got hit by a bus. Not literally, but figuratively. On a sunny Saturday morning I wandered down to the shop to get the paper, milk and bread, but something far more important caught my eye. On a large poster outside the local dairy was the headline: "Crowe: Cricket not for Maoris".

Naturally, once inside the shop I was astonished to see I had made it on to the front page news of the *New Zealand Herald*. Cricket reporter Richard Boock had picked up on a column I had posted three weeks earlier. The column referred incorrectly to Maori not being good at concentrating. Boock didn't hold back on his outrage. Not surprisingly, Boock was supported by New Zealand Cricket.

My post said: "Not many Maori make good cricketers because they don't have the patience or the temperament to play through a whole day, let alone over a test match."

New Zealand Cricket operations manager John Reid said the comments were not representative of the national organisation. "I can say I do not agree with that comment," he said. "And I certainly wouldn't like it seen as representative of New Zealand Cricket. It is most certainly not accurate."

My first reaction was: why has Richard Boock done that? We got on fine; he was the brother of my former team-mate Stephen; I respected him as a journo and we had never had a problem in the past. It was an old column on a new website, probably not heard of in New Zealand, until now. Why didn't he call me to alert me, or ask me if it was true, if that was what I meant to say? Why would he go for me so cruelly? I felt sick.

I logged online and read the column again, but I knew immediately that this was not my opinion or words. However, Boock was quoting accurately from the story under my byline and I was mortified because there was nothing that I could do to change it. Stupidly, I never proofed this particular ghost-written article, probably because it was the very last one and I forgot to check it. As a result I opened myself up really badly.

My point to the ghost writer was that Darryl Tuffey, the New Zealand seamer, had had such a positive impact during the tour that he would hopefully become a cricket role model for other Maori and Polynesians to aspire to. Historically, Maori and Polynesians enjoyed the more physical contact sports, such as rugby and league. Cricket, with its long duration, did not hold the same attraction. I praised Tuffey and wanted more to follow in his footsteps.

I had no choice but to front the media and apologise. I never blamed the ghost writer for completely messing with my comments and meaning. Any fool upon seeing that draft would have corrected it. But I didn't proof it and in a flash I was worldwide news for having a racist view.

Huhaana, my pregnant partner at the time, was part-Maori. Why would I say that knowing my partner would be offended, let alone anyone else who read the awful comments? For a few days it was headline news and dominated talkback. Prominent Maori sportsmen and friends Michael Campbell and Phil Tataurangi took exception to my supposed comments, as did many. It was truly a dreadful time in my life. I took such a hammering over the next week that I finally rang *Wisden*, which owned the website and pleaded for it to make a statement that revealed the truth, that I didn't say those words or write them. However, *Wisden* did nothing and I licked my wounds instead. In short, I was negligent and unlucky. Richard Boock made sure I got the message and reminded me of my responsibility next time. It hit me hard emotionally and I felt deeply humiliated.

But, on my father's grave, I never said or believed those hurtful comments about Maori.

* * * * * * *

Finally in this section of hair-raising oddities I want to settle one more thing – my sexuality. Everyone is entitled to their own sexuality, but to label a person as something he is not is blatantly disrespectful. Where and why people drummed up this stuff about me being homosexual is something I will never understand.

Was it just plain envy and vengeance? Where did the Aids rumours come from – my hair loss or perhaps while I was recovering from salmonella?

I am a heterosexual. I have got friends and acquaintances who are homosexual, but isn't that the case with everyone? Yet tagging me as gay was some people's attempt to be vicious towards me and was a wrongful slur on homosexuality.

Being labelled something I'm not and with a defamatory tone has left me disillusioned to say the least. Enough said.

Back to the proper story.

CHAPTER 9

Skylarking: Paying the Price

Christmas 2008

If you can't play in the middle, on centre stage, to entertain the watching fans, the next best thing is to tell the story of the event. Or, as we say in the television business, "produce" the live event. I loved producing live television. It's pure drama, it's unpredictable and it's a real reflection of our lives.

So working for Sky Television in New Zealand was a huge opportunity and joy, a satisfying vocation following retirement from playing cricket.

My first thought when I went to work was, "What do the fans want?" I learnt in the marketing department about creativity – asking the market, listening to the fans, communicating and planning ahead. From Nate Smith, the chief executive, I learnt about the key words: "live, local and exclusive". This set the scene for the type of production we would make.

Then there was David Hill, a Channel 9 cricket production pioneer, who reminded me of the tools for compelling and sustainable production – cameras, sound effects, common sense and 10 per cent improvement every time.

In the Sky sports department, however, I learnt very little after the initial years. That was simply because we hardly ever communicated. Under Kevin Cameron, director of sport, the three executive producers – Tui McKendrick (league and others), Andy Fyfe (rugby) and me (cricket) – rarely sat around a table and discussed ideas. It was odd. We just boxed on in our own little corners looking after our own silo and the business at hand. Only Nate Smith would wander around the building and offices and inject some sense of belonging and sharing of information. On the flip side, Kevin did allow us our freedom to create, but we lacked unity of spirit and family togetherness; a real shame.

Nate Smith left in 2001 and a massive void was created. We missed his warm, open, communicative, sharing style. After he left, life at Sky became "corporate". As a public company, profit margins were everything, budgets were a priority and creativity was deemed expensive. Out went any feeling of being in a family and in came the bean counters, the almighty bottom line, the political threats and the gradual feeling of worthlessness.

By 2005 I was almost done. I had my own issues at home and then I had young James Cameron pull off a coup against me.

He approached me to say the crew didn't like my management style which, coming from someone who had never managed, was a bit rich. Maybe he was put up to it by others. I was still learning about management of large groups and budgets and felt there had been improvement, but I came up against an ambitious resistance in James. I didn't argue, frankly. One, because I didn't have the headspace, and two, because once that's the perception, what can you do? Also, I saw the silver lining of looking for other avenues.

I weighed up the situation and focused on my child and issues at home. I removed myself from touring with the production team and stayed home and worked out of the office, which was enjoyable. I hated being on the road, having done it so much during my life, so I was quietly happy with the turn of events. James took over and did it his way.

In 2006 I created a new production idea in an attempt to carve a niche for myself in the industry and to provide a new avenue away from cricket. I launched a 12-documentary series called *The Chosen Ones*. This idea was conceived in July 2005, when I got lucky in attending the United States Open golf tournament at Pinehurst, North Carolina.

My trip included playing golf with brother Jeff in Florida, then heading north to see one of the great golf courses in one of the most exciting and brutal of golf's Majors. The US Open had last been staged at Pinehurst in 1999, when Payne Stewart won in dramatic style. Tragically, he died in a plane accident four months later. From that day, Pinehurst became a spiritual home for golfers paying homage to Payne.

As soon as I walked into Pinehurst I felt it, too. It was eerie to have towering pines all around you, an amazing golf course beneath you and a feeling of walking with a higher spirit. It is very hard to explain, but it was palpable.

The only New Zealand player in the tournament was Michael Campbell. He had qualified at the last minute and took his place in the field behind the Big Five – Woods, Mickelson, Goosen, Els and Singh. Cambo had started to hit some form, so I kept a close eye on his play in the early rounds. With steady scores of 71 and 69, Cambo made the cut, sitting inside the top 15. It augured well for a ripper weekend.

At no stage had Cambo noticed me walking only metres away. I knew him well enough, and I knew to leave him to focus, as I would have asked of my friends or supporters watching on. Cambo had his head down and was playing his guts out. When he holed an outrageous bunker shot at 17 in the third round to move to even par for the tournament, Cambo was well and truly in the hunt to win his first Major.

The rest is history. He hit the lead after four holes on the final day, kept in front the whole way and strolled in, fending off a late-charging Tiger Woods to win by two strokes. I was in Heaven. To watch this drama unfold in front of my eyes was an honour and a privilege. We partied with Cambo all night and I flew home inspired to say the least.

Once home I began writing a book as well as producing a 90-minute documentary on the Cambo win. The doco was called *Cambo – the Chosen One*.

It then made me ponder that there were many New Zealanders who could be called by the same title. So we set about *The Chosen Ones* series determined to do justice to some of the finest sports achievers in our country. We aimed at many of the main sports, including a mix of team and individual sports. Ian Smith agreed to conduct the interviews and Ian John, a well-known producer of local movies, advertisements and documentaries, took over the director's chair.

I selected 12 great New Zealanders for their legacy, influence and unique stories –

Watching Michael Campbell's fabulous win in the US Open was one of the highlights of my life. Here we celebrate his famous victory.

Brian Lochore, rugby; Tawera Nikau, rugby league; John Walker, athletics; Danyon Loader, swimming; Chris Cairns, cricket; Irene Van Dyk, netball; Tab Baldwin, basketball; Steve Williams, Tiger Woods' caddie; Stephen Fleming, cricket; Sean Fitzpatrick, rugby; Ruben Wiki, rugby league; and Lance O'Sullivan, horse racing. Over the next year or so we had the honour of meeting these fine people and telling their stories. It was fulfilling television to make and be proud of.

Every July 1 for the next three years from 2006-08, I met with John Fellet, Sky chief executive, to discuss if there was anything else I could do in Sky away from cricket and the Cameron sandwich – father Kevin and son James. He listened and acknowledged there was a problem, but nothing ever eventuated.

That is until Christmas 2008. I had been on leave in Adelaide, speaking at a function as a former New Zealand captain and watching the test between New Zealand and Australia. There wasn't much to watch, because New Zealand got smashed early on the fourth day in superb conditions. With that defeat New Zealand dropped to the lowest world test ranking in its history. It was a bitter pill to swallow.

After the game I received a phone call from Roger Mortimer, a high performance manager who looked after Hamish Carter and Sarah Ulmer, among others. He told me he been asked to observe the New Zealand camp and while doing that had noted that John Bracewell allowed a team of consultants called "Leading Teams" in the dressing room throughout the tests. At the end of each session, forms would be handed out for players to fill in. They were asked to critique themselves and their peers.

Roger described the situation as macabre, watching young men, lacking confidence, being exposed to a programme that appeared to render them worthless. Apparently, it got to the point where young players were even judging older ones and reading it out in the dressing room. On the field they appeared to play with no heart or nous and looked fearful in the heat of the battle. I was appalled at what I was being told.

As it turned out, Doug Golightly of Radio Sport rang me, knowing I was holidaying in Adelaide, and asked to talk about the test. In hindsight I shouldn't have, but Doug was a mate and I felt like a chat. During our live interview I mentioned I had been informed of the Leading

Teams crowd in the dressing room, and voiced my indignation at it all. Doug couldn't believe it and played it back strongly in response. Before I knew it I was peeling off some big statements about the demise of New Zealand cricket under Bracewell.

Three days later I got a concerned call from Kevin Cameron, asking me to see John Fellet immediately. I dropped what I was doing, walked into the office, sat down and was fired from my role as executive producer of cricket.

John and Kevin were in no mood to discuss it, or mess around with it. In front of John were two letters – one from Justin Vaughan, New Zealand Cricket chief executive, and one from Heath Mills, chief executive of the Cricket Players Association. John told me they had made strong complaints about my comments on radio and demanded action. They felt Sky should be a strong ally of New Zealand Cricket and be treated accordingly. Basically, John wanted us to be New Zealand Cricket's cheerleader. But it was a one-off mistake, an exception to the rule. I had spent years forging a strong relationship with Doig and Snedden, but clearly it caused a severe reaction from John.

So Vaughan and Mills got action all right. I was removed immediately. The new project I had been seeking at Sky was given to me. I was to be demoted to running the Rugby Channel, a replay channel which regurgitated old rugby games around the clock, and showed European rugby during the middle of the night. I was taken aback. John tried to soften the blow by saying it was a job promotion. Then John offered me another softener – to continue commentating. I suggested that was a total contradiction. If I was to be fired for making one comment, why would I be allowed to continue to commentate? It made no sense. I guess they just wanted to have their cake and eat it. At that point I realised it was all very odd. Talk about confusion.

I received no support, no warning and no second chance. Something in John snapped, and that was it. I apologised to him, saying I wasn't thinking as an executive producer, purely as a concerned former player. He simply said: "Marty, play with the cards you are dealt," implying that sport is cyclical so it was best not to fret, and it wasn't our business to worry about someone else's performance. I looked into my bare hands and visualised a pair of twos, a rather bad hand, I thought. I said: "But we can't just sit by and watch them ruin a sport we've invested so much money in ($10 million a year in rights and production for New Zealand alone). John said: "Yes we can sit by. That's why we take out five-year deals, so we can ride out the bad years."

I said: "The game will be buried here in five years, John," and I walked out.

John Fellet was no Nate Smith. With Nate it was so easy, but with John it was like a poker game. He would walk past you in the cafeteria and look right through you. I would try to break down the barrier by wandering by his office with a Pepsi Max, his favourite drink, looking for a fun chat about baseball or basketball, or giving him interesting books about baseball legends like Clemente and Torres. Chats lasted a few minutes, but I always sensed he had better things to do. Fair enough. It was a burgeoning company and something was always happening. In the end it comes down to what makes you comfortable. With Nate, I loved his storytelling and that's how Sky basically worked in the early days. As a medium it took pride in telling the story, especially of sports. With John, it was about profit, the bottom line that pleased the shareholders. They played their part for Sky in different ways and were successful. For me, it was the story-telling, the making of television, that interested me far more than profit and the making of money.

Within a week or so James Cameron was the new executive producer for cricket. I didn't want to fight Sky, so I gave up the thought of mediation and accepted my lot, seeing the silver lining of a change and a new opportunity. I went on leave and licked my wounds. I wasn't ready to leave Sky because I still loved making television. So I shut my mouth, kept my nose clean, pulled up my socks, toed the line, and put my head down and my arse up!

In my quiet moments I was pleased not to have to deal with the Camerons again. James had got the promotion he wanted and could work hand-in-hand with his father. The best news was that I didn't have to deal with New Zealand Cricket again. I thought that producing rugby, our national sport, wasn't going to be such a bad gig anyway.

CHAPTER 10

Guardian Angel: Lorraine

February 14, 2009

It had to be Valentine's Day that we got married. There was no other day that would be good enough. We chose a private residence, bused in 70 friends and family and had the best day planned – a beach ceremony and a pool party to follow. But for the only day that month it rained non-stop and we went into plan B mode inside.

This was just as good because of the remarkable house we were lucky enough to use. A friend of China Gillman, my great friend, had lent us the house for the whole weekend to celebrate our greatest day. It was the same venue where Lorraine and I had spent our first romantic weekend together three years earlier.

Our story is a fascinating one, if I say so myself. It's about two young people who were thrust into the limelight, unprepared in many ways, and followed their dreams.

On July 11, 1983, Lorraine became the first and only New Zealander to win Miss Universe. She was just 19, a gorgeous Pakuranga girl, brought up in a loving family environment by a regal man, Lloyd, who was an outstanding cornet player, and Glad, the mother of four thriving daughters, Sue, Jenny, Lorraine and Carolyn. When Lorraine flew to St Louis, Missouri, for the Miss Universe pageantry she had no expectations of grandeur and fame, and was just grateful for the opportunity to see the world and represent her country and family. But she won and it changed her life. Mostly, it was her bubbly, genuine personality that won the day, and that smile. Lorraine has always been an outwardly positive soul and she wooed the judges and the world with her naturalness.

On that same day in 1983, I scored my maiden first-class century for New Zealand, batting at Lord's against Middlesex. I was 20 and finally began to believe I was good enough.

What special memories I have of our wedding day. Here Audrey, Jeff, Deb, Lorraine and I pose for a happy family photo.

Seven years later Lorraine and I met in Auckland, although we both lived in Wellington. She was four years married and I was single. We were brought together to film an in-house video for the National Bank, showing all staff how to groom and dress for work. We spent three days shooting the video in Auckland, enough time to form a firm friendship. We kept in touch from time to time while I was in Wellington, but once I got married and moved away, we lost track of each other.

Fast forward to 2001 and my 39th birthday. For some reason I was in Wellington with great friend Ash Fogel, who mentioned Lorraine was doing some modelling for his business and that she was separated. I rang her to say "Hi", and we arranged to meet for a chat. As we settled down for a catch-up, we both uncannily produced a half-bottle of Pol Roger champagne from our bags. We laughed at the synchronicity and celebrated a birthday cheer. The next night we did a movie together, *Captain Corelli's Mandolin*, and then a late snack. I noticed she was very shy and preoccupied being with me in a public place. She looked on edge because of the probability that people might talk. She noticed in me a bit of flighty confidence, but a lack of grounding.

The next day she rang to say that she enjoyed the catch-up, but didn't want to take it further because she felt we both weren't ready. While it was a blow to my ego, she was right. Lorraine was still raw from her separation and she wasn't prepared in her heart to enter into a relationship so soon. She probably sensed I was not ready for a relationship either.

Now the story moves to November 8, 2005. Months earlier I had moved out of the home I'd shared with Huhaana and was flatting with China. I had begun therapy and made a new start in life. I hooked up with Ian Smith and some mates and flew to Christchurch for some golf, horse racing and a bit of fun. We stayed at Clearwater Resort for a few nights and I bumped into an old friend, Petrina Miller, who had also come down for the meet at Riccarton and was staying next door with friends. I invited her group to pop in for a drink and as I was opening a bottle of wine, in walked Petrina and Lorraine.

Immediately I caught her smile and felt a connection. We had a laugh and a chat till three in the morning and then parted ways. My final comment was: "I would love to do another movie with you." She nodded and we exchanged numbers.

It was an off-chance meeting that led to a summer romance in two cities, Wellington, where she lived, and Auckland, where I lived. I commuted every second weekend to stay with Lorraine and her two lovely children, Hilton and Jasmine. We were in love and the weekends were special.

Her life was high-profile in small New Zealand and she often faced the difficulty of being a reluctant performer in the public eye. She coped well and focused on her two children and her health and came out of her troubled time a truly remarkable person.

We spoke of our journeys, the ego world and the pitfalls of celebrity life. We spoke of a desire to find peace from it all, to be in spirit and truly connected to family and friends. We had so much in common.

Lorraine had gone through six years of being alone and re-discovering her own spirit and who she really was. She was strong and ready for another relationship, although meeting another sportsman was probably not on her list. But as chance would have it, she noticed in me a growing spirit and replenished soul and so she gave me a chance.

We soon discovered the compatibility that would provide the foundation for our relationship. We had the same priorities – our loving children, supportive family, loyal friends, nature walks, positivity, R&B soul music, romantic movies, healthy food and quality wine, getaway travel, white sandy beaches, fashion, art, candles, sleeping, cooking, small parties, barbecues and so on.

We took our time and slowly grew together through our fortnightly rendezvous and occasional trips away. We put our children first and made sure they were safe and loved. Motherhood is everything to Lorraine, and she is a champion at it. As it has been for me, raising children has been the ultimate experience in her life.

During 2006 Lorraine entered the hit TV show *Dancing with the Stars*. She was partnered with professional Aaron Gilmore, a lovely, honest man with a young family. He proved to be the ideal mentor and partner. The series ran 14 weeks and they trained 30 hours a week. It was a major challenge for Lorraine, not only the physical workload, but the fact she was re-entering a very public spotlight. She thrived on the dancing, learning 10 new Latin and ballroom dance styles. She had already learnt the art of Argentinian tango, but this was a different set of rules because it was performed live in front of a large studio audience in Television New Zealand's Avalon base.

It soon became clear that Beatrice Faumuina, the 1997 world champion discus thrower, would be the bookies' favourite. Lorraine and Aaron were initially ranked as outsiders on the TAB books, but soon became the public's favourite with their combined style of flair and flow across the floor. They made the final and took out the title. I flew down every Saturday to look after Jasmine, massage Lorraine's feet and watch out of shot in the Avalon studio. It was a nervous but exhilarating time. I couldn't help but admire the courage and commitment of a beautiful woman, very much the love of my life.

Lorraine showed an inner calm and a spirit that inspired me. She talked a lot about Wayne Dyer, the American self-help author and motivational speaker, and Oriah, who wrote three amazing books on personal well-being. I was soon following her lead and focusing on

finding a similar peace within. I continued my therapy work and that helped fill in many gaps in my life. The angel in waiting had become the guardian angel.

Those were incredible, surreal days. We often still say: 'Wow, those were the days."

After two years of commuting we started to consider moving in together. The dilemma was which city. Lorraine's family were all in Auckland, as was Emma, while Hilton was ready to stay with his father in Wellington. After much consternation, Lorraine and I decided to move Jasmine with us to live in Auckland. Jasmine would be able to further her ballet aspirations and we could start a new life near our immediate families.

In late 2007 we drove from Wellington to Auckland and unpacked just before Christmas in a new home we had bought in Kohimarama. The first year had its adjustments, but we soon settled into a hard-working mode, Lorraine with her image consultancy and me at Sky TV, while Jasmine settled into a new school.

Lorraine loved being back among her own family, especially seeing her mother and three sisters regularly, but she badly missed Hilton as he entered adulthood, as well as her close friends of 21 years in Wellington.

We threw ourselves into our various family lives, the one where we lived with Jasmine, and the other two homes where Emma and Hilton lived. We made the best of it through constant communication and visits.

Our wedding day was magical. As the rain poured down, a lucky sign they all said, Lorraine and I shared our vows in front of them all. We were surrounded by love and joy as we became husband and wife for life.

Everything I had dreamed about was now a reality, a beautiful marriage, a thriving family, a secure (if not fun) job, steady health, and a growing enlightened soul and spirit.

I was grateful for a second chance. I was living the dream.

What more could I want?

Left: Who wouldn't have voted for her! Lorraine and dance partner Aaron Gilmore. *Photo, Neil Mackenzie*

Lorraine and me on our wedding day. The world couldn't have seemed brighter.

CHAPTER 11

Shifting Goalposts: Rugby Channel

Winter 2009

When I told Lorraine I was in charge of the Rugby Channel, she was taken aback. She had spent the previous 20 years surrounded by rugby (her former husband being an All Black) and it seemed it was back to haunt her again. I felt awful and vowed not to let rugby have the same effect on our lives. It was to be just a job.

Over the summer of 2009 I reflected on what I had done wrong to be sacked. I made a mistake by speaking publicly. Even though I was on holiday as a former New Zealand cricketer, I had no excuse because I was also the executive producer at Sky. I acknowledged I had got it wrong. I also acknowledged that I had a new opportunity to embrace and that I would throw everything I had at making the Rugby Channel something cool. So I was pleased with the outcome, but wary of the way it was handled.

Immediately, I asked marketing for assistance to find out what the market, and in particular the subscribers, thought of the Rugby Channel. They obliged and ran a survey asking a variety of questions, taking polls and testing the market for likes and dislikes. It was invaluable and straight away I got a feeling for what the fans would be attracted to.

First, I removed what they hated – constantly repeated games from the past with no context or analysis. They were boring shows with no relevance or energy, and with old graphics and old music. The channel had been running six years, but nothing had changed in its look or content. A core of 40,000 subscribers supported the channel all year. They were the die-hards who wanted rugby, rugby, rugby, around the clock.

Marketing asked questions about presenters. Unprompted, the majority asked why Keith Quinn, former Television New Zealand commentator, wasn't involved in rugby presenting or commentating any more. Internally, there were objections to his inclusion, but my attitude was whatever the fans wanted, they should get. They were the people paying good money.

With Quinn and rugby, it was the fans' almost unanimous call that he be involved in the Rugby Channel. After all, he was the voice of rugby. Ultimately, it wasn't about what I or anyone at Sky thought, it was about what the fans wanted.

I signed Keith immediately. He was to become the face and voice of the channel, along with former All Black prop Bull Allen, who appealed to the younger fan base. Together Quinn and Allen provided a massive shift in the appreciation of the channel. They provided the personal touch, the passion, the humour, the history and the fundamental joy that rugby gave New Zealanders.

Keith opened for us with a nice warm feel-good show called *Test Match Stories*. This series invited former All Blacks to talk about the tales of the tours, the characters and the camaraderie of the mighty All Blacks, along with footage going back to the 1950s. Keith was outstanding and the show became a feature of the build-ups to live All Black tests.

During 2009 I received an email from Ken Laban, former league player turned rugby commentator. He offered three ideas to give the Rugby Channel a point of difference: women's rugby, Sevens and First XV college rugby. He also mentioned touch rugby as a growing community sport.

Sometimes in life, good ideas hit you between the eyes. The words "First XV" had that effect on me that day. I knew it was a magical idea. I began gathering stories about great First XV rivalries, compelling local derbies, and put them to air on our new weekly show *RugbyCentre*. It started to resonate with the viewers. We all knew that First XV rugby was the lifeblood of the game in New Zealand, but we had never seen it live on television, apart from the very rare game many years ago.

In April 2010 we launched live First XV coverage, from all around the country. We embraced the Saturday afternoon slot that had become vacant owing to night rugby. We built the coverage from scratch, turning up to schools and building scaffolds to broadcast off, designing a run-down that would enable all the schools' rituals to be incorporated into the broadcast. We chose two callers to commentate, plus a colour analyst alongside – three broadcasters instead of the two that Sky used for most other rugby games.

Leading from the front were Quinn and Allen, closely supported by John McBeth, Steve Davie and the pioneer of the idea, Ken Laban. The team gelled beautifully, sharing the coverage up and down the country. The schools made each visit memorable. Making the live television was great fun. Crowds flocked to the games, the media jumped on the bandwagon and Sky itself acknowledged a new champion with subscriptions climbing to 75,000. Sky also upped the budget so we could cover 35 live games by 2012. We'd started with 25 in 2010 and that had grown to 30 in 2011.

The true sports fan loved it: watching the best schoolboy rugby, the traditions, the rivalries, the free-flowing spectacle as young men went out and played for their school jersey. Reunions sprung up from all over,

The Rugby Channel's front row of commentators, Keith Quinn, left, Ken Laban and Bull Allen.

sponsors lined up for inclusion, and the fans were happy to subscribe ($2 a week) to see it all.

Keith Quinn became a true champion in my heart. Never have I worked with someone so genuine, loyal, passionate, flexible, knowledgeable, devoted and inspiring in his humble, self-effacing way. He had no ego. He had only love for what he was put on this planet to do, to call rugby games. I was a lucky man to feed off such a skilled operator. For three years I felt privileged. The others were no different. They all gave it everything and thoroughly enjoyed the ride.

I felt pleased that I had responded well to my sacking from cricket production, had tackled a new role and come up with the right results. I hoped that it would put me back in a good light when it came to new opportunities within Sky. But the reality was that no-one knew where they stood. There was zero communication and sharing of vision, so it was a simple case of boxing on in one's own silo. So box on is what I did. But getting boxed in was going to be the over-riding issue.

CHAPTER 12

Mid-life Madness: One Last Time

Winter 2011

Call it a midlife crisis, but in mid-winter 2011, I crazily set the goal of wanting to be playing good senior club cricket at the age of 50. My rationale, if there was one, was to drive myself to a high level of fitness, while believing that batting at the other end with a young rookie would be helpful to whoever that might be.

So I announced the "going back" to Cornwall Cricket Club, my first club, and booked in for a personal trainer, a muscle balance specialist, an optometrist, a nutritionist, and a weekly net session.

It was a blast. First, Brett Howes, my optometrist, put me through the exact same hand-eye and balance tests he performed on me in 1992. There were two tests, one where I stood at a board with flashing lights and chased the moving light with my hands, the other standing on a wobble board reacting to the moving light in forward, back or sideway motion. He pulled out the results from 1992 and declared that in 2011, I was 25 per cent faster than 19 years earlier. How?

Brett said my eyes were stronger than ever, my hand reactions were faster and, unbelievably, my balance and movements were better, too. We assumed that the latter was because of a successful knee operation that stabilised the knee and gave me better balance overall, compared to 1992, when my knee was shot.

One of the reasons I felt compelled to play again was purely because the knee and body in general felt pain-free, compared to the latter part of my career when the body was on the brink. I had trained relatively hard in the Body Tech gym over the past five years and so I thought that while it was a huge gamble, there was nothing to lose.

I stated very clearly from the outset that the one issue I had coming back to play competitive cricket was going to be running between the wickets. I hadn't run or sprinted since 1995, so that was a major hurdle to overcome. My joints were simply asleep, having been inactive for so long. But with four months' solid work in front of me, I felt it was worth a crack. It seemed highly probable that it would end in tears with another injury, but I wanted to give it a go.

I absolutely loved the net sessions, chalking up more than 25 hours during the first three months. My technique was still there, but the quickness of feet not so. However, I worked on the footwork and sprinting side of things and felt it was coming together. I was batting well and felt mentally fresh and strong.

Yes, inevitably I had injuries along the way. The first was a popped left hip flexor because of a silly exercise that only a 20-year-old should do. I decided to go with a fitness programme that suited my 49-year-old body and to be flexible for each workout. If I felt good I worked hard, if I was stiff, I worked a bit easier, did more stretching, and so on. Then I pulled a left hamstring doing my first series of sustained sprints: totally understandable. After the hamstring came right and the fitness improved I took a week off and went to Fiji, but in the warm weather I over-trained and came back too stiff. Stupidly I played tennis and pulled my left groin running back for a lob.

By November 5, I was ready for the first match of the two-day competition that I had targeted. Trouble was, the Cornwall coach didn't want to pick me, so I played in the reserves instead. That brought a few complications because there were no umpires assigned to the game. Player umpires were used at that level. That can be fine, but the TAB, sensing the public were interested, placed odds on the number of runs I would score. That put a bit of pressure on everyone, because there was bound to be a few bets placed by people interested in the game. It was all meant in fun.

Second ball into my comeback I was hit well outside the line of off stump and given not out. Well, it caused a mini-riot from the opposition. Then the abuse came thick and fast as I batted out the remaining 45 minutes of the day for a steady and unspectacular 15 not out. I gave them a serve about showing the game a touch of respect as we walked from the field, but I was more frustrated and agitated with the Papatoetoe No 1 pitch, which was … well, a shitheap. How anyone, especially young talent, could prosper on such rubbish was difficult to see. Ironically, a $15 million indoor centre was only 70 metres away. I hoped that other senior club pitches were in better shape. Otherwise it could be an unpleasant summer.

So that was my first day back. I made it back to the Cornwall bar that night and cajoled the coach to pick me in the premiers for the second round of matches. He duly did, so I reached my first goal of playing premier cricket again, at the age of 49. The big goal for me was to be playing well enough to be justifying my place at the age of 50, the following season. It wasn't meant to be a one-off attempt, but I had set myself three years before the body would surely pack up for good.

Mostly, I enjoyed training and coaching some of the young guys at Cornwall. Practising with them felt like a great way also to instruct them, showing them what I knew, not just saying it.

In my comeback premier match, against Parnell, I fielded well, taking two sharp slip catches. Then we had an hour before stumps to survive. Early wickets fell, so I walked out against a newish ball and a fresh, young tearaway named Lachie Ferguson. It was a brilliant feeling to be out in the middle again, competing with bat in hand.

After ducking and weaving the first two balls aimed at my throat, I pushed a full ball into the covers for a quick single to get off the mark. Four strides in, I felt the left quad pull. Damn it. I tried stretching it out, but it was torn, three balls in and another injury to the silly old fart. Four serious muscle injuries in four months, all upper left leg, all compensating for a croaky right knee.

The quad injury was going to put me out for weeks. But something inside me said I should stop then and there. I batted with a runner in the second innings, scoring a fluent and pleasing 20 before getting a good delivery that hit the shoulder of the bat and ballooned to gully. My last competitive innings was over. For a brief period I proved to myself that all the hard work on my technique was not in vain, that I saw the ball really well and that I could still bat. Problem was, I couldn't run. At the end of the match I announced to the team, and those in the media who were interested, that I was pulling out for good. Simply put, the body kept breaking down, which was always on the cards. But after only three balls it was highly embarrassing. I felt stupid.

I walked away quietly to lick my wounds. Then I got an email from my cousin Russell. He was training hard for a series of movies and had lost a lot of weight and had also undergone a diet of supplements to support his training. He sent me the concoction he was taking and highly recommended I give it a go.

The key, he said, was to take masses of fish oil, glucosamine, D4, and selenium daily. So for the next month, until Christmas, I did. Then once my quad was right I hit the tennis court. It was incredible. I ran, twisted, turned, jumped, sprinted, slid and played for hours without even a hint of a tear or a strain. I was in the best shape I had been in for 20 years.

On January 7, I walked back into the nets at Cornwall and made myself available for any cricket going. Two days later I was back for another session. This time, though, we would play a practice Twenty20 game on an artificial wicket. Our quickest bowler opened up and started to beat the bat. Straight away an edge flew to me at first slip and I caught a screamer. In the third over, with the same quick operating, another edge was taken. This time it climbed up and away to my right side. As I followed it, it caught the end of my left thumb. The ball went through to the right hand and stuck, but as I fell to the ground it bobbled out of my right-hand grasp.

I looked at my left thumb and nearly died. It was a mess, smashed in four places, a multiple fracture, and a highly complicated break. That was it, out for good. I was devastated. I never went back to Cornwall again that summer. Instead, with my left thumb in plaster, I played tennis three times a week, never got injured, ran like a teenager, played like a man possessed and loved every minute of it.

I just wished it was with a bat in my hand.

CHAPTER 13

Turning Five 0: Redundancy

Winter 2012

In the final years the only time I got to speak to Kevin Cameron was in our six-monthly performance and development plan meetings. Every time he marked me down for a lack of communication. I chuckled because it was a touch hypocritical. Sometimes he caught himself with the contradiction and remarked on it. The meetings lasted a few minutes or so and that was it. I often asked how to improve my communication skills. But in the end if your bosses don't want to talk, share and work closely with you, then they won't.

Putting that aside, Kevin's work ethic was his badge of honour. He worked like a Trojan. Give him a major event like an Olympics or a Rugby World Cup and he was unbelievable in pulling it all together. He was the finest in the country at orchestrating that kind of sport production. It was part of the reason why we never saw or heard from him – he was head down organising things in minute detail. From 2005, he moved on from being our day-to-day leader to being the master of special events.

Mind you, it staggered many of us why Sky invested in an event like the Olympics, which lasts only 16 days and supposedly cost $20 million or thereabouts, when the pay TV model was always to invest in a competition that lasted a minimum of six or eight weeks, but ideally 26 weeks, like the NRL. That gave marketing, sales and promotion a chance to build up awareness, a proper following and momentum, and to secure new subscriptions and advertising. Apparently Sky lost $15 million on the 2012 London Olympics, despite it being a high-quality production led by Kevin. The consistency of sacrificing creativity for the bottom line went out the window with that project, which became an ugly contradiction. Life at Sky was indeed interesting. We had defeated the free-to-air opposition and now we appeared to beating ourselves.

Soon enough change was in the wind. Richard Last, a sales rep from way back who had started as an installer in the infancy of Sky, worked his way up the corporate ladder and was sitting tall as the new director of sport content and programming. Kevin was being stripped slowly of his 20-year stranglehold while he focused on expensive major operations. Richard Last became the golden boy with plenty of power to wield. Good luck to him – he had obviously worked hard to get to where he was, but the feeling around the traps regarding his appointment was cold.

It was fascinating to watch as the politics and games began between Kevin and Richard. It appeared Kevin didn't want to give up anything, especially as he had built Sky Sport from scratch, but Richard was ambitious and hungry and wanted the limelight. I got more than a few minutes one time when Kevin was keen to tell me about Richard's manoeuvres. Then the official changeover was announced. Kevin was retiring at the end of 2012 and Richard was taking over. The interesting thing from the sports department's point of view was that Richard had no experience whatsoever in television production, and he didn't like or even follow sport very much, with the exception of his beloved Chelsea football side.

Apparently, that was the whole idea – to come in fresh, strip out the excess fat, the creativity and the spending and just do the basics. The clock was ticking, the good old days with Nate Smith were long gone. I wondered where I would stand amid all the changes.

Still, I carried on my creative thinking, trying to find ways that fans, Sky and the Rugby Channel would all benefit. I proposed to Richard Last a three-year plan, with forecasts, to offer the fans a 12-months-a-year diet of live, local and exclusive coverage around three new rugby brands at three different times of the year. First XV was established from April through to October, but Sevens rugby wasn't. It was played domestically, but under no structure – a few tournaments played here and there to get ready for the annual Sevens finals in Queenstown, but no incentive to truly compete. I worked closely with New Zealand Rugby Union to set up a Sevens league. Each tournament would offer qualifying spots for 16 teams to participate at the finals. This was scheduled from late November until early January.

The third part of the puzzle was for the Rugby Channel to cover a new competition under a "Super A" brand I created. These were the five "A" teams of the New Zealand Super 15 franchise teams. I devised a competition in which most "A" games were curtain-raisers to the main local derby Super 15 games. When the top teams were out of the country, the fans could still go and watch the A teams, the up-and-comers, compete in their own competition. The benefit I felt the televised competition would have would be to expose the talent, coaches and referees coming through, as a stepping stone to Super 15 rugby. It would put New Zealand ahead of everyone else in the rugby world. The tournament would last two months, finishing in early April and ease nicely into the start of the First XV coverage.

The New Zealand union did well in getting the Sevens going in late 2012, but Richard Last wanted the matches on Sky Sport, not exclusively on the Rugby Channel, and he didn't really get the "A" idea. With the Rugby Channel being stripped of these new ideas and the chance for growth, it dawned on me that either I was going to stagnate, or my role would diminish in the new regime. I needed something new.

Richard Last began slicing and dicing, dividing and conquering, and recruiting to fill the voids. A new head of production role would be created to fill the gap that he knew nothing about. I applied with confidence. My references were kind and supportive.

Keith Quinn said about me in his reference: "In 40 years of working with other TV producers, Marty is one of the best, if not the best, I have worked with. His organisation and planning is comprehensive and deep. The people who work for him 'know where they are' and can plan accordingly. His enthusiasm, innovation and consistent commitment make him a pleasure to work with. He covers all bases."

Nate Smith, former Sky chief executive, retired in Westport, Connecticut, wrote: "Marty embodies the quality that businesses often dislike but desperately need – the desire to change something before it gets stale. I saw that way back when he saw the world of cricket needed a shorter formatted game. Did all the ideas tested last? No, but it did move the code forward in its thinking. Marty may not always say what people want to hear, but that is why he would be the perfect choice."

Martin Snedden, having just completed running the greatest sports event in New Zealand history, said: "For Martin, sport is in his blood, part of his DNA. He demands excellence of himself, and those around him. He is not satisfied with just 'doing the job'; he wants to do the job the best way possible. That was true of him as a cricketer, and from my observations, is also true of him in business. He is intelligent and a thinker. He identifies issues and finds solutions. I watched him do this when he took on and triumphed over possibly the most fearsome fast bowling attack in history, the West Indies. Then he did the same when faced with a completely different challenge, spin in Asia. It wasn't only his natural talent that got him this far. It was his ability to work out how best to use that talent to nullify the opposition. His approach when head of cricket at Sky was the same. Cricket in New Zealand, and consequently the broadcasting of it, is full of challenges and problems. Martin vigorously identified issues and looked for solutions. He and I had many robust debates about those. I loved having someone with his approach to partner with. It was never about life being smooth and comfortable. It was about facing up to and solving impediments to high performance. Martin is not afraid of risk."

Richard Last didn't want to know about robust discussion or a partnership. Needless to say, I didn't get the job. By all accounts it had been promised months before to a relocating South African.

My reason to stay at Sky for so long was simply because I saw it as the only place to produce live sport in New Zealand. Every year, it seemed, the free-to-air networks lost further ground in being producers of sport. Sky therefore became the only bastion. As time went on Sky became a strong monopoly, so we all stayed.

I was content working for an organisation that fulfilled my passion and initially offered a freedom of expression to televise live sport. I was happy with the "doing". As I did playing cricket, I just wanted more. I wanted to grow to be the best I could be. I was a romantic fool to think that way, but playing cricket and making television were the only two jobs I had experienced, so there is no doubt I was a little narrow-minded in my outlook.

When Nate Smith left Sky in 2001 the fun disappeared. In hindsight, I spent a decade waiting for it to return, but I was naïve. As I have mentioned, bean counters took over to satisfy the shareholders and that was that. Those around me said similar things and felt the same. The soul of the place had slowly vanished. I assume a few of the large burgeoning organisations have this problem. It's a shame if that's the case. People stay for the security of a large, safe place, or they love the work, or the politics. In my case, I was realising that I wanted none of the politics. In the end it was the lack of adventure in me to look beyond television and cricket that left me stuck, stalling for time.

I kept telling Lorraine that I lacked purpose and that Sky made me feel worthless. I was becoming more and more restless and needed a new challenge. But what would it be?

As I contemplated the future, I also took time to reflect on the past. There were many ground-breaking moments at Sky of which to be proud. The list of new sports or competitions we launched over a long period was a highlight. Kevin Cameron carried the company over many humps and on to many milestones. I respected and admired him immensely for that. I was grateful for his early influence.

When I watched the documentary *Weight of a Nation*, the story behind the All Blacks winning the 2011 Rugby World Cup, I was hugely impressed. It was one of the best productions to come out of Sky. Directing and producing it all was Kevin. Putting on his working hat again, away from the executive role, he was in his element, making compelling television. He proved again that he was the one of finest television producers New Zealand has ever had. It was great to see him sign off from Sky doing what he was born to do.

In the ranks, there are many fine directors, producers and presenters to be proud of, following Kevin's footsteps. However, in the environment that exists now, whether they are being used properly is questionable. They are passionate people, but they feel they also aren't being heard from enough, and aren't encouraged to express themselves truly. World Cups and big events brought out the best in these folk for obvious reasons, but day to day, month to month, that essential, passionate feeling appears to be becoming more and more subdued.

In my view, Sky began to lose some of its relevance. It was losing touch with its core being: creativity, freedom of speech and nurturing the honest integrity of good, genuine people motivated to move their audience, to entertain and inspire, and to tell the story of sport. It had become purely a money-making business and in doing so had started to lose that true connection with the fans, and with its own workers. And though there was talk of change, of work being done to form a mission statement, I never saw it.

Ultimately, we all spoke of working for a sausage factory, a same-shit- different-day mentality. It was the end of an era. Where Sky goes from here will be intriguing to observe from the outside. It is extremely fortunate to have a monopoly in a small market, but if making obscene amounts of money is the absolute priority, then that's a real shame.

For me, one thing was certain: my time was nearly up and working fulltime at Sky was not going to be an option. Richard Last was on the move.

Indeed, as I started my 16th year at Sky TV (13 as a fulltime employee), I felt a lack of inspiration. Was it to be another year of being left alone by the bosses, no communication or sharing of ideas with fellow executives? Or put another way: same shit, different day.

With Richard Last having landed the director of sport job and Kevin Cameron to retire at the end of the year, change was in the air. Everyone sensed Last was planning and scheming, but no-one knew exactly what. You couldn't get a straight answer out of anyone. All I kept thinking was those words from John Fellet in late 2008: "Marty, play with the cards you are dealt."

On May 23, I got wind of something when Last said in the second of our newly arranged private one-on-one meetings that the executive producers in the end offices were underworked and overpaid. I looked up in surprise and saw he wasn't kidding. It was rubbish that we were underworked and overpaid. He had no idea what we did to make all the productions we had to. I felt I was doing everything I possibly could to make the Rugby Channel the best it could be. So did Last have a plan or was he just winding us all up? I rang Grant Fox for advice; his was a commonsense voice I always respected. He simply said: "Go talk to John Fellet." Later that day I met John and asked him if my time was up. Emphatically he said absolutely not, that he saw me as a long-term employee, following behind Last. I walked out hugely relieved, rang Grant, thanked him and told him I needn't have worried.

For months, Andrew Fyfe, the executive producer of rugby on Sky Sport channels, was paranoid and had been predicting we would all be fired by Christmas. I confidently bet him a bottle of wine that he would be wrong. On September 19, about mid-morning, I was sitting in the cafeteria having a coffee with my excellent producer, Andrew Hawthorn, when an email came through on my iPad. As I read it, my body went cold.

An awful chilling feeling enveloped my entire being, and my breathing shortened. I pushed the iPad to Andrew and he read it, too. Our eyes met and we both acknowledged the moment was significant and serious. All four executive producers were being summoned to Rick's office first thing Friday morning, September 21, the day before my 50th birthday.

I was up first at 8.30am. In a short presentation, it was explained that the four executive producer roles were being discontinued and a restructure would take place, offering three places as supervising producers, a role that was explained in detail. I quite liked the sound of the new role, with its emphasis on supervising up to eight different sports, events and shows over a calendar year. It looked challenging and motivating. Then the salary was mentioned – almost half the figure the executive producers were on. I was puzzled and confused. It was too much of a drop in salary for any of the existing executive producers to accept, unless they had nowhere else to go.

Legally, Richard Last was creating a divide in roles so he could open up the role to the whole market if he wished. Or perhaps Last simply wanted to see the last of a few of us and bring the younger brigade through.

It was becoming clear that I was not wanted, and nor were the others, with the exception perhaps of James Cameron, easily the youngest of the four. He had been an executive producer for only three years, after he took over cricket from me in 2009. I walked away fairly stunned, convinced that it was all over. I went to lunch with my 10 best mates in Ponsonby at Moochowchow and we celebrated the big Five 0 and drowned out thoughts of the impending redundancy with a superb feast of amazing food and wine.

The next day, September 22, I turned the halfway mark. I was hung over physically and mentally confused from the day before. The big day itself was a blur and uneventful, just a quiet family lunch to toast the milestone. But the cloud hanging over me was obvious. The next day was worse; I was listless and grumpy.

Lorraine and I were all booked to head off to Bali for a holiday on the Tuesday for my birthday treat, but I needed one more meeting with Last. I told him that I wanted to apply for the new job, but he quickly stipulated the salary would not change at all, that if it was him he would hate the drop. No kidding, I thought.

Last said Sky didn't want to lose me, so opened the question of redeployment. He mentioned it would be great to have me back in the commentary box. During our trip to Bali, I convinced myself it was time to go and try a new venture.

I wrote up a new business plan under the simple company name of MC – Martin Crowe – Consultant. I focused on the consultancy roles I wanted to play – mentor, creator, media and general consulting. I split them up into four pillars of the company and used M and C words in the creative pitch.

It looked promising and exciting to think of new challenges and adventures. Part of the new plan was to write my second book, so in the quiet and warmth of Bali I started to jot down the skeleton and bones of my "Second Innings", following on from my autobiography in 1995.

Arriving home on Sunday evening, October 7, I felt refreshed and invigorated. The next day I had two doctors' appointments – one a consultation for the removal of my upper wisdom teeth, the other for a second opinion on swollen glands I had recently discovered in my neck.

Before going to Bali, I had a needle biopsy to check them out. It had come back as good as gold, just a mild infection. But my fine doctor, Anna Twhigg, wasn't so sure. She booked me in to see a head and neck specialist, Mark Izzard, upon my return.

The day after I got home, Mark had a good nosey around the glands, neck and nose and asked very casually if I could pop in for a CT scan the following day. I didn't think anything of it. I was just back from a glorious holiday, wanted time with Emma, and had a few things to do around the house. While the redundancy issue was still on my mind, it wasn't stressing me any more.

The next day the CT scan was done and I carried on life as normal. Then the following morning, while I was dropping off Emma to tennis, the car phone rang. Emma was still in the car when Mark Izzard came on the line.

"Marty, I've got the results back from the scan."

CHAPTER 14

In a Heartbeat: Cancer Diagnosis

Wednesday, October 10, 8.45am.

In a heartbeat your life can change. In one word.

Cancer. Or try another, a more specific word.

Lymphoma. An incurable blood disease.

The CT scan had found other swollen and enlarged nodes in my stomach, as well as throughout my neck, my left armpit and my left groin. Again, my body went cold and breathless. I looked at Emma and she said: "Papa, what's lymphoma?" Thankfully Mark didn't mention the C word. I kissed her goodbye and raced home. I googled lymphoma, knowing it wasn't good news.

Yep, I had cancer. I was stunned looking at the iPad and reading about it. As I looked down, Lorraine came up the stairs with that beautiful smile, not suspecting anything, and then I burst into tears. I couldn't speak a word. Instead I handed her the iPad and as she read she knew what it meant. The smile was replaced by that quiver around the mouth, as our eyes met we sank into each other's arms and cried. Jasmine came in and Lorraine summoned up some remarkable strength and told her daughter the basic truth. She took Jasmine downstairs so I could breathe and then I just collapsed on the bed. It is truly painful to know you have a deadly disease. To what extent I didn't know, but just the word cancer sends a shudder through your body. Lorraine rang my mum and my sister Deb, and I tried to speak to Emma's mother, Huhaana. It was hard piecing any words together.

Mark ordered a surgical biopsy the next morning to remove a core sample from the neck to determine the extent of the cancer. A few days later Mark rang with the news of the biopsy. It was follicular lymphoma. It was treatable, but not curable. What also rocked me was the timing in relation to the impending Sky redundancy.

Just as in early 1996, when within days my cricket career was forced into retirement and my first marriage collapsed, it was a classic case of when it rains it damn well buckets down. I was facing multiple stresses. Again.

I felt so bad for Lorraine, who had been through a year of supporting loved ones with the same problem. Worse, she lost a close long-time friend only months earlier. Her stress levels were already high, so this was the worst nightmare.

Lorraine and I decided that if we didn't release something publicly it would get out and circulate, become rumour and gossip and the media would start hounding us.

So on October 15 at 8pm we released the news. The statement simply said that I had follicular lymphoma, wanted to be left alone in my hour of shock, and to contact Louise Henderson, our business manager, for any queries.

First thing the next morning, I went around to wake Emma (and Huhaana) and explain what was happening before she got to school, where naturally word would have spread because it was public knowledge. I explained that I had a disease that would be treated, but I would be a bit sick for a few months. Emma looked calm and assured by my voice. She felt safe and she would handle it okay. I dropped her off at school and gave her another reassuring smile. Underneath I was in shock at what I had to tell her.

As I went home, I tried to gather my thoughts and calm down. But the reality was so severe that I just released it all. In those moments you become paralysed with fear. The fear of dying and leaving behind the ones you love so much becomes a flash in your mind. All I could do was lie still and breathe deeply.

I started to read specialised books and went on online to find out about lymphoma. After a few days I knew about the various lymphoma types and the treatments and potential percentages of success. Reading that I had an average of seven years to live or a 60 per cent chance of making remission was not very heartening. My concern was what grade I had, or what stage the disease had spread to. Was it in the bone? Was it in any tricky places? That was all to be revealed after further scans and biopsies over the next few weeks.

Immediately, I had a real problem. I had tinnitus, a loud high-pitched ringing in my ears. It happened as soon as the shock of the cancer news hit me. Out of the blue I began to experience an awful, unrelenting sound that I couldn't shut down. My sleep went out the window. I tried everything – ear plugs, iPod on through the night until I finally dropped off to sleep, or listening to loud white noise from radio static. I was in a state of panic at times from the horrible tinnitus.

Basically, my neck and shoulders were carrying so much stress that the nervous system in that whole area broke the threshold and sparked off the hideous screeching din. It was like the sound of a wave of cicadas. The problem was that the sound connected into the beat of my heart and became a pulsating orchestra! I drowned it out with constant music and meditation.

When I was in a quiet place I decided I had no choice but to listen to the orchestra as if it was music, even laughing at the absurdity of it, and therefore removing the stress of it. Soon it started to subside, become less of a nuisance. But it never went away.

The scans and further tests were exhausting and stressful. On top of that I had to have two wisdom teeth removed as well as a broken molar, so as not to interfere with any future treatment. That set me back a week.

During this time I went back and read the 25,000 words I had written in Bali. I was shocked to see all the stress right there in the pages. It occurred to me that I was obviously ill because of what had transpired over the previous 20 years, but in particular the amount of emotional turmoil I went through and I how I handled it, or didn't handle it. It was all emotional stress.

I then searched for books of stories of cancer survivors, those who had been through hell and back. I needed to understand the emotion that was involved in creating their illness and their reaction to it. I ploughed through heaps of books and gained inspiration for what to do, how I could manage myself. Slowly, a plan was forming in my mind and I knew I had to start making decisions about what help I would need to get through.

I was overwhelmed with support from all over the world. It came flooding in and it hit me very emotionally. Former team-mates and opponents made tributes, almost as if I was on the verge of dying or had already died. Greg Chappell, Barry Richards, Mark Nicholas, Ian

Botham, Tony Greig and Ravi Shastri, to name a few, all rang from overseas. It was all positive and appreciated.

All my loved ones were there. Deb, my sister, was simply amazing. She was there with stacks of loving support. Jeff rang in concerned from Florida. Poor Mum too. She was no doubt beside herself with worry, but kept calm and loving. Lorraine's family were fantastic, as were my close mates, who gave me room, but also a shoulder when needed. Lorraine was unbelievably strong.

I couldn't lose with this team around me. All I needed to do was select a team of experts who would guide me through this period and assist in the healing. Most of all I needed expertise about how to deal with my emotional state, the present one and the one I would need in future. Clearly the old one hadn't worked. I was trading that one in.

I soon came to the conclusion that my cancer was entirely an emotional problem. That's what hit me like no other feeling of the many millions I was going through. I truly believed that was the case with me. To my mind, the reason I became so ill stemmed from my problems of being thrust into the limelight so early and missing out on normal emotional development over the following 30 years.

Too often I failed to come up with the right emotional response to the obstacles and challenges that life inevitably throws at you. It happens to us all, but I couldn't handle it emotionally. What I did was suppress the emotion instead of releasing it and letting go. I would take it all so personally when really it wasn't meant to be personal. It was just stuff that I should've ignored. Then I began constantly internalising it in my mind, going over and over it. I never learnt to express those emotions properly, so as time went on I became more reluctant to do so. I was in the spotlight in a small country, where showing emotion isn't always easily accepted or understood, so I kept it within. That wasn't healthy.

My follicular lymphoma was a slow-growing, indolent blood disease, a snake in the grass, moving slowly and quietly through my body, infecting all the nodes that are supposed to fight back. The lymphatic system has a natural highway of stopping points and if they are infected, it causes long-term havoc. I suppose when the snake senses you have dropped your guard emotionally and have become stressed, it wakes up and moves to the next point. It builds an empire of small malignant stations it can control and grows from there. And you would never know because it happens ever so slowly.

Who knows when this all started? Most probably, when I really started to feel stress in my life back in the mid-1990s. Of course, there would have been periods of months, even years, where life was so good, like when Emma was born or when I fell for Lorraine, and the snake would have just slept with nothing to feed off. He would probably just roll over and lie in the sun and rest up, happy to wait until Uncle Stress popped in again.

My last year at Sky was another period of stress. The constant worrying as to what was happening, leading to my unhappiness in the Mt Wellington offices. My life needed a change and a pick-up, but instead the snake had moved fast enough in the last 12 months to raise his head by putting a lump in my neck, then a few more. We found the snake after a few scans and a good look around and he was everywhere through my lymphatic system. So my desired change came in the biggest shock any human can get.

On October 29, 2012, I found a book placed on my bed by Lorraine, passed on to her by Deb. The book was called *Cancer: Don't buy its terror tactics*, by Diana Newcomb. I started reading and found Diana was a cancer survivor. She had identified the reasons behind her cancer as being emotional. As I read the words I stopped and looked to see where this woman was from. Incredibly she was from Matakana, just minutes away from my sister and only an hour from my home. I googled her and saw her counselling web site and emailed her immediately. She replied within an hour. I was booked to see her four days later.

In that moment I felt an edge of anxiety lift and that I had, through this woman, indentified the very core issue to my own survival and healing. My emotional being was about to get a long overdue overhaul.

The journey to my real truth had just begun. Lymphoma had come as a real wake-up. Then came the other: Sky Television.

At Sky, Richard Last completed his cull. On November 2, all four executive producers were made redundant. This happens in life and it's how you respond that's most important. I was happy enough. My break in Bali in early October had given me the chance to work out that this was an excellent opportunity to leave and start afresh.

What I hadn't banked on were the mind games Richard Last wanted to further play concerning me. On September 21, he offered me redeployment of some sort, but wouldn't exactly elaborate, except the mention of "commentating". The form of redeployment would be as a freelance contractor doing some work for Sky, because "Sky doesn't want to lose you," he kept saying. I took it as goodwill gesture and while in Bali had emailed him and John Fellet some ideas, suggesting commentating and continuing to produce First XV rugby could be the two main roles I could play.

Yet by November I still couldn't get any idea of what exactly they were offering. Oddly, I received no word from John after my email from Bali, not even a get well note regarding my cancer when it was known. On November 2, I popped in to see him, to say Last was being difficult. But John was distant and not forthcoming as he had been previously. He comforted me to say his father had also had lymphoma and lived to an old age and I gave him a great book about Howard Cosell and Muhammad Ali as thanks for my time as an employee.

Richard Last knew I needed a decision about deployment because my cancer treatment was the priority and that I didn't need any unnecessary stress to upset the start of that treatment. Instead, he delayed, dismissed and fobbed me off. He even sent an email to everyone at Sky saying I had signed a freelance deal and would be around the offices in the future. Yet I had never seen or heard one word of any proper contractual or official arrangement. The news got leaked to the media and all of a sudden I was down to be commentating for Sky come Christmas.

I was livid and stressed by such arrogance and corporate stupidity. When I finally got an offer via Tex Teixeira, the new head of production, late on November 5, I was offered only a 10-month contract with a clause allowing for a one-month notice termination at any time for any reason. The remuneration was insulting and I realised I had been played all along in what seemed like a ploy so I would remain positive and quiet about the redundancy, because the media had wind of that, too.

On November 7, I had had enough, walked in to Sky, cleared my desk, walked into Tex's office and told him to tell Richard Last to shove the freelance contract. I walked out never to return. It was the most liberating feeling I had had for some time. Last had inadvertently presented me with the freedom to walk and be owned by no-one, let alone by Sky. He had made it so untenable that my decision to walk for good was crystal clear and vital to my well-being. I was letting go of my fears and negative emotions around work. They paid me a redundancy after 13 loyal years as an employee and I left with head high ready to throw myself into my treatments, ready and willing to get rid of the first snake, this hideous cancer.

Two snakes. Surely it couldn't be a case of three in a row?

After the first six weeks of recovering from the shock of knowing I had follicular lymphoma, I revisited my haematologist, Richard Doocey, on November 29. I had had more blood tests and was waiting for the complete prognosis as to what treatment lay ahead.

Under the microscope the cells were not dividing and multiplying. The snake was lying still. The tumours themselves were all under 3cm, the biggest being 2.7cm in my neck, and there was no sign of it in my bone marrow. That was great news. He said I was being placed in the "wait and watch" group and to check in with him every few months. He said whatever I had been doing in the last month was working and to keep it going. I described my natural "complementary" approach to him in detail, and waited for his verdict. He said it sounded good, especially the approach to stress through counselling and meditation.

Discipline was my mode of operation. Every day I would need to do any number of things to ensure my health was improving. My first activity every day as soon as I woke would be to meditate quietly on my own, either listening to meditation CDs on my iPod, or to sit still and affirm to myself the positive statements that I needed to carry me through the day. I felt that gave my mental state a chance to be quiet and to shut down the ego voice before it got going, before I was exposed to the goings-on of the outside world.

This session was vital to heading off the constant chatter that often invaded my head space as a matter of habit. I began the process of letting go unnecessary stuff that lived within me. That's where the discipline came in. Whenever my ego voice would start up the talk and the constant questioning, I would reply with the words: "I don't care." That way I removed the conversation.

I needed to be disciplined enough to continue to nip it in the bud. It had dominated my psyche for 30 years, so it wasn't going to be a pushover. I had to respect the ego was always lurking inside and that only discipline would keep it at bay.

It was critical that I got into a routine to remove all the stress I was feeling from all corners.

Once I was awake and the tinnitus started, I got up straight away and made myself a cup of green tea and got stuck into my meditation. The green tea set up my body with something invigorating and clean. After a half-hour of meditation I would head out for some exercise – a quiet walk with Lorraine along the beach or through the forest up at the farm were my favourites. Once that was done and I began to feel hungry I started my all-important diet for the day. Fresh fruit or freshly squeezed juices were the two obvious ones. Now and then I tried the Budwig diet, which consisted of freshly-ground flaxseeds mixed with cottage cheese, while adding an assortment of nuts, honey and cinnamon for flavour and crunch.

Completely out of my diet went flour, sugar, grain and dairy products. I removed red meat and cut back the red wine to just a glass a month. I relied heavily on fish for protein and ate leafy green salads or steamed vegetables daily. Snacks included apples, nuts, kiwifruit, pineapple, blueberries, strawberries and protein smoothies, which contained flaxseed oil.

My supplement intake was a large smorgasbord of vitamins and minerals, mainly vitamin C, B, D, magnesium, curcumin and selenium, plus a variety of products like co-enzyme Q10, Salvestrol, Resveratrol, mushroom, alpha lipoic acid, omega 3 and fish oil, as well as daily probiotics and digestive enzymes.

Twice a day, I drank a mixed concoction of baking soda, lemon juice, water and honey or molasses, which helped to alkaline my stomach and remove all acid. That tasted awful, so I blocked my nose and gulped it in one. Discipline for that was tough!

I did a few colon irrigations and also tried intravenous vitamin C and K3 to boost my immune system and, in particular, my energy. Once my energy was back to near full strength, I cut down the complementary medicines and focused mainly on curing my illness with a positive attitude and a shift in my thinking. I knew controlling and reprogramming my thoughts and emotions was going to be a key to my recovery.

For too long my mind had been guilty of thinking and believing the worst. That fear factor, again. But that was okay because my awareness was alive and I could tell when my mind was drifting and the ego voice was tricking me into deluded notions.

Interestingly, through a decade of my best batting I had applied a disciplined approach to my concentration in the middle, not allowing negative thoughts to infiltrate the task of watching the ball. It occurred to me that for most of the time since I'd retired I hadn't used those techniques in everyday life.

I guess the acute focus you get when a bowler is steaming in was the difference, plus the fact that it needed to work for only a few hours over a given period of time. I could switch it on and off when I wanted. When it came to my meditation and moments alone, there was no reason why I could not apply the same technique.

The more I thought about it, the more I realised that much of what I did as a batsman I could apply to my healing – discipline, visualisation, goal-setting, removing negatives, staying in the present moment, concentration and a steely determination and will to keep going, especially during the tougher days. I could do that. I would enjoy it.

My counselling with Diana Newcomb was massively important. She gave me the insight I needed, the tools and the information, the positive boost that I could do it, though it would take time. Her own struggle was the core to her total commitment to healing herself and her devotion to helping others. I wanted to be like that, to serve others. I wondered if I could one day be someone who could communicate to others who needed a push, or a helping hand. I felt it was a possibility.

Diana introduced me to the writing and philosophy of Stuart Wilde, an Englishman who became widely followed for his books and lectures on self-help and human potential. I immediately resonated with his strong beliefs and findings.

Everything around me started to appear differently. I saw things in people, in nature, in life in general, that generated love and goodwill, compassion and understanding, laughter and joy, peace, harmony and tranquillity. I even saw it in myself.

I liked this way of life. Deep down, I knew I was going to love life, without the emotional fear.

CHAPTER 15

Nasty Snakes: Open Wounds

Summer 2013

Despite my positive intentions to begin the all-important work, I couldn't believe what was around the corner. One more snake in the grass emerged. It was my old foe returning to taunt me like never before.

Cricket, to which I had devoted most of my life, was lurking with vicious intent.

On Friday, November 30, I was truly feeling on top of my game, doing everything I could to ensure a healthy road ahead. I had a good understanding of what lay ahead and felt a sense of liberation that I was finally free.

I couldn't have felt better considering all that had happened. I had clarity over my illness and on my new journey to find true peace, I had walked out of Sky for good, reinvigorated and free, and I had just that morning resigned from the talent scout job I was doing for New Zealand Cricket, something I had decided to do pre-diagnosis.

Then on Sunday, December 2, Ross Taylor rang me and my world changed again. He had just returned from Sri Lanka and suggested he wanted to withdraw from cricket. Shocked at hearing such a sad statement from a young man with the world at his feet, I asked him to explain what had happened for that to be even on his mind.

What he revealed was sickening. Ross told me the whole story since the appointment of Mike Hesson as the New Zealand team coach.

In the first three months, during the world Twenty20 tournament and the Indian tour, Ross felt Hesson had not shown him any public support or respect. Because of Hesson's attitude, it became clear to Ross that Hesson's long-term management plan didn't include him as captain.

Much of what Ross told me then has since been made public, but hearing it straight from my friend, from a good, honest New Zealander, who had tried so hard to do his best as a cricketer for his country, had a profound effect on me.

I learned about the meeting that had taken place on November 13 in Ross' hotel room in Galle, just three days before the start of the Sri Lanka test series. Hesson, Bob Carter (assistant coach) and Mike Sandle (manager) had walked into Ross' room and let him know in a plain, unambiguous manner that they did not rate him to continue as the test

Ross Taylor was a victim of the Machiavellian manoeuvrings of New Zealand Cricket, but at least the public seemed to understand what had gone on. *Photo, Fairfax*

captain. Apparently he was more of a follower than a leader.

That wasn't the end of it, said Ross. The following day, Hesson confronted him again and told him he would not be recommending him as captain for the tour of South Africa that was to follow a few weeks later. Ross said there was little he could do but nod and continue trying to prepare for the first test.

I tried to understand the motivation behind what Hesson and others in the team management had done. Ross was locked in as captain for the series against Sri Lanka. Did they want him to resign then and there?

New Zealand lost the first test when a second-innings collapse gave Sri Lanka the game, after an even first innings. Ross focused on the second test, in Colombo, and responded magnificently. He scored 142 and 74 and led his side to the first victory by New Zealand in Sri Lanka in 14 years. Ross was hailed as a hero at home.

But now he was back in New Zealand filling me in on the manoeuvrings that had taken place behind the scenes, and I felt sick. I felt desperately sorry for Ross and his story revived old feelings of my own travails with New Zealand Cricket over the years.

There followed weeks of public statements, claims and counter-claims, revelations and apologies. Bit by bit, more of the full story became public. I got more involved behind the scenes than I should have, given my fragile state of health. I had an email exchange with New Zealand Cricket board chairman Chris Moller, and I spoke to chief executive David White by phone when he was in Dubai on cricket business.

Gradually it dawned on me that despite some fine words to the contrary, New Zealand Cricket was hellbent on removing Ross as captain and replacing him with Brendon McCullum. There was to be no proper debrief, no calm assessment of the situation. At about this time, director of cricket John Buchanan (formerly the coach of the champion Australian team), who had backed Ross as captain, urged New Zealand Cricket to show more "integrity, trust and accountability". I could understand what Buchanan was getting at - I really couldn't see enough integrity, trust or accountability coming from New Zealand Cricket.

It appeared the push for a change of captain was coming from Hesson, but White and the New Zealand Cricket board seemed more than happy to go along with that.

There was a cursory conversation or two between New Zealand

Cricket and Ross, but it was clear the decision had been made. The whole thing was appallingly handled. White and Moller held a press conference and tried to run the line that there had been a misunderstanding, that Ross had been removed as captain only for the limited-over matches, that he was still wanted as test captain.

That story didn't wash in the court of public opinion. For one thing, if Ross was fine as test captain, what was the pressing need to confront him about his captaincy on the eve of the Sri Lanka test series? For another, how could he be a perfectly fine test captain, but so poor in other forms of the game that he had to be removed immediately? The words of New Zealand Cricket sounded more like spin.

Ross turned down the test captaincy, feeling it was untenable to continue after the way Hesson and New Zealand Cricket had treated him. Over the next few days, Ross spoke freely to the media and gave his version about everything that had occurred. In response, New Zealand Cricket stated fairly much the opposite. Ross was asked by media outlets if someone was lying and responded: "Definitely."

John Buchanan, a supporter of Ross Taylor. *Photo, Fairfax.*

I was proud of him. He continued to show his mettle as a man. The public judged that he was speaking truthfully. Few people who followed cricket bought the White and Hesson angle that there had been a miscommunication regarding the test captaincy. They looked ridiculous.

I was very fragile about this time. I took it very personally and felt my world cave in. My emotional stress level was flying through the roof. Lorraine was extremely worried, given the situation with my cancer. It wasn't just Ross I was crying for. I was reliving my own nightmares of 20 years earlier. New Zealand Cricket had done it again. I tweeted my disgust: "NZ Blazer burnt, Dec 7, 2012. RIP." It was a metaphor for my complete severing of ties with the worthless organisation that New Zealand Cricket had become in my mind. I vowed that it was finally all over and that I could not have any involvement ever again. My health was at stake.

Throughout the rest of the summer, more aspects of the debacle emerged. These included:

- Ross received an emailed apology from New Zealand Cricket a fortnight after the news of the debacle broke.
- Shane Bond, the bowling coach (who had strangely not been present during the infamous meeting in Ross' hotel room when he was told he was not up to the required standard as New Zealand captain), wrote to David White to express his feelings about what had occurred. According to published newspaper accounts, a portion of Bond's letter read: "I believe the coach has been dishonest in his assertion around the miscommunication of the captaincy split with Ross. At no time in my conversations with Mike Hesson, that mostly included Bob Carter and/or the manager, was the captaincy split ever discussed. It was clear to me that Ross Taylor was to be removed from all three formats." I doubt Bond ever intended the letter to become public, and it must have been embarrassing for him when it did, but it was revealing all the same.
- Mark Geenty, The Dominion Post deputy sports editor, reported in Fairfax newspapers in late March that Bob Carter had approached Ross on the eve of the second test against England in Wellington and apologised for the way the captaincy affair had been handled. This tied in with what Ross had told me privately.
- At the end of the cricket season a long document, prepared by John Parker, after consultation with many other New Zealand cricket figures, was released. It was an ill-advised thing to do and really helped no-one. Some of what was in the document was correct, some was merely speculation. It achieved little because it was initially released anonymously, though Parker then publicly said he had

released it. My involvement with Parker - in about mid-December 2012 - was relatively brief. I had a short conversation and then an email list developed which I eventually asked to be removed from (and was), because I had my health concerns to worry about and focus on totally.

At a time when most New Zealand cricket followers were trying hard to move on after the unsatisfactory rumblings behind the scenes, the Parker document merely stirred up things again, and not in a positive way. It was clear to many of us who had been involved with New Zealand cricket that there needed to be change, certainly at board level. But I was doubtful if Parker assisted the situation by releasing his document. In fact, the board appeared to be accepting of a significant change down the line, so the main goal of improving the game overall appeared to be moving slowly in the right direction anyway.

Throughout the summer I watched Ross trying desperately to find his place in cricket again. He was so rocked by what had happened in and after Sri Lanka – not so much losing the captaincy, but the manner

Chris Moller, left, Mike Hesson and David White – three key figures in the Taylor affair. *Photos, Fairfax.*

it was done – that he made himself unavailable for the team that toured South Africa. While Brendon McCullum took over the captaincy, Ross stayed home and licked his wounds, trying hard to regain his joy for cricket.

In South Africa, the New Zealand side suffered two beatings in the test matches, but did much better in the limited-over forms of the game, winning the ODI series 2-1. Against the top team in the world, it was a most encouraging performance. McCullum himself batted bravely and several other players stepped up. What the team lacked, especially in the tests, was runs, and it was obvious that having an in-form Taylor back in the ranks would be a big plus.

Ross took a long break then returned to top cricket, first for Central Districts, then for New Zealand in the Twenty20 and ODI series at home against England. One remarkable fact was that every time he went out to bat he received fantastic crowd support, and often a standing ovation. It was the New Zealand public's way of telling him they believed him, felt for him and supported him. It must have been difficult for McCullum to keep being reminded of the public backing for Taylor, but it was a result of a situation that New Zealand Cricket had manufactured.

Ross looked a little at sea at first, though he fought hard and battled to a century in the second ODI match, in Napier. In the tests, he was clearly struggling. Gone was the commanding batsman on top of his game. He played one significant innings, 41 not out, to help save the test in Wellington, but otherwise was off the pace.

At the end of the season, he was named in the New Zealand team to tour England, but I really wondered what the international future held for him. He just didn't appear comfortable in a team in which Mike Hesson was the coach. Too much trust had been destroyed.

As I thought about Ross' problems during 2012-13, I reflected on the way another friend of mind, Mark Greatbatch, had been treated in recent years. Mark, one of our better test and ODI batsmen, has tried hard to make a contribution since retiring as a player. The good work he did, especially as a coach, in Central Districts, was followed by other positions. He was coach of the New Zealand team for a period in 2010 and has had other stints as a national selector and, for a time, as the man in charge of a selection panel also including Glenn Turner and Lance Cairns.

But for reasons that don't reflect well on New Zealand Cricket, Mark has been pushed and pulled, all seemingly on a whim. Promised jobs have not eventuated, or positions he has held have been abruptly terminated. The treatment he has received has been shameful at times.

People will call me blind, but there is no getting away from the fact that two of my friends, Ross and Mark, were both shafted. I make no apology for my loyalty to two fine men.

But it wasn't just those two. When you look back at our game over the past couple of decades, it is difficult to name a player who walked away from the game happy, celebrated and feeling worthy.

Too many long-serving servants got short shrift. Ken Rutherford got the same treatment at the end of his career as when he started. Danny Morrison was dumped unceremoniously after saving a test against England at Eden Park. Remember Nathan Astle's and Chris Cairns' departures? Or Fleming's sad exit? Or Shane Bond and the ICL rubbish? Or Lou Vincent, Andre Adams and Scott Styris and their departures? Young blokes entered the New Zealand Cricket system hungry, talented and ambitious, but left stripped of any worth, deflated and disillusioned.

I just hope that players from the next generation get a better send-off, a pleasant memory to savour. I hope that at least Ross Taylor is treasured as he should be.

Again, as with Sky, I felt a total liberation that it was all dead and buried. I had severed all ties with New Zealand Cricket. If there hadn't been such cruel treatment of one of my best friends, I probably would have remained hopeful of helping our floundering game, feeling it was my duty. It would have proved totally foolish and a continuation of the same insanity.

That it was over, for good, was the best treatment with which I could start. The key, however, was to make sure I never put myself in that situation again, or reverted to behaviour that would lead to resentment. While Sky and New Zealand Cricket were guilty of their attitude, I was no different. I had to change my ways – fast.

So there it was staring at me: three nasty snakes, three open wounds. To remove in one fortnight two snakes – Sky and New Zealand Cricket – that had dominated my life for so long was very important.

Ultimately, Sky and New Zealand Cricket represented pursuits that didn't fit with me; Sky with money, New Zealand Cricket with power, or the misuse of it. Anyone who knows me well enough will know that those two pursuits are not in my make-up. I learnt my lesson about money being a distraction when I got my first manager, and pride of performance has always meant more to me than needing power. For long periods, Sky and New Zealand Cricket represented my love and passion. Neither organisation did so any more. Therefore, while it was acceptable for others, it wasn't for me. I needed to remove them from my world completely.

One snake remained: lymphoma. I welcomed it for the message it delivered, but I wanted it to go, its message received.

On December 16, 2012, I realised just how much turmoil my mind was in, and wrote this to myself:

"My scheming ego self is a tough nut to crack. Give it the right subject and it will run riot, delivering its unrelenting diatribe. It is wicked and untrustworthy, unhealthy and unforgiving. Feed it and it will grow. Deny it and it will die.

"I realise that my spiritual self must step forward. Therefore I must discipline my ego mind and shut it down. When the little black thing (ego) starts chirping out questions and statements I must respond with, 'I don't care'.

"My struggle will continue unless I apply concentration to the task in hand. By drifting off to listen to the ego self I lose control. Use the discipline, the concentration, the affirmations and techniques that you used to use when you batted to shut out the ego voice. Shut it down.

"Have the courage to accept that it must change and that you can change it. Get to the place where you feel the words 'I am what I am', and that this is your truth. Replace struggle with peace and silence. Learn to unlock your silent power. Be non-judgemental, be loving, be compassionate, be understanding, be in harmony with nature and all around you, and the higher self.

"Remove the negatives with positive affirmations. Affirm that your being is still, is at peace, is secure. 'I am what I am'. 'Peace of mind is mine'.

"Focus on love for Lorraine, Emma and family. Focus on a healthy well-being and physical energy. Focus on what's important. Let the rest go.

"Today is the start of that discipline. Hold on to the cords that let one's spirit in, relish the silence and stillness, nurture the love and kindness around you, trust the unknown, embracing a new peace and harmony within."

On Christmas Eve I felt a nasty burning in my stomach, but it passed quickly. However, it was back on Boxing Day, and that time the stomach pain had me worried. I thought it might be because of a week of Christmas indulgence. I had had meat for the first time in eight weeks and two glasses of red wine on December 21 and a glass of wine each day after that. The stomach pain lasted 48 hours and then passed again.

I enjoyed a relaxing week up north over New Year, but then uncannily, while watching New Zealand being bowled out for 45 at Cape Town after McCullum had for some crazy notion decided to bat first, the pain returned.

Because it was the third time, action was required. So I drove back to Auckland and booked into see Mark Izzard for tests the next day.

That night the pain became severe, accompanied by nausea and the desire to vomit. Lorraine drove me to Auckland Hospital and the staff decided to check me in as Mr Vincent Brightside. That was novel, but the pain wasn't. They concluded I didn't need surgery, but that I would stay in overnight for tests on my lymphoma and digestive system. After having a gastroscopy – a camera search in the stomach – the next day the tests discovered "erosion", the start of an ulcer, on the duodenum, in my small intestine.

The following day, as Lorraine and I drove back up north for a quiet few days, I received a call from the haematologist on duty. The news was that I had a new and significantly large tumour in my stomach, near the duodenum. I was gutted, literally. The tumour had come from nowhere and grown to almost 4cm.

I knew in my heart that the new tumour was again down to emotional stress. There was no doubt the New Zealand Cricket-Taylor-McCullum drama had stirred me up, on top of the Sky redundancy, but the reality was that I had never been able to remove the emotional stress from the day I'd heard I had cancer. Such was my normal behaviour, the emotion I felt was overwhelming me and causing further problems.

I was back to square one. Worse still, the pain was becoming constant.

The disease in the cells was dividing and multiplying rapidly. I immediately rang Dr Doocey and he booked me in for an emergency consultation.

I was in desperate need of chemotherapy to reduce the growing tumour. Thankfully all the other lymph nodes were stable, but the new stomach tumour needed to be zapped so I could ease the pain. Ultimately, the chemo would kill everything and hopefully I would start again, with a chance to repair and restore.

One thing that really bothered me was that my voice was losing all its strength. It was dying as if sapped of all energy. It had become a weak horrible rasp. It reminded me of when Dad was diagnosed with his cancer and had only a few weeks to live.

The fear was back. I was back in the hands of my nemesis – my raw, fearful emotional state and chaotic mind.

CHAPTER 16

Letting Go: Let the Restoration begin

On January 24, 2013, Lorraine walked with me into Mercy Hospital to begin chemotherapy. Only metres from the main door I pulled aside and broke down. Lorraine grabbed me and held me tight. She knew how devastated I was feeling, learning I needed chemo. She knew I was not willing to put anyone through the next four months, but that I had no choice. I felt guilty. I felt humiliated that I hadn't controlled my emotions calmly enough to stop the illness. Maybe I never had a chance anyway. Maybe it was just more useless emotion I was feeling, a hideous spiralling of unnecessary emotions and feelings one after another.

Lorraine looked at me and said: "We will be fine, but you have to let go and accept it and slowly rise above it." She half-smiled that beautiful smile and I nodded: "I know." I was quiet all day, nine long hours of steroids and the body reacting, then more steroids. Finally the red poison, the chemo called R CHOP, was slowly, intravenously, injected into my body.

Going through chemo was not a good feeling, but I was over my feelings. They were becoming bloody annoying. I even heard my inner voice say that I was dying, that maybe I would be too much of a burden to the others and to myself. And so I began a mode of ignoring the inner chatter, these pointless emotions rising. I just shut them down, like I did when I took guard and faced the best bowling in the world. I put the game face on and that was that.

For the next seven days I went numb emotionally, while physically I began to waste. By the sixth day, I was incredibly weak. I'd lost 13kg over the previous few months, so felt completely listless and had a sense of not caring. But I wasn't depressed, or upset. I wasn't contemplating death either. For the first time in my living memory I felt and thought nothing. I took it as a good sign.

In those moments you accept your lot – the four months ahead, the lack of energy, the inability to offer anyone anything. That's the way it is. All those around me accepted that, too. The one thing I was not going to do to was to complain. I stuck to my mantra of this being a gift. I had asked for all this and now I needed all this and so I was bloody well going to accept all this.

I had watched a very sick Paul Holmes in an exclusive interview, in what felt like his final hours, talk of his life, what he had focused on throughout his career and therefore what he had missed out on with his family. He didn't have major regrets, but wanted the Lord's mercy for some things along the way that he had misgivings about. I thought he was incredibly brave to acknowledge out loud his need for mercy. I admired him for having the courage to say it.

Awareness, even in one's final hours, is not too late. For me, my awareness was hopefully going to give me a chance to write my own script, live my own life and fulfil my own spiritual needs for many years to come. More than anything I wanted to live a quality life with Lorraine, Emma and my family, but this time without the emotional fear or self-sabotage. I wanted to feel at peace when I eventually died. I wanted to leave my human nervous system and body with remarkable spiritual and soulful experiences, not false ego-driven ones. That was my motivation. As sick as I felt, especially once the steroids wore off, I was affirming the good work I had done over the previous month, despite the stomach tumour appearing. I needed to acknowledge that to keep the spirits going.

But while doing that, I wasn't quite able to recapture the discipline I had mustered previously. It was a battle to get into meditation mode. I would try, but I would drift off to sleep, or my thoughts would wander and I wouldn't have the energy to bring it back. Diana insisted that was okay and natural under the circumstances and that once the energy slowly returned, so would the discipline.

I tried to stick to those normal, immensely satisfying daily routines of having a slow walk and a chat with Lorraine, or picking up Emma and taking her to tennis or school each morning. It was exhausting, but it was enormously important.

My voice was getting worse and worse. It was an immediate signal to all I spoke to that I was struggling. It got down to a squeak, so having long conversations, even in counselling, was not enjoyable. I visualised the day when I might stand in front of hundreds of people and speak strongly and calmly about life and all its challenges. Again it was just a touch of motivation to reach out to something and aim for. This book was a voice, too, and I felt better every time I wrote, but I longed to be able to speak properly again.

By February 8 I was through my first course of R CHOP chemotherapy. The "R" stands for Rituximab, which belongs to a group of drugs called monoclonal antibodies. These are used to try to destroy some types of cancer cells while causing little harm to normal cells. Rituximab is used to treat several different types of B-cell lymphoma. It locks on to a protein called CD20, which is found on the surface of one of the main types of normal white blood cells. The body then quickly replaces any normal white blood cells that are damaged. "CHOP" stands for Cyclophosphamide, Hydroxydaunorubicin, Oncovin and Prednisolone. The first three are chemo drugs, Prednisolone is a steroid. Incidentally, CHOP is also my brother's nickname, so it was nice to know he was close at hand!

I looked back on the first course of R CHOP. For the first five days, when I kept taking the steroid pills, it went okay, but then it went slowly downhill. Once the steroids wear off, the body really does shut down. From days 6 to 10 my body was unable to function at all. I couldn't speak, because my voice went completely, I couldn't walk, or do much at all. At least I could eat, but my appetite was limited and I easily dropped a half kilo a day.

During those days I surrendered to the chemo doing its vital job.

I had decided going into chemo that I would hold off on taking any complementary supplements or treatments. I figured, after much reading and asking a few specialists, that for the chemo to truly work I needed my body not to resist, not building any strength at all, so it would be totally at the mercy of the poison drug. By stepping out of the way I was giving chemo every chance to kill everything in its path. I wanted the cancer removed, so I could enter remission for the long term. Despite my desire for energy, for relief and for any sense of being normal, I had to surrender and do nothing except cop whatever the chemo was dishing out.

Not having been through it before, I was a little thrown by the extent of the discomfort. It was a bit like the week when I had glandular fever in Hong Kong in 1992, but this time around I knew that it was only round one of six, a marathon not a sprint. I didn't pick up the phone much during this time because I couldn't speak and didn't have the energy.

I dragged myself off to watch Ross Taylor at Eden Park, but soon felt so wasted that I worried about driving back. Going through chemo on days 6 to 10 was not going to be my favourite period, but having gone through it once and felt my energy rise on day 11, I was pleased to have clarity about what chemo was all about. I could plan my weeks ahead knowing exactly what I would feel and what I was capable of.

The same applied to resuming counselling and meditation. I just couldn't concentrate through the rough period, but was relieved to pick it up again once I perked up a bit more. Exercise, too, became a necessary and enjoyable activity, and it was nice to be back reading and writing every day.

Importantly, through renewing counselling and meditation I began the process of forgiveness. In one of my sessions with Diana, she asked me to choose someone to forgive and see positively through visualisation. Geoff Howarth popped up in my mind, so I chose him. Through the session I began to see all the good qualities in him – his smile, silky batting, strong tactical leadership, a nice man. I saw him doing his best despite his own troubles, the pressure he was under. I had never seen him that way before. My resentment drifted away, and I developed a feeling of forgiveness for him and an understanding that he was only doing his best at the time. I

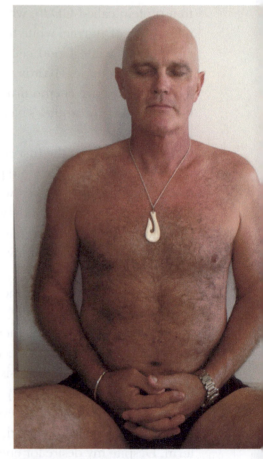

My body changed totally while I was undergoing chemotherapy. I lost my hair, lost a lot of weight and even lost my voice.

had reacted to him in the only way I knew how then, but it was time to let it all go. I forgave myself for reacting and harbouring those emotions the way I did. I let it all go, like a hot air balloon flying off into the clouds. The negative emotions towards Geoff were gone and I knew if I was to see him again I would see him for the positive qualities he possessed. It was a massive moment for me.

I continued this visualisation of others, John Bracewell being a key one. Each time, I sensed I was truly healing myself, removing the toxic emotions that had manifested so long deep in my stomach. Forgiveness of all that happened, of the people involved, and of me, was a necessary and critical process in my healing. As Diana said, it was going to be a work in progress. I needed to be diligent and disciplined when it arose, going to painful places, facing them full-on and removing them all. The raw emotions of Sky and especially New Zealand Cricket were still bubbling away, but were nowhere near as bad as a few months earlier. I was moving slowly into a quieter place of clarity and peace.

Clarity was indeed a beautiful tonic. Knowing what was coming with the chemo gave me mental strength. I could visualise it, imagining coping with that awful feeling of being wasted and the surrendering. And I got a clear picture of how I would feel at the end of it. Without all that, I knew that fear would return. I was over fear that paralysed my life. I ignored the thought as soon as it entered my head, imagining I would grab the thought as a piece of paper and screw it up and throw it away.

By the end of round two of chemo in early March, I was fully aware of the vigil, the necessary evil of injecting R CHOP into my body. It was pretty simple; the first 10 days were horrific as the poison moved swiftly through my body, killing the weakening cancer cells and hopefully sparing a few healthy ones.

While feeling lifeless, I resorted to basic meditation and some reading, but even exercising was hazardous. I was a zombie through this period. All my hair had fallen out, the taste in my mouth was metallic, the nausea was constant and my tinnitus did my head in. What was really tough was not truly connecting with those I loved, being unable to give much more than a weak smile here and a cuddle there. Conversation was draining and afternoon sleeps became mandatory.

I wrote less, wary of too many mistakes, too weary to find insightful thought. Through "the trough", as the doctors called that 10-day period, I just let it be as much as possible. At times my ego voice would pop in for a chat and ask: "Can you really endure another 14 weeks of this?" That's when I would slip on my iPod and drain out the chatter with some theta brainwaves meditation or a Deepak Chopra sutra. Surrender. That's all I could do in those darker times. Then I'd come out of the trough and enter the last 10 days. There would be massive relief as I ventured back into some sort of normality.

Going through chemotherapy was going to be tough, but if it didn't kill me I would come out so much better in the end. The process of going back into the past and forgiving was also going to be tough. That had begun and I could already see the fruits of removing those unwanted demons. It was all part of the healing process.

Ultimately, I had to ask myself some hard questions:

Do I really fear being a failure or being successful again?

Of course I want to be the best I can be. But maybe the shift is in serving others, not serving my own selfish needs or ego. Can I not just be, and do, and be happy? Do I need feedback and judgements to feel worthy? No. If I give out love it will come back to me and I can find and live my peace through that.

Do I want to live?

Of course I want to live. But I want to live a life that is fearless, that is without judgement or scrutiny, let alone have any negative emotions of hate, resentment or grievance. I am so tired of that life, of fighting, of ego, of trying to win opinion and of needing acceptance.

What I truly look forward to is the opportunity to start a new life, write a new script, read some new lines and enjoy new experiences ahead.

That constant mind chatter has to be over. My judgement and fighting days have to be done and dusted and the resentment and the grievances all in the past. I am ready, I am so ready.

Removing some of that raw emotion instead of suppressing it, quietening the mind instead of feeding it and reaching a natural balance is my destination. Finally, just being me and accepting it.

I have to get to the point where I can say: "I am what I am. I accept that."

I will.

PART TWO: FOR THE LOVE OF THE GAME

Introduction

This part of the book is purely about cricket, a bit about what's going on in New Zealand, but mainly about cricket around the world. It is where I call upon all I know about the game, the issues it faces, the future, the lessons from the past, the history, the great players and teams. In this second innings of the book I focus on all that is great about test cricket, the protagonists, the movers and shakers and the dream teams from the main nations that have played test cricket.

I spend time talking about the major issues that face the game – Twenty20, IPL, technology, the spirit of cricket, chucking, the future tours programme and the scheduling of the international calendar using three formats. I love what the game stands for – its integrity, cricket's reach to fans who pay good money and where the game fits into society.

I begin this second part with the crisis facing New Zealand Cricket and its place globally. In particular, I expand on the saga of Ross Taylor and Brendon McCullum, another example of poor New Zealand Cricket administration. I look closely at these two personalities and the need for them to stand side by side. I also look at the influence Stephen Fleming has had on our game, and how influential he could become. Finally, in a reflective mode, I look at a group of New Zealand cricketers who touched my heart and epitomised everything I loved about playing for my country.

I hope you enjoy my top 100 test players of all time and my Dream Test Match story, conjured up from my love of the game. There are also dream teams from each country and a special Bible for batting purists about how to score a test century – what the century-makers do.

There is much to tell in these next pages. But first let's start with the latest saga, one of the saddest stories in New Zealand cricket history.

CHAPTER 1

New Zealand's Dilemma: Taylor or McCullum

New Zealand Cricket can't afford to mess with our best players. But they do it time and time again. Lately, they have messed around with two fine players, Ross Taylor and Brendon McCullum, and even pitted them head to head in shameful circumstances.

The Too Easy Kid

Ross Taylor is one of the most honourable and easy-going men I have met in cricket. His only fault, which doesn't qualify, is that he is a little shy. His most common reply to me whenever we have spoken is to say: "Too easy, Hogan, too easy." So I now call him "Tuisi". He is "The Too Easy Kid".

Mark Greatbatch tells of the time when Ross, aged 12, invited him into his school dressing room and asked him to be a mentor for the day. Ross wanted to learn. Out of the blue, never having met the man, he rang me in 2006 and asked for private coaching lessons in Auckland. He flew himself to where I lived and we got cracking on the fundamentals of how to play the best attacks in the world.

I was impressed by his approach and manner. He became a trusted friend; there was no business arrangement, no commission, no fee – just an occasional exchange of wine, mostly from me because whenever I dared him he delivered another ton.

It was a privilege to help a man fulfil his dream and achieve his goals – to score more hundreds and runs than anyone else, to be the best the country had produced. I couldn't think of anything better for a young man to aspire to. I gave him everything I had to help him.

First, he needed some straight talking on basics, the lesson being that their everyday application was non-negotiable. He took it in. He knew he had the tendency to self-destruct occasionally, to hit out, but we didn't dwell on that so much, because in time that would disappear naturally. In the meantime, it was also his strength.

What we really focused on was having an impregnable defence to the best ball by the best bowler. If he could keep that out he would occupy the crease and put pressure back on the opposition all day long. The key was identifying what was a great ball. We worked hard on sensing instinctively the length of the ball that was trouble and he soon became a better player.

His first test century, in just his third test match, against England at Hamilton in 2008, was near perfect. He played straight all day, and his punch straight driving was sublime. It was a master-class in position, power and placement.

One of many things I admired was his ability to ignore those around him, especially mediocre coaching staff, whom he understood knew nothing of the fortitude required out in the middle of an international match. He shut them out and stuck to what he knew, what he was learning himself. In the modern era, that is a very important attribute.

Ross doesn't need crutches because he has in-built belief. However, he does need feedback of sorts, because there is little time on the circuit to step back and do the checks and balances. When he feels something is off he calls on the team he has selected. That's impressive. If it's something in his batting he calls me and we work through it. If it's in another area he goes to the expert who can assist him. It's his livelihood he is nurturing and he wants his dreams kept alive.

Only a few times have I raised my voice to get his full attention, to shake him up for proper effect. Once was via a text after he slogged out at Lord's in 2008. In no uncertain terms, I told him that he had played like a club cricketer. In the next test, in Manchester, he scored 154 not out. That's how he would respond, if severely pushed. The other time was just before the home series against Pakistan in late 2009. He looked too casual in his preparation. He spoke loosely about the upcoming challenge and I decided to give him another rev up. Roger Mortimer was in earshot as I gave him a blast about his preparation and attitude. I said he should be looking to prove to all that he was the best batsman in either team throughout the series. He was taken aback by my outburst, but absorbed it and responded, with two outstanding 90s against impressive bowling.

In March 2010, in Hamilton, he did it again against Australia when he needed it. He smashed the fastest test hundred in New Zealand history, an innings of fierce determination and brute force. It was frightening when he got a little angry.

Now and then when he got stuck or bogged down, instead of being patient, his youthful fearlessness kicked in and he would lash out with the "Samoan sweep-slog". Sometimes it backfired, other times it sailed out of the ground. I kept encouraging him to hit straighter, but only his inexperience under extreme pressure cornered him into hitting across the line with his mighty bottom hand. Mostly, though, he survived. His eye was so good, his ability to get so low and under the ball unique, and his power immense. His hockey ways never left him, but it was only a matter of time before he would shed the recklessness and replace it with absolute poise and control.

He is naturally fit and strong, but realised he had to work harder because his hamstrings didn't carry him for long enough. He loved his food, but his desire to be the best he could be meant the appetite had to be tamed.

We both love red wine. He wanted to create a legacy with his batting, just as any winemaker wants to with his vintages. He gradually matured and got smarter, more sophisticated in his approach. Success followed.

He was always a natural leader and led with vigour from the front. He used only the exact number of words necessary. If two were needed, then two were delivered. He lived by principles and values of honesty, loyalty, integrity and compassion. You were never in the dark, or misunderstood his motives. That is leadership.

Captaining New Zealand was not something he chased. When Brendon McCullum was relieved of the vice-captaincy for whatever reason in late 2009, Ross quietly and humbly accepted the role of stand-in captain should Daniel Vettori leave the field. He saw it as an honour and nothing more. He was confident enough and had a feel for it, having skippered at other levels. He just got on with it. He might have preferred to focus more on his batting, but he was asked by Vettori to do the job and respected the situation, put his team first and acted. Not surprisingly, his personal performances improved. He looked at home.

After 18 months as stand-in, or vice-captain, he felt ready to become

If Brendon McCullum and Ross Taylor were in step, it was no fault of New Zealand Cricket. *Photo, Fairfax*

the official captain when Vettori announced he was standing down from the role. Ross won New Zealand Cricket's ill-advised head-to-head captaincy race with McCullum. He didn't fuss about it, just walked in and spoke of his vision. He didn't need a PowerPoint presentation or a detailed dossier of theories and promises. He won a fair race.

John Wright was the team coach and was there to guide him. Ross led a poorly skilled team, down on batting overall and short of bowling experience. He knew the enormity of the task and mucked in with Wright and gave it his all. His batting improved even further and soon he was averaging 50 as leader, up from 40 as just a player.

He led the team well in Hobart for a glorious win, the first in 26 years in Australia. Yet around him there was trouble, especially among some senior players. McCullum couldn't buy a run against a decent attack, Ryder was imploding when the going got tough, and the rest were out of their depth.

Ross boxed on, knowing the mission was long term. He was determined to drive straight ahead and drag a few with him. He saw in Martin Guptill and Kane Williamson two young and talented players around whom he could build a batting line-up. He hoped McCullum would get over the captaincy decision and waited for the penny to drop with Ryder – those two were critical.

Then he lost John Wright and in a flash Ross' vision became blurred. All of a sudden Mike Hesson, a young 37-year-old coach with no first-class playing experience, was calling the shots. Ross' leadership became exposed to a coup that would rock the game in New Zealand.

The Tattooed One: Brendon McCullum

Many people, including cricket selectors, get confused by the definition of a vice-captain. Some take it to mean that the vice-captain is the one who will eventually take over the captaincy and is therefore being groomed under the existing skipper. Often, therefore, vice-captains are selected far too young. Other vice-captains are thought of as simply the perfect lieutenant for the skipper, the ideal support and ally.

The reality is that the vice-captain is the captain in waiting. He has to be ready to captain and captain well at any moment or he should not be appointed. Basically, he is the second-best captain in the team. It is preferable that he has some captaincy experience, so he knows what to do as soon as the job is handed to him.

There are many examples. In Australia, they do it best. Greg Chappell followed brother Ian, Mark Taylor followed Allan Border, Steve Waugh followed Taylor, Ricky Ponting followed Waugh and Michael Clarke followed Ponting. Their only blemish was when Kim Hughes resigned prematurely and Border took over reluctantly, but in time steadied the ship superbly. For the West Indies, Viv Richards followed Clive Lloyd after Lloyd had a decade in charge. Before Richards became vice-captain, the West Indies had the experienced Deryck Murray to stand in for Lloyd. Alastair Cook has succeeded Andrew Strauss in a smooth transition.

In contrast, hearing Tim Southee touted as Brendon McCullum's deputy in 2012-13 was a real worry. Sure Southee would no doubt be a loyal subject to his mate, assisting here and there. But if McCullum were injured on the first morning of a test match and Southee became the captain, with no prior experience, who wouldn't be concerned?

When Stephen Fleming lost the test captaincy in 2007 and it was handed to Daniel Vettori, there was no surprise (apart from Fleming being sacked). The intriguing appointment was who would be the vice-captain, knowing that Vettori had on-going injury problems. The obvious choices were either Scott Styris or Jacob Oram. Both their positions seemed assured and both were well equipped, with Oram having had good experience with his province. But for the tour of South Africa in late 2007, John Bracewell chose 26-year-old Brendon McCullum. It seemed a bit odd that someone less mature would be chosen ahead of the experienced Styris and Oram, but the rationale may have been that Fleming was not far away at first slip and could guide McCullum. Who knows? Perhaps Styris and Oram were asked and turned it down.

McCullum had previously shown his leadership potential as the New Zealand under-19 skipper, leading a team that included Ross Taylor to victory over South Africa in a three-test series in 2001. He had the wicketkeeping duties and batted at No 6, where he excelled, scoring three tons in four innings and averaging 151. He was the standout player of the series and had leadership quality stamped all over him.

By late 2007 he was established as one of the world's best wicketkeeper-batsmen. His keeping was brilliant, and his batting at No 7 proved repeatedly to be the difference. So it made sense that at some stage he would become the heir apparent to the New Zealand captaincy. Bracewell may well have made an inspired choice.

Vettori carried on and managed to stay on the field. Only in October 2009, in the Champions Trophy final against Australia in South Africa, did McCullum get the chance to lead the side. He chose to bat first, scored a duck and New Zealand made barely 200, losing by six wickets.

Shortly after, Andy Moles, the coach of 11 months, was sacked, and there was a change of vice-captain. On the team's return from Abu Dhabi, following a 2-1 ODI series win over Pakistan (in which McCullum was named player of the series) a major reshuffle occurred. Moles was replaced by Vettori as coach and no vice-captain was named. Deeper investigation revealed that Ross Taylor would be the on-field captain should Vettori be injured, but not the official vice-captain. Therefore, Vettori had a portfolio of captain, selector and coach, with no vice-captain. It was the weirdest scenario.

In the media and public's mind it seemed that player power was the reason for the demise of Moles, but no-one knew why Mccullum was no longer vice-captain. Taylor, when asked if he would accept the on-field duties, replied that he was somewhat reluctant.

His batting apprenticeship was still a work in progress. But when pushed by Vettori and Co, he was happy to help. Taylor was quickly into action in the opening ODI against Australia in Napier in early 2010 when Vettori pulled up injured. He scored 70 and led the side to a thrilling victory. It appeared Vettori had found a vice-captain with whom he was comfortable.

McCullum expressed his disappointment with what had gone on. He seemed to feel it was his right to be the next captain and on paper that would have been correct. He was three years older than Taylor and more experienced. He must have been annoyed at times because he constantly became the player the media and public seemed to criticise first.

After the Napier win, orchestrated by Taylor, New Zealand dived into a dismal run of losses. Under Vettori they went on to lose the next 11 ODIs. McCullum was having a lean trot and players were dropped left, right and centre. The selectors, including Vettori, looked lost, as did the players on the field.

By December 2010, the New Zealand Cricket board, under new chairman Chris Moller, moved to sort out the debacle. It promoted Mark Greatbatch, the batting coach, to chairman of selectors, joined by Glenn Turner and Lance Cairns, and finally got John Wright to accept a two-year deal as head coach.

Vettori was no longer coach or a selector, but held on to the captaincy. Meanwhile Taylor and McCullum kept looking at each other sideways, perhaps waiting for the next bizarre episode, which as it transpired wasn't far away.

By that stage, McCullum probably resented the whole business. Vettori was a conservative and defensive skipper, which didn't seem to wash with McCullum's natural style. McCullum's "brand" as a cricketer was growing quickly in the crazy world of the Indian Premier League. It was McCullum's slashing blade that set the inaugural IPL alight in 2008 with a once-in-a-lifetime 158 not out against my team, the Royal Challengers.

From that moment, McCullum became an overnight millionaire.

He left long-time manager Leanne McGoldrick, who also managed Taylor, and jumped into the powerful clutches of fledgling manager Stephen Fleming. Perhaps instinctively, McCullum was positioning himself for the long-term. What was missing for him was the New Zealand captaincy.

One of the issues I had with McCullum was his overwhelming desire to be an opening batsman and give up the gloves. His reasoning was that his knees were failing him, so he couldn't keep in all forms of the game. Something had to give. But I still see him squatting at slip all day, or diving around the covers, so I don't know the answer. He looks fit, but only he knows his body.

What seemed obvious was that he would have gone on to be one of the world's best wicketkeeper-batsmen, even better than Mark Boucher, or batsmen-keepers (depending on the main role). He would have ranked at least alongside MS Dhoni and Matt Prior, who became world leaders.

His ability at No 5 or 6 would have served New Zealand so much better than it did as an opening batsman. It would also have served him better as the vice-captain to be the wicketkeeper at all times and play that understudy yet pivotal role. But that's all history.

On January 4, 2013, McCullum became the 28th test captain of New Zealand. In Cape Town he won the toss and chose to bat. His opposite, Graeme Smith, did a double-take on hearing his side had first use of the wicket to bowl on. By lunch on the first day South Africa had already lost Smith lbw for one. But in 19.1 overs New Zealand had been bowled out for 45. No-one in the commentary could understand the rationale for electing to bat on a fresh, greenish pitch against the best attack in the world on their home soil. New Zealand went on to lose both tests heavily and McCullum's dream of being in charge had become a tough baptism of fire. He then dropped down the batting order and rallied his team to a breakthrough ODI series win over South Africa, the world's No 1 team.

As an opener, he didn't have the technique to survive the very good ball by a good test match bowler often enough. No-one doubts his strokeplay when he is instinctive, but too often he premeditates his response to a ball that just isn't there.

His stance, balance and eye level are all fine when the bowler runs in, but at the last instant he hitches his hands into his stomach and bends his back more, forcing his head a fraction to the off side, his right eye moving to align with mid-off not the bowler, thus affecting his balance. As the bowler delivers, his balance is slightly askew, so his front foot falls to counter the imbalance. The result is he finds himself in a stuck position, in which he either plays around the front pad or nicks off with an angled bat.

When opening, his defence doesn't have the solid base or balance with which to see out the danger ball on a length around off stump. When he attacks, he is better because the balance is quickly restored, but you can't attack all day. For 75 per cent of balls faced in a test innings, your ability to defend (and therefore not score) is called upon. McCullum is definitely better suited to the middle order, when the ball is older and bowlers are tiring. His attacking ability is then utilised.

The challenge is finding top-order batsmen who can set up the innings for McCullum's ability to come to the fore, as Adam Gilchrist's did for Australia. The memorable debut of young Hamish Rutherford against England in Dunedin seemed to be a step in the right direction.

It was noticeable that when McCullum permanently dropped down the order against England in early 2013, he was not only technically better, but he was able to get in against the older ball and dominate, as we all know he can. His batting during the one-dayers and the tests was breathtaking at times. As a result, his captaincy became better and he looked very comfortable as a leader.

When looking at their respective merits, Taylor and McCullum both have much to offer. They are fine athletes, highly skilled stroke-makers and have a determined streak. Where they differ is in approach. Taylor doesn't say much unless it's needed; McCullum is a natural talker. At the crease, Taylor is technically sound, has a better defence and plays straighter, with the occasional heave. He has the brute force and power to hit hard, especially to leg.

McCullum in the middle order has the tools to play well and intimidate the opposition when his balance is right – his footwork can be electric and his range of strokes is unique.

As captains, they have had to direct young, inexperienced, but promising bowlers. Taylor was aggressive when his young bowlers had good sessions, but he was cautious and selective at times when he had to control the damage. However, he won two tests away from home and both times his batting and captaincy were outstanding. He proved he could do it. McCullum is naturally attacking and proactive and that is a good trait. The bowlers need to show control to allow that, and they did so superbly against England at home in 2013.

Batting in the middle order is a vital part of McCullum's captaincy because he can perform to a high standard, adjusting to the situation. A captain must perform, end of story.

McCullum has more experience, is older and has been around for a decade. He was always the natural choice. Taylor would acknowledge and accept that and support McCullum in every way. What was not acceptable was the callous way both were treated, but in particular how Taylor was removed as captain.

This begs the big question: who decides who should be the captain? Should the coach or the board decide? Or should it be left to the independent selection panel that used to do it? Does Mike Hesson, despite his inexperience, get to decide who the captain should be over everyone else?

John Wright and John Buchanan, the director of cricket, preferred Taylor as captain a year earlier, when the captaincy interviews were held. But when Wright resigned as coach, did that mean the new coach, no matter how inexperienced, could change the captain? Should Hesson's preference wipe out a whole year's work?

Wright resigned, citing a difference of opinion with Buchanan, who was appointed after Wright had already been positioned where he was comfortable and felt he could operate best. Buchanan had introduced a new system, dropping the independent selection panel structure and instead employing Kim Littlejohn, a fellow Australian. Littlejohn had no top-level cricket background, but would provide the computer data, and joined Wright in forming a selection team of two. Nothing felt right for Wright, and he departed.

Then a panel including Stephen Fleming (McCullum's business manager) appointed Hesson (McCullum's good friend) to the coaching role, which included a job description of being the head selector as well. That was surely taking it all too far. It was one thing to drop a balanced, experienced, skilled and geographically spread group of independent selectors for a panel of only two (the coach and a computer analyst), but to appoint a coach with no first-class playing background and just a short-lived coaching stint with Kenya as international experience didn't stack up.

My criticism is not so much of Buchanan and his plan, but of the board, which had minimal cricket nous. The board continued to ignore the independent selection panel structure that had generally served New Zealand well until 2003. To me it was time to go back to the basics, part of which meant calling on the available experience and resources within our country.

Surely it was more prudent to choose a coach to coach, selectors to select and a captain to captain. As for choosing the captain, that would be done by the selectors, after selecting the team with board approval. Having a coach as a head selector in the dressing room can create a fear factor among players. This isn't a baseball franchise in a 30-team competition when, if a player is not wanted or doesn't fit in, he can up and leave and find another team. No, this is the national team, the only team to aim for. In that scenario, if the coach doesn't like you, it's bad luck because your career might be cooked.

It would require a very experienced coach to coach and select a struggling national cricket team without causing further insecurity within the team. People like Andy Flower or Gary Kirsten, very experienced former players and successful international coaches, have succeeded with strong teams, but can it work with Mike Hesson?

To my way of thinking, by having a cross-section of expertise working together, with clear demarcation lines as to their roles, you can create a unified, stable and skilful structure. Further, you can build community support in which former players feel involved, and can contribute their knowledge and experience. That way you are relying on a collective of credible opinion.

One thing that continues to disappoint former New Zealand players is the lack of inclusion, respect and gratitude.

Maybe coaches can't function these days without having the final say on everything. It's not the environment I would like to play in. I would always prefer to play under a captain who had the vision and responsibility to make the main decisions.

Cricket Australia has recently gone through similar problems with coach Mickey Arthur, also a selector, creating tension within the ranks, and captain Michael Clarke doubling as a selector. It confirms to me that the coach should stick to coaching and the captain to captaining.

New Zealand Cricket will say that Mike Hesson has done a fine job in light of the good performance against England in the three-test home series in March. It was a good effort, not only for Hesson, but for McCullum. His batting was a revelation down the order, and his captaincy fed off that success. He showed he was a worthy leader.

But New Zealand Cricket has a long way to go to right the wrongs done to Ross Taylor. Ross played inconsistently against England in the tests. He wasn't helped when Bob Carter, the batting coach, in a private conversation before the second test in Wellington, apologised to Ross for the Sri Lanka timing. Ross was disappointed it had been brought up again at that time. He then played like a man resigned and defeated. The morning after the third test, Ross revealed to a radio station that he hoped the truth would be heard in the weeks ahead, because he was still not comfortable in the team. Ross' statement was ill-timed, but sadly what he said was true.

The change of captaincy was handled so poorly that the game in New Zealand suffered. Ross's career was left at the crossroads, because of the lack of honestly and openness on New Zealand Cricket's part. Ross could be one of our very best, and that's where his focus must lie. To recover fully and regain his best form, Ross has to feel some trust has been restored. New Zealand Cricket should show some accountability and do everything it can to rebuild that trust.

In hindsight, if McCullum had stayed as vice-captain from 2009, and then become captain in 2011, Ross would have been a fine vice-captain to him, a perfect stand-in if necessary and a successful batsman for the team. All that is in question now. Instead of being pitched in a head-to-head battle, Taylor and McCullum should have been working side by side. I hope they can in the years ahead, but it's a big hope.

CHAPTER 2

The Influential Leader: Stephen Fleming

He sits in his office, computers and exchange rates at the ready, seemingly with the world at his feet. He will be planning the next encounter, the next project, the next move. He is tall, powerful, dark and handsome, and has hands the size of large buckets. He is influential, he is a fine leader. He is Stephen Paul Fleming.

Fleming is well connected; he controls cricket in Chennai, and has tentacles in Christchurch, Auckland and Wellington, too. He is responsible for many players' livelihoods. Plus he has the ear of the New Zealand Prime Minister. In 2011, he accompanied John Key on a diplomatic trip to India and was more widely recognised than the Prime Minister. His reach in the political world exceeds most politicians.

Fleming was raised by his mother, Pauline. The two forged a special bond. He became the man of the house early on and never gave it up. He learnt to stand up and lead the way and he's never looked back. His story is a fascinating one.

Cricket soon became his outlet, his release. He quickly showed poise for the occasion. His career in the game was mapped out and it was pre-ordained he would become a legend.

In Christchurch, he built a strong group around him... Chris Cairns, Craig McMillan, Nathan Astle and Chris Harris. They played together in age group and provincial teams, dominated attacks and worked their way up the ladder. Fleming learnt the art of delegating and when necessary, leading from the front. This he did with aplomb.

Selected for New Zealand at 21, he flourished, getting off to a flier in his first test. Then he settled in for the long haul. His batting looked classy. But just as it needed fine tuning, he was handed the New Zealand captaincy at 23. Once in charge, he led the way and the rest is history, even if his batting never reached the heights it might have.

While there was a certain enigma about his batting career, there was certainly none about his overall leadership and tactical nous, or his catching, in both of which he was consistently outstanding. Perhaps it isn't surprising that with bat in hand he didn't leave a lasting impression; instead it was leadership that was his legacy.

With his batting you were always left with the feeling that his very best form was just around the corner, and that a run of big hundreds would flow from his heavy blade. You always had the thought that his true natural talent was about to blossom into a glorious extended run. We were happy to wait, but it never really came.

Analytically speaking, on home soil in conditions he knew well, he averaged a disappointing 33 in 54 tests, scoring just two centuries in 89 walks to the crease. If you look deeper into that home record, in his second innings of a home test match, Fleming averaged under 22 from 35 innings. It dropped to 15 from 15 innings in Auckland and in Christchurch.

He was much better than that, so it was frustrating for those who knew his abilities at close hand and no doubt for himself. Yet he averaged an impressive and much more respectable 46 overseas, including three superb double tons in different countries. This was Fleming showing his true self, away from home.

In particular, on the subcontinent where the high humidity saps the energy levels to the extreme, he averaged 65. In the second innings he averaged 74. Clearly, he was comfortable in the heat and especially on slow pitches. Conversely, in all his second innings in England his average was 19 from nine innings and, in Australia, a miserable 11 from seven. So in summary, it seemed that on the faster, seaming, bouncier tracks of New Zealand, Australia and England he couldn't sustain his balance or move his feet quickly enough.

To average barely 40 (40.06 to be exact) in tests in an age when a dozen or more of his contemporaries were averaging above 50 was significant. To score just nine test hundreds when many of his peers got into the 20s was also disappointing. To never make the top 10 ranked batsmen in the world just about sums it up, really. But why? What stopped him from truly fulfilling that huge promise he always carried as a free-flowing left-hand batsman?

There is no doubt that by inheriting the captaincy at the tender age of 23, he subconsciously gave up the chance to truly focus on his batting development. In truth, he missed two or three years of his batting apprenticeship. Instead, and rightly so, captaining New Zealand became his priority.

His early consistency of getting a start then changed to bigger peaks and troughs. Still the golden run eluded him. In the end he holds the worst conversion rate of fifties to hundreds in test history. Of those who have scored 50 fifties, Fleming converted only nine, the next worst being Alex Stewart, a wicketkeeper mainly, with 15.

For whatever reason, Fleming appeared reluctant to set milestones or targets, instead claiming, as he once told me: "I just want to bat for the occasion, do my best, play for the team." Steve Waugh, on the other hand clearly used targets, sub-goals and points during a long innings to drive himself past comfort zones and into a wider realm.

Batting is an individual pursuit, a contest between yourself and the bowler. It requires personal targets and stepping stones, as well as obvious awareness of the team situation. Instead, Fleming got himself out for sixty-odd on more occasions than we wish to remember. It was as if someone just pulled the plug out from the wall socket. The head went up, so did the ball and the innings was over. It happened all too easily, for no apparent reason.

In the end he didn't quite set a high enough run-scoring standard for the team. He definitely didn't set a Waugh or Ponting standard, or a Dravid or Kallis standard, or even a Vaughan, Langer or Chanderpaul standard. And believe me, he was just as capable as most of those fellows, most certainly the latter group.

Overall, batting has cost New Zealand the most. Simply not enough runs to play with. It's been the heavy bats, some poor coaching, a lack of precise mental preparation and, in particular, the emphasis on biomechanic theory. No other New Zealand batsman, with the exceptions of Mark Richardson and Ross Taylor, have averaged over 40 for more than a decade now. Yet, the captaincy and bowling had been of a very good standard by comparison.

Fleming himself will say that there weren't enough runs and in particular will regret those missed centuries, but he will emphasise that he had more important things to do. The responsibility of leading your country occupies one's mind, let me assure you.

Interestingly though, what will he say to the next generation of batsmen as to the right mental preparation now that he can reflect on his career? Will it be: "Bat for the occasion and do your best. Play for the team"? Or will he add, from experience: "Aim to be a top five-ranked player, score as many 100s as 50s and match the records and feats that your opponents and contemporaries have created"?

His greatest legacy will be his leadership – his man-management ability, his tactical acumen and strategic planning. He was absolutely inspirational from 1999-2003, the best in the world. That was a time when he was on top of his game and truly in charge.

Overall, there is no denying his impact over 10 years as skipper. When he retired, Fleming had captained New Zealand in more tests (80) than anyone else, and was

Stephen Fleming was a superb captain, but in the end his batting output was not worthy of his talent.

second overall in test history (behind Allan Border, 93). He also held the overall record for the most matches captained in ODIs (218). There is no question he will rank up there with the best when the captaincy roll of honour is read out. He was truly an influential leader.

What about the lasting image of Stephen Fleming the player?

He was a fine batsman, slightly unfulfilled, a steady and at times charming presence. But I will probably remember him standing at first slip marshalling his troops superbly, then seconds later plucking an extraordinary catch out of thin air – something he seemed able to do in his sleep.

In 2009 I produced a one-hour documentary on him as part of *The Chosen Ones* series on Sky. It was titled *The Elegant Ambassador*, a description of his fine work representing New Zealand, of the respect he had gained as a leader and a man around the world and of the elegant way he went about it. The film was a glowing portrayal of a fine career.

Fleming, since retirement, has been incredibly busy. He cleverly moved out of being just a player for Chennai in the IPL to become their all-conquering leader, the head coach. It was as smooth a transition as you could imagine. He recruited well and coached them to early success and still enjoys the spoils of that success.

That was a clever strategic move, something he has become adept at.

In Wellington he set himself up as a player agent looking after Brendon McCullum, James Franklin, Jeetan Patel and Tim Southee, to name a few. He is in business with McCullum.

When John Wright resigned in April 2012, Fleming made a mistake by agreeing to join the interview panel to appoint the New Zealand coach to replace Wright. As a player agent it was a misguided decision, fraught with conflicts of interest. As a result when Mike Hesson was appointed and then Ross Taylor sacked for McCullum, it created waves of criticism. Fleming's reputation for unflappability took a hit.

Influential, strong leadership has been missing in New Zealand Cricket since John Anderson and Martin Snedden departed. It's time for new blood and a clean slate.

Stephen Fleming may well have a desire to become a leader of New Zealand Cricket one day, but if he does he will need to remove any conflicts of interest. He would be an asset to the organisation, because he is powerful and well connected. But he would need to be on top of his game.

And hey, if he ever needed a hand, there's always the Prime Minister to call upon!

CHAPTER 3

Reminiscing: The 80s Mafia

The name "mafia" suggests a sinister tone, but to be fair to Stephen Fleming, who created "the 80s Mafia" tag, I am sure he meant it in part as a dig and partly out of respect. The name was born when Fleming and his men took on New Zealand Cricket by creating a Cricket Players Association and demanding better pay and conditions.

At some point in the first few years of the millennium, Martin Snedden was New Zealand Cricket chief executive, John Bracewell was head coach, John Wright was in High Performance, Jeff Crowe was New Zealand team manager, Ian Smith, Jeremy Coney and I dominated the television commentary team, Stephen Boock was a New Zealand Cricket board member, Glenn Turner and Richard Hadlee were national selectors and others were working at national age-group level. We were everywhere! It obviously bothered Fleming and his men.

It shouldn't have. The 80s Mafia were a fine bunch, the best I played with. Underlying everything was a natural love of the game. The 1980s was still primarily an amateur era. Most of the team had other jobs. "Real jobs." The combination of professional and amateur was its strength. County cricket pros Glenn Turner, Geoff Howarth, Richard Hadlee and John Wright brought a new approach to the old ways.

They taught those coming in or those not exposed to the game outside New Zealand that the opposition could be beaten. The pros had competed one-on-one with the world's best in England day-in and day-out and therefore there was hope that collectively we could do the same at test level.

The era started in the summer of 1979-80, when the all-conquering West Indies toured New Zealand, after completing a series win in Australia. They were led by the towering Clive Lloyd, spearheaded by fast bowling greats Andy Roberts, Joel Garner and Michael Holding and batting legends Gordon Greenidge, Desmond Haynes, Lawrence Rowe, Lloyd and Alvin Kallicharran. Viv Richards had a rare series off, suffering from an eye disorder. They arrived as overwhelming favourites and left bitter, beaten and disillusioned. Somehow New Zealand beat one of test cricket's best teams 1-0.

It all started in Dunedin, bitterly cold Dunedin. The Windies, used to the heat of Australia, did not know what hit them. The pitch was low and slow, the opposite to Perth and Brisbane. Then there was a fresh, hungry and focused Richard Hadlee, starting to hit his very best form in test cricket. Hadlee, known as "Paddles" for his splayed feet, was the major difference. He exploited the low, skiddy bounce by claiming seven lbws among his 11 wickets in that first test. No-one on either side, with the exception of Desmond Haynes, scored any runs. New Zealand chased 104 and got there by dint of a leg bye, with a wicket to spare. It was one of the biggest shocks in test history.

The Windies regrouped and arrived in Christchurch determined to stop this nonsense and level the series. Their determination soon turned to anger and hostility as they became annoyed at the umpiring and resilient New Zealand batting. The umpiring had stirred them somewhat in Dunedin, but in Christchurch it sent them through the roof. While skipper Geoff Howarth was playing his finest test innings in a fine all-round team batting display, Colin Croft was in a showdown with local umpire Fred Goodall. In a moment of bizarre anger Croft, steaming in to bowl to Hadlee, barged Goodall in the shoulder and sent him sideways. The Windies refused for some time to play on after tea on the third day and eventually the test was drawn.

At Eden Park, the two teams were as distanced as they could be, but the rivalry was intense and the match closely fought. In the dressing room for New Zealand was a 17-year-old specialist fieldsman by the name of Crowe. Me. I was plucked from a peaceful teenage existence into the hottest kitchen in cricket. For a week I witnessed not only the inner workings of the New Zealand side I hoped to play for one day, but also the hostility of the West Indians.

New Zealand sensed a rare and glorious series win. The confidence was high and the team was improving, even from Dunedin. There they had seen Hadlee singlehandedly steal the test. In Christchurch Geoff Howarth, John Parker and Jeremy Coney joined the battle with sterling and spirited performances. Hadlee stamped his growing status as a world-class all-rounder by registering his first test century.

At Eden Park it was the turn of Gary Troup, the local tall left-arm fast bowler, who stole the show. He took 10 wickets in the match, a career-defining performance, and in doing so ensured a draw and a historic series win. I watched at close range the ecstasy and the pain of the two sides. New Zealand had arrived at a pivotal point in its history. It was the ultimate boost. Led by the tactically astute Howarth and spearheaded by Hadlee, the team found a steely resolve, tasted success and wanted more. In the dressing room I noticed a nice mix of characters and personalities. These were the men who have become labelled the 80s Mafia:

Glenn Turner was not around too much because of his self-imposed exile. He did not play test cricket again for New Zealand after 1977, except for a couple of matches against minnows Sri Lanka at the end of his career. He had his reasons and they appeared valid. He did, however, play for New Zealand at the 1979 and 1983 World Cups. I was to experience Glenn mainly in his coaching roles from 1985-87 and again in 1995.

Turner's absence meant that **Bruce Edgar** stepped in to open the innings with John Wright and together they blunted the best attacks in the world, in all conditions. "Bootsie" Edgar was tenacious and brave. He fought like hell, never giving his wicket away. He was thoughtful and quiet, but immensely proud. I admired his work ethic and attention to detail. He had a hard job and never complained. Instead he began to blossom and in no time showed his amazing mental toughness and resilient technique. His greatest innings was against the Australians, when he scored a match-winning 161 at Eden Park in 1982. He tore Lillee and Thomson apart at various times with rousing hooks and cuts. He defended Alderman with great care and swept Yardley with daring precision.

I was very much taken by Bootsie's batting and in particular his preparation for a test match. He would armour up and have hours of short-pitched balls either thrown or bowled at his head. He stopped when he felt he was ready. If not quite right, he would soldier on. Preparation was an important part of the 80s mantra. My personal highlight batting with him was when we shared a double-century stand at Lord's in 1986 and it saddened me when he fell just short of a well-deserved ton. He was a beautiful outfielder and a kind, respected teammate. You couldn't fault him.

John Wright was true grit. The look on "Shake's" face when he padded up was a study in psycho-cybernetics. What was he thinking? Could playing cricket be so hard, so tortured? Yet despite his demeanour, he was in heaven, loving the heat of the battle and the toughest challenges. When you joined him in the middle, he never faltered in his steely determination to give the opposition nothing. He would simply say: "Hogan, fight, believe in yourself; you will be great." He was in the war zone the whole time. Not a lot affected his concentration – the wind never bothered him, nor did the sledging or humorous banter, or the pace of the new ball. But what did was a small ant moving behind the umpire, near the sightscreen. That really got his nose out of joint. If he was distracted from seeing the ball clearly, he wasn't happy.

When his eye was in he was a seriously fine player. In my first series, in 1982, he followed Edgar's example from the second test and cut the crap out of Thomson in the third test, scoring a ripper 141. His other

John Wright was always up for the battle. Here he avoids a bouncer from Ian Botham.

notable innings was in his golden summer of 1990, when he led New Zealand to victory at the Basin Reserve with a faultless 119 not out in a serene run chase against Australia. He compiled 12 worthy test tons. It should have been more. Sadly he tripped up on 99 twice, once at the MCG in 1987, and again in a disappointing loss to England in 1992. He also stumbled on 98 at Lord's in 1990. Those were rare misses for a truly gutsy player. Shake could not be shaken easily.

Geoff Howarth ("Mr Stirred but not Shaken") on the field, as captain and batsman, had a rich period from 1978-81. He was an experienced tactician and, of course, could build his attack around the great Hadlee. Howarth could bat. His twin hundreds against England at Eden Park set him up for a stellar period with another ton in England following, then big hundreds against the West Indies and India. The 147 against the Windies was pure and courageous. At the crease he kept very still, played fast bowling on his ear and had a nice style to watch.

John Fulton Reid, the left-hander from Auckland, was a special player. He took over from Howarth at No 3 and in 19 tests accumulated six fine test centuries. I had the pleasure of batting with him for Auckland and loved his poise, calmness and lateness of stroke. He was as fine a player of spin as you could ever bat with. His batting in Pakistan and Sri Lanka in 1984 and then back in New Zealand against Pakistan in early 1985 was unbelievable. He was an intelligent cricketer and went on to become a fine administrator. John was top drawer, one of the best in my book.

Later in the 1980s, **Andrew Jones** became a worthy successor to Reid. For me "Jed" was my perfect foil. I loved his batting. His attitude was brooding and stalking; he was so focused and so himself. He couldn't give a damn what those watching thought of his talent or style. Instead he demanded respect and always got it with massive periods of unbroken concentration. His batting in the series against Sri Lanka in 1990-91, with more than 500 runs in three tests, was out of this world. Our record partnership of 467 in that series was my testament to what I thought about batting with him. If I wanted someone to bat for my life it would be Jed Jones every time. To bat with someone that long you truly get a sense of their mettle. Jed showed how committed he was to the cause. We were losing and the only way out of trouble was to fight each and every ball. One mistake would kill it, but he never relaxed. He just kept going, urging himself on. We hardly ever spoke in the middle, just a grunt or a nod was enough. There were no niceties, just simple urges of devotion. I liked it like that and so, in an odd way, he was a joy to bat with.

Jeff Crowe, who showed true grit when facing the West Indies on their home patch.

"Chopper", my brother **Jeff Crowe,** was a class player. That he never really showed it in New Zealand conditions was a shame yet understandable. When he left at 17 to venture to Adelaide he lost his game on slow low tracks and learnt a better one on fast hard ones. That's why when he toured the West Indies or Pakistan, for example, he was world class. His century against the all-conquering Windies in Jamaica had to be seen to be believed. He smashed them at their own game, peeling off 113 in three hours against Walsh, Garner, Marshall and Davis. Before the ton at Jamaica, in the third test at Barbados, Jeff joined me in the middle on day one after the seventh ball with the score 1-3, Howarth, Wright and Rutherford all dismissed for ducks. He immediately scored a single off Marshall and we swapped ends. For the next 94 minutes, under the most pressure you could imagine (series tied at 0-0), he defended Joel Garner without scoring a run! Garner bowled with hostile pace and bounce and Jeff got in behind every ball, knocking most of them into the gully. His 94-minute scoreless period was a world record at the time. The way he took it on the body, resisting so long without scoring, was truly courageous. At the other end I had my hands full facing Marshall. Jeff was dismissed after three hours for 20, but used that experience to produce his century a week later – one of the three best innings I ever saw. (The others were Gordon Greenidge's 214 in Auckland 1987 and Greg Chappell's 174 in Christchurch in 1983.)

In the dressing room he was much loved, mixing with the various personalities with absolute ease. That made him a natural captain, but sadly his back-foot technique was exposed in New Zealand and he was dropped.

Jeremy Coney, "Mantis", was a unique team man. He batted at No 6 and had the uncanny knack of trusting the tail to bat with him, often producing heroics, as we witnessed at Carisbrook in 1985 when he had a last-wicket stand of 50 with Ewen Chatfield against Pakistan. He stood at slip and recited Shakespeare while plucking catches out of the air off the pace of Hadlee. He stood in the bar and sang Beatles songs, arms and legs moving to the beat (while his hand never quite reached the bottom of his pocket to buy a round of drinks!). He borrowed a club bat to make his test debut, bowled autumn leaves and broke vital partnerships. He told outrageously funny stories and made impromptu speeches with incredible skill and flair. I batted with him a lot and enjoyed many fine partnerships – we scored our first test centuries together against England at the Basin in 1984, attacked the Windies in Guyana in 1985 and counter-attacked against Australia in Christchurch in 1986. He had a fascinating way of brushing off a pressure situation, often complaining of a headache and a "what the hell" approach. It worked. He was great theatre in the middle and fun to watch; his jump shot, his back away ramp, his look away hook, his Basil Fawlty running style were all unique to the Mantis. He was an enigma – deep, intelligent yet quite extroverted. Overall, he was a valuable contributor on and off the field.

Richard Hadlee was the supreme being on a cricket field. Wow, he could play! Pre-ordained for greatness, he followed the script and more. His bowling was freakish. No action before or since has had the same fluent smoothness and economy. It allowed him to bowl to the very highest level at the age of nearly 40 – incredible. He programmed his mind to deliver on every promise. He budgeted

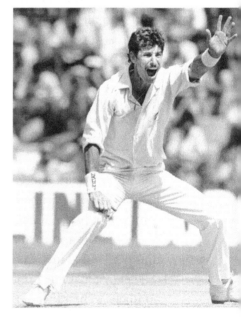

Richard Hadlee was our champion.

how many balls were to be bowled, how many wickets he would take, how many runs he would concede. It was daring to do so because it was so different to anyone else. Many never quite understood the Hadlee way; I couldn't get enough of it.

When he bowled to a Viv Richards, David Gower, Javed Miandad or Greg Chappell, he was in Heaven. It brought out the best in him every time, especially when playing the Aussies or in England. When he bowled to a No 11 he had his goals and the job needed to be done swiftly, with little blood or damage. His batting was pure on his day – natural swing, keen eye, and up for the challenge. Paddles was our king of the throne and without him we were just also-rans. He took us to rarefied heights.

Wally Lees was a fatherly figure, always warm and encouraging, humorous and a good listener. He didn't play a huge amount, conceding the keeper's spot to a younger buck, but he gave plenty in terms of his presence and management of people. He would become the best coach I played under, from 1990-93.

Ian Smith ("Stockley") was a natural. He could play golf, soccer… you name it, a true talent with a hunger to match. He loved the atmosphere of the 1980s team because it gave him that sense of being a drummer in a cool band. His role as the wicketkeeper meant he was central to all we did. If he was up, we were too. Often he was brilliant and breathtaking in his duty. With the bat, he was downright dangerous. That 173 he smoked all around Eden Park against India in 1990 was surreal – 169 in a session! I roomed with him on many occasions and we became close. He was like another big brother in a team of fatherly figures. Stockley is in my all-time great New Zealand side.

Stephen Boock was the best New Zealand spinner I faced. He got me out more than any other bowler. He was underused by New Zealand, but when he did succeed it was a treat. Evidence of this was against Pakistan in Hyderabad in 1984. The Pakistanis were fine players of spin, yet he had Zaheer, Javed, Mohsin and Mudassar all confused with his loop, drift and turn and finished with 7-87. His unique run-up gave him perfect balance and position to deliver the goods. He was a plucky cricketer, very determined and competitive, but also kind and caring like an uncle. When I went through a rough patch in my first test against the West Indies, it was "Boockman" who encouraged me, quietly affirming the positives, the way forward. When I got in at Guyana he promised, via notes from the pavilion, he would help me to my double ton. He hadn't banked on a rampaging Michael Holding and a new ball. When he got out to the middle, his bat had not moved when the middle stump went cartwheeling first ball. But it was the thought that counted. I think he was New Zealand's finest left-arm spinner, even if the records don't support that. He was denied many times the chance to show his skills owing to the conditions at home.

The other spinner was **John Bracewell.** "Braces" was a tough cookie on the outside. He displayed a bit of bravado as if he was strong and macho all the time. But we all saw a man who was, as we all were, like a duck on water – sweet and secure on top, but paddling like mad underneath. He needed the team support, as we all did. He was a fine all-round cricketer – he embraced all three disciplines and had magic moments in all three against the very best. His off-spin was at times devastatingly brilliant. He spun the ball hard, got bounce from his tall action and was lethal against left-handers. His habit of removing Allan Border with unplayable deliveries was a highlight for him and the team. In the test against Australia in Auckland in 1986, Braces was in his element, sledging the opposition and ripping them out not longer after. Yep, on turning tracks he was a handful, as he proved again in Mumbai in 1988 with another large haul and victory. When Braces stopped fighting himself and those around him and focused on his skills, he was a terrific asset to the team.

Lance Cairns was a special man. He looked a club cricketer the way he bowled and swung the bat, and yet he delivered like a superstar. New Zealand cricket fans identified with "Lancer" and he was genuine hero material. I just loved his simple messages of support. When Howarth was firing off his spittle, "Lancer" just shrugged and said: "Don't worry Hoges. Let it go." It's a sad thought that I never did, but I never forgot Lance trying to father me the right way. His strength is well-known, but his subtlety was his real forte. His use of the slower ball, adjusting his grip to make up for his lack of pace, was a joy to watch. His 10 wickets at Leeds in 1983, when Hadlee took none, showed his class. He, Chats and Paddles won us many tests.

Ewen Chatfield ("Charlie Chats") was the banker in the team. He was the one you could rely on every minute of the day. As honest as the day is long, he manned up to the task, delivered and hit the spot like an

Ewen Chatfield, a dream team-mate.

Olympic archer. The "Naenae Express" was his favourite tag. He was a true Wellington boy who would bowl into any wind, providing the perfect foil for Hadlee. Chats received the biggest cheers of anyone I played with, and that was just for his walk to the batting crease! People loved him. He "died" momentarily at Eden Park when felled by a bouncer from Englishman Peter Lever, so every time he ventured out he carried the hopes of the fans that he would not only survive, but score some rare runs. When he scored 21 not out (from 84 balls) in that unbelievable last-wicket stand at Carisbrook to beat the Pakis, I cried in admiration for the achievement. It was just the enormity of what he did with no-one behind him if he made one error. He played one of the great innings, all things considered.

Chats was a champion man, a truly reliable team-mate and a nagging back-of-a-length, precisely accurate bowler, who could run in all day. You just can't beat that, really.

Martin Snedden was the brains of the team. He was always an outstanding thinker and analyst of situations. He was measured, calm and totally unemotional. That showed often on the park. In a pressure moment he was the one to throw the ball to. That was the case in the test against the West Indies in 1987. Hadlee and Chatfield set the scene in the first innings, but in tougher bowling conditions in the second innings, "Sneds" produced the crème de la crème. His 5-66, including removing Viv Richards in full flight, was his finest hour. He was a steady player, nothing flash or eye-catching, but he thought his way through and competed well.

His batting was a great example of that. He never gave an inch. He got behind the ball, defended with his life and gave many sterling displays. His best was with Mark Greatbatch in the famous draw at Perth in 1989, the other when he scored a duck over three days at Nottingham, when rained intervened. Sneds was the smart one and you need those types in certain situations. I thought he was marvellous in all he offered.

Mark Greatbatch played his first test against England at Eden Park in 1988. He took to test cricket immediately, sending the ball to all parts of the field while smacking a swashbuckling 107 in the second innings. He joined three other New Zealanders, all lefties – Jack Mills, Bruce Taylor and Rodney Redmond – in scoring a century on debut. (The list has grown since, the latest being another left-hander, Hamish Rutherford, against England in 2013.) "Paddy" played with passion. He was vocal and spirited in his approach to the opposition. His only way was to be in their faces, either batting or in the field, where he showed amazing agility.

His greatest moment was the one-off test in Perth in late 1989. With two days to bat to save the test Paddy, batting at No 3, knuckled down better than any New Zealander before or since and occupied the crease for a record 11 hours to score 146 not out. That was on top of his four-hour 76 in the first innings on day three, so effectively he batted three consecutive days, a touch under 15 hours in total, with just one mistake. The opposition was Geoff Lawson, Terry Alderman, Carl Rackemann and Merv Hughes, a potent attack in anyone's book. Paddy never quite lived up to those early heroics, simply because he had climbed such a high a mountain in Perth.

No-one in the history of the game has been more exposed in his first series than **Ken Rutherford** was. He was a lamb to the slaughter. To be 19 and told to open the batting against Garner, Holding, Marshall and Walsh in their neck of the woods in Trinidad in 1985 was a nasty and unnecessary assignment. He started his test career much as I did, with 0, 0, 4, 0, 3, 7, 0. How do you ever recover from that? How do you ever reconcile the record books when you start from so far back? Imagine how damaged his belief in himself was.

He did recover to post some superb knocks – centuries at Wellington, Colombo and Christchurch – but his consistency never matched his talent. One innings I will never forget was his 307 scored in two sessions at Scarborough in 1986. He tore the Brian Close XI to shreds, in particular the deceptive Dilip Doshi. It was an incredible display of raw talent, showing what New Zealand missed. If only.

Three other players featured in the 1980s: **Trevor Franklin, Evan Gray** and **Danny Morrison.**

Trevor was a sturdy opener, following in Edgar's footsteps. Just as he was finding his way he was literally cut down by an airport truck at Heathrow, when he had his leg pinned to a wall. He nearly had to have it amputated. That he survived and went on to score an emotional century at Lord's on the following tour of England says much about Trev's character. His fitness was always hampered by the accident, but his spirit is there for all to see on the Lord's honours board.

"EJ" Gray was a real trier. He gave it all, whether with bat or his left-arm spin. He simply had limited opportunity and was third in the queue behind Boock and Bracewell.

Danny Morrison may have been limited in height, but he believed he could bowl like Hadlee and Lillee and ran in with great intent. His bowling may not have reached the heights of those two greats, but "DK" (the same initials as Lillee) had a huge heart, despite having only one lung. His finest moments came in the 1990s, but he learnt his trade alongside Hadlee and mentor Martin Snedden in a three-year apprenticeship. When they retired in 1990, Morrison had to take the reins, which he did with honour.

For quite a while I was the youngest in the team. I batted at No 4 behind Reido or Jed and above Chopper and Mantis. I was surrounded by strong support when out in the middle. Once Howarth departed, I loved the dressing room. It was full of humour and laughter, with massive amounts of time just sitting around at the end of a day sharing stories and a cold beer. That was my favourite time. I loved going next door to fraternise with the opposition, too, to pick a few brains or break down the fast bowlers' myths. I hung out with Cairnsy, Stockley and Chopper a lot. We played golf and visited vineyards when we could. But I felt equally at home with them all. Cairnsy was the patriarch, keeping the peace, while Shake was the motivator, preaching the oracle about how we were "better than they are". Paddles was the mastermind, plotting and planning the next move, and Chats was the organiser, the ideal assistant manager, Sneds the lawyer. We all had specific roles on tour from social committee to flag, balls or scorebook carrier to tickets controller, and we each took pride in every contribution on and off the field.

The 80s Mafia didn't lose a test series at home from 1979 till 1992. It became our duty to hold on. A well-fought draw might result in a win in the next test. We played each test as part of a series, knowing our moment would come.

Paddles had us all target our opposite number and try to beat him. He took on Imran, Botham, Dev or Marshall. I would take on Gower, Border, Viv Richards, Javed Miandad, or Vengsarkar. It was a massive challenge and one we thrived on. It helped us focus on our own game and deliver for the team cause.

We wore the black blazer everywhere we went. That was our badge of honour. The cap was nothing back then; we all wore floppy hats to protect us from the unrelenting sun. We were called the New Zealand team, not a stupid marketing name like Black Caps. We were paid little and never complained because it was part of the privilege, the sacrifice. Paddles kept the car in 1986 (the prize for the player of the series against Australia) and most of us were content for him to do so. It was a rare break in unity.

Paddles and Mantis didn't talk for a few days in Christchurch in 1987. It was during the famous win over the West Indies. It was quite funny watching Shake act as a conduit and relay messages back and forth. But while egos were bruised, it only galvanised the team to achieve a glorious victory, arguably our finest.

The golden run at home finished when we were beaten 2-0 by England in 1992. As captain I felt the disappointment the most, but I said to the team that a new era must begin soon. Only a month later we bounced back to nearly make the final of the 1992 World Cup. Throughout the 1980s, the crowds flocked to watch us defend our territory. That flowed over into one-day internationals as well, where we continued our winning ways.

Those who played won't forget the 43,000-strong crowd that spilled over on to Eden Park when we took on against Greg Chappell's Australians to open the 1981-82 tour. The Underarm match in Melbourne had sparked fervour in New Zealand and many jumped on the bandwagon to support us. Record crowds jammed in to watch the ODIs against England the following year, and the circus rolled on. They were glorious times for all.

Overall, the 80s Mafia were a select lucky few who came together at a time when professionalism met amateurism and the chemistry worked. The senior players carried the day and the young guys toed the line and learnt the ropes. Players knew their roles, who they were up against, and what it meant to wear the blazer.

The 80s Mafia were a fine battalion for the cause – loyal, sacrificing, skilful, courageous and determined. It was an era of massive memories and moments, friendships and foes.

Those were the playing days, but what has that fine bunch been doing more recently for Fleming to tag us so? Well, they are very busy indeed and are rightly involved in supporting the game in many areas because they have the drive, care and expertise to assist.

Glenn Turner is still on the scene, most recently as a talent scout under the Buchanan structure. Turner is an astute and knowledgeable figure, probably best suited to the board level, where he could ask the right questions and encourage the correct kind of debate about our game.

Bruce Edgar, who lives in Australia, was on the short list for the chief executive role eventually won by David White. He would have been an outstanding choice with his honest, intelligent and communicative style, as well as his expertise in the game at the highest level.

John Wright has headed back to India to coach. It was such a shame he lasted only a year or so as head coach of the New Zealand team. Let's hope he returns one day to assist a new generation.

Geoff Howarth lives in England, and has done since he coached the New Zealand team, but no doubt keeps in touch with the game that has been his life.

John Fulton Reid plays a significant part in the administration of New Zealand sport, mainly with Sport New Zealand (formerly Sparc), which replaced the Hillary Commission in assisting sports with funding. He would be a fine board member.

Andrew Jones lives in Auckland and is not involved with cricket, but whenever I catch up with him his ideas are clear and well thought out, and I know he would be an outstanding selector.

Jeff Crowe is one of the top two ICC match referees, travelling the world controlling international matches. He has overseen two World Cup finals. One day, I hope, he will return home from Florida. If he does he will be sought after to join the administration of New Zealand Cricket, such are his mana and qualifications.

Jeremy Coney lives in England and continues to commentate from time to time, something he is very good at. He would always be welcome back on our airwaves, providing good banter with his old mate Bryan Waddle.

Richard Hadlee is retired in Christchurch, after giving so much to the game. Following his fine career he did eight years as a selector. He would be a great voice on the New Zealand Cricket board.

Wally Lees, since being unfairly sacked as New Zealand coach in 1993, has not been seen in any official capacity within the game, but can be heard commentating on radio in the Deep South when an international tour is on.

Ian Smith continues to enhance television sports coverage with his fine anchoring of our live cricket broadcasting on Sky, and his sideline work during rugby matches in winter. His cricket commentary is the best we have: insightful, astute, yet very engaging and chatty.

Stephen Boock has had a rocky ride recently with New Zealand Cricket. He was an excellent board member for a while, and should have become chairman following Alan Isaac, but was surpassed by a rugby man. He then applied for the New Zealand team manager's role and surprisingly missed, but found a position as president of New Zealand Cricket. At least he is still involved.

John Bracewell is in Gloucester, where he runs the cricket department. Had he moved on from New Zealand following the semi-final placing in the 2007 World Cup, he may well have carried on coaching for another country. By the end of 2008 the opportunity had passed and he headed back to county cricket. But he is young enough still to coach internationally, or he may return home and coach new generations, as has Wright has. We need that kind of experience.

Lance Cairns has selected at under-19 level over the years, then had three months as a national selector before Buchanan's new structure led to him being put out to pasture. He is a part-time scout at present. Lance has a brilliant brain and good old-fashioned values, as well as an eye for the creative. He is vastly under-estimated.

Ewen Chatfield drives for Corporate Cabs in Wellington, but should be involved and would be an excellent selector or scout, especially identifying seam bowling talent. He is such a hard worker that he would always be a great asset to the game.

Martin Snedden, since finishing his job as 2011 Rugby World Cup boss, has become the chief executive of New Zealand Tourism. However, surely it won't be long before he is back helping to run our game. He would be an ideal board chairman, someone who is respected the world over and who knows the ins and outs of the game after his successful previous stint as chief executive.

Mark Greatbatch has been desperately unlucky in his efforts to offer his best to cricket here. First, he was wrongly replaced as my vice-captain in 1992 after coming home from Sri Lanka and the bomb-blast saga. More recently, he was removed as a national coach after only 11 months, then wrongly removed as national selector thereafter. I will never understand it because he is a fine man, with genuine integrity. In Hawke's Bay, where he lives, he is always seen coaching and helping young kids with their game. His knowledge is vastly underused.

Ken Rutherford has not ventured back to New Zealand since leaving in 2006, but his bright mind and overseas experience would be welcome here. He keeps a close eye on things these days since his son Hamish, an opening batsman, was promoted into the New Zealand team.

I will add Dipak Patel in here, because while he didn't play much in the 1980s, he is probably seen as part of the mafia. He runs an academy in Howick, Auckland, and has been involved with the under-19s. But his road has been blocked recently, for no apparent reason. He is a fine spin bowling coach and, of course, could bat a bit, too. He'd also be an excellent selector.

So I have broken our omerta, our code of silence, and I am proud to reveal our secrets. We were a special collection of talent and personalities, coming together to represent New Zealand with pride on the cricket field. We enjoyed the honour and the badge we borrowed while in that privileged position. We weren't perfect. We made mistakes, but our intention was to grow and build on the foundations of success we were fortunate to experience. The record speaks for itself, and the camaraderie lives on, the legacy set in stone. Even Stephen Fleming would have to respect that.

CHAPTER 4

Timing is the Thing: Twenty20 Hype

England, May 2003

Life evolves, and change is inevitable. Some handle it, some don't. Life can be simple, or it can go crazy and become complicated.

Normally, when life moves and evolves at a consistent, even pace, situations can be handled better. Growth can be measured and obstacles overcome. But when it gets fast-tracked, that's when it can get complicated and uneasy.

Time, in the literal sense, is what guides us. What do we make of those 24 hours in a day, seven days a week and so on? As life evolves, how well are we using that time?

Over the past few decades we have seen the incredibly fast-changing evolution of many things – computer technology, medicine, science, global warming, media, entertainment, nutrition and intelligence, just to name some obvious ones.

On the incredibly tiny scale of cricket, when I heard the words of Nate Smith, Sky chief executive, say, "Marty, can't you make cricket three hours instead of 30?" a seed was sown in my psyche.

The kids of the mid-1990s were already into many other distractions and activities, such as computers, PlayStations, television and lots more social interaction. Less sport was being played from high school on. Teenagers didn't see the point of playing a game all day.

Nate Smith knew this from growing up in the largest sports nation in the world, the United States. He knew the optimum time frame in which to stage live sport. It was between one and three hours. Playing a game over days, even a working week, didn't make sense to him. Television in the United States had for a long time built its model around the three-hour time frame. Could cricket adapt to such a model?

With Cricket Max we found it could. We found that the three-hour time frame was brilliant to fit around, like going to the movies. We found that the entertainment factor was improved, holding the viewer until the very end. The Max experiment was to become a phenomenon very quickly.

In the winter of 2002, I spoke to Martin Snedden, New Zealand Cricket chief executive, about what was blocking Max from becoming a global game. It was still working well in New Zealand. However, New Zealand Cricket was not growing the format. Instead, since Chris Doig and Neil Maxwell had departed, Cricket Max had started to be downgraded by New Zealand Cricket. From a weekly Friday night slot over eight weeks during 1997-99, it had been cut to a season opening weekend in 2001.

I was getting agitated and confused, because the basic positive signs were obvious, but it needed another injection of enthusiasm and focus from the organisers, New Zealand Cricket. With my concentration on Sky's international cricket coverage, I was not directly responsible any longer for staging the events. So I called Snedden for a review and to understand why he and his marketing department were cooling off on the format.

Snedden's feeling was that for the ICC and its members to embrace Cricket Max, the Max Zone had to be dropped. It was seen as too radical in principle and in execution when setting it up on every ground. We decided that for the next Max tournament the Max Zone would be dropped and a more conventional format adopted instead – same name, same two innings each and same free hit on a front foot no ball.

Annoyingly for me, as already described, the New Zealand Cricket

Nate Smith, Sky chief executive and a man who really understood televised sport. *Photo, Fairfax*

Players Association strike caused the cancellation of the upcoming Max tournament in November 2002. With no players, there was no cricket and Max got hit first. Sadly, it was never played again.

Six months later, the England and Wales Cricket Board (ECB) announced a new format and its plans to launch "Twenty20", a 20-over per side game played during the twilight hours at the height of England's summer season. The board prepared well over three years. It surveyed diligently, and presented it so professionally that when it was launched in May 2003, it went off like an atomic bomb.

Twenty20, designed by Stuart Robertson, a marketing man within the ECB, was a simple derivative of the 50-over game – one innings each, fielding restrictions the same but reduced in direct percentage and four overs maximum for each bowler. The only innovation was that it adopted my free hit idea for any no ball.

The key to Twenty20 was that its designers had locked in on the three-hour time frame. They had seen what we had done with playing 20 overs per side and confirmed it was ideal. Their difference was that as with one-dayers, they adopted one innings each. To this day I will never agree with one innings cricket.

Cricket, which was invented centuries ago, started with two innings to provide everyone with a second chance. That is the essence of the game. Too often I had seen and played in one-day matches that very quickly became one-sided and boring.

With Max, you always had chance to come back and with the Max Zone the game was often never over until the last ball. In the 150 or so first-class Max games played over seven years, 45 per cent went to the last over. The players' and spectators' attention was held to the very end. I also liked what Nate Smith beautifully summed up: "If my favourite player got run out without facing a ball and wasn't to bat again, I would head home!"

The success of Twenty20 reverberated around the world. New Zealand Cricket scheduled it into its domestic programme for 2003-04 and dropped Max. South Africa picked up the ball and ran with it, too. I wasn't surprised or terribly upset by the switch. Yes, I was a little disappointed, but I could see it coming from both the ECB and New Zealand Cricket points of view. The ECB had the clout and backing to make it rock and roll, while New Zealand Cricket could see no-one else playing Max and backed off it. Yet we had been very close to getting the game right until that players' strike. Ironically, Max was an attempt to increase player pay packets, and yet it ended up being shut down by those very players.

When Max was cancelled in late 2002, Stephen Fleming rang me and gave a sarcastic apology. That was probably the most disappointing aspect of the whole thing. I quickly learnt that the new breed of player wasn't that grateful for small mercies.

As for Twenty20, I was privately pleased that what Nate Smith started, I inspired and Rob Hellriegel marketed was being treated deadly seriously all around the world. We may not have owned the patent to the new phenomenon, but we sure knew where it all started – back at Panorama Rd, Penrose, in little old Auckland.

The "baby" that Nate Smith wanted to get rolling eight years earlier was about to take cricket into orbit. Three-hour cricket was set to revolutionise the game globally. The effect would be massive, a quite astonishing transformation in the history of the great game. But not all of it would be gentlemanly.

CHAPTER 5

IPL Launched: Royal Challengers Saga

During the inaugural IPL in 2008, the Royal Challengers Bangalore franchise showed a dark side, revealing a murkiness of private enterprise, ego, deception and, at times, plain bad sportsmanship.

Dr Vijay Mallya, chairman of United Breweries (UB Group), paid more than $US100 million for the Bangalore franchise during the IPL tenders for the eight franchises.

United Breweries, which owned more than 100 liquor brands, had Kingfisher, the biggest beer brand in India, as its flagship. Mallya also owed an airline branded Kingfisher.

He bought the IPL franchise to promote his UB brands. For example, Royal Challenger is a popular whiskey and so it suited being the naming sponsor of the new IPL franchise based in Bangalore, where the UB Group headquarters are.

I was rung in March 2008 by the captain, Rahul Dravid, and chief executive, Charu Sharma, and asked to become involved in the management team for the first year. It was an exciting invitation, especially because I had so much admiration for Rahul. Also, I was intrigued by the development of the new enterprise using Twenty20.

I took leave without pay from Sky for eight weeks.

Over the next few weeks Mallya, Dravid and Sharma planned and then attended the first live cricket auction (each team had salary cap of $US5 million) and bought a team to represent the Royal Challengers Bangalore.

On April 18, 2008, in front of 60,000 screaming fans at Chinnaswamy Stadium in Bangalore, and a massive television audience, the official opening was held, followed by the first match, Royal Challengers Bangalore against Kolkata Knight Riders. It was a dramatic night indeed, because Kolkata launched a blitz on our bowlers that will long be remembered.

In an astonishing display, Brendon McCullum smashed the bowling to all parts, scoring 158 not out from just 73 balls. He hit 13 sixes and 10 fours. It was an innings that set the IPL alight.

Only an hour after the Royal Challengers had lost, Mallya summoned Rahul Dravid and me (as the chief cricket officer) to his after-party and debrief. Rahul wisely didn't show. Unwisely, Mark Boucher took his place as my wing man.

Within 30 minutes, Mallya was yelling at those around how he had "had" wicketkeeper-batsman McCullum at the auction. "He was mine!" he screamed. Then he complained that Dravid and Sharma had denied him and that McCullum had ruined his big night. He vented all this in front of me and his wicketkeeper-batsman, Mark Boucher.

Boucher, to his credit, skulled his beer quietly and walked off muttering under his breath: "I have no respect for this man." I sat there and said nothing. When I walked away, I thought as Boucher had. Was that to be normal behaviour for our owner every time we got beaten by a better side? Annoyingly, it was. For the next seven weeks, I received texts and phone calls from Mallya, often after midnight, demanding all sorts of things. The bluster came thick and fast.

Charu Sharma, a lovely man with a genuine love of cricket, was unceremoniously sacked as chief executive. So, too, was coach Venkatesh ("Venky") Prasad, the former Indian medium pace bowler and then the Indian bowling coach. This happened the morning after our fifth loss in seven games, following another Kingfisher after-party at UB Headquarters.

Upon hearing the news at 11am on May 6, the day we were to fly to Kolkata, Rahul and I started damage control. If Venky was sent packing, we could off too, we felt. Venky wasn't even in the country in the lead-up to the IPL, or anywhere near the auction, yet he was a scapegoat. Charu's father had just died, so the timing of his sacking was especially cruel. We felt Charu was best out of the debacle, a chance to grieve in peace.

Amrit Thomas, United Spirits Group's vice-president of marketing, quickly realised Rahul and I meant what we said and backtracked, sparing Venky, but confirming Charu was gone. From my standpoint it was becoming a murky business indeed.

It got murkier when the news of the sacking of Charu and Venky got leaked to the media. Venky got the shock of his life on the Hyderabad tarmac en route to Kolkata to learn via texts from friends that his head was on the block, and that the media was reporting he had been sacked. Thomas got to him at Kolkata before he boarded the bus and assured him it was a media beat-up. Thomas then stood in front of the team at the hotel and told them about the situation with Charu, saying he had resigned for "personal reasons".

Thomas, a nice enough man, was the assigned corporate dressed up in big smiles and in the Royal Challengers shirt he wore day and night. But he appeared under pressure to deliver the message of doom. Venky went at him later that night, while Rahul and I sat seething at the way it was unfolding.

Discussing Twenty20 batting with my captain, Rahul Dravid.

There were still seven matches to go. We were only halfway through the tournament and already the team was sunk, on and off the field. In Mohali, Rahul and I spoke of resigning with dignity and grace, but we held on.

Thomas turned up in Delhi, just before the fifth game, and from then attended all our team gatherings, practices and selection meetings. He had been sent in to work the oracle, to avoid further embarrassment as the team staggered from one loss to another.

Mallya demanded victory, despite having bought a team that was too tired and slow, too injured and old, for the hustle of Twenty20. The team looked more like a test unit.

Some of the key players, such as Anil Kumble, Rahul Dravid, Zaheer Khan, Dale Steyn, Mark Boucher, Shivnarine Chanderpaul and Jacques Kallis, were more suited to the longer version of the game. They were fine players, capable of adjusting to different formats if given the time, but most had recently played in gruelling test series and the fatigue factor was significant. We had only two days before the tournament began and our big-name players were exhausted. The local Indian players – there had to be seven locals picked per match – couldn't pick up the slack at all, which wasn't the case of many of the other teams, notably Rajastan, Delhi and Chennai.

Thomas claimed we weren't practising enough, or using enough data and stats to force the message home. He knew little about cricket, or sport for that matter, but had taken charge of the Royal Challengers. My role was becoming redundant by the day.

Tagging along with Thomas was the IPL entertainment director, Venkat Vardhan. He was the henchman with the deep, croaky voice. Why a rock concert promoter was at all our meetings and in our dressing room was beyond me, but he played an increasingly dominant role, too. I began to feel that a significant moment in cricket history was being overshadowed by ego and corporate intrusion.

From that point, no matter how hard our players tried, you could tell their hearts weren't in it. Getting paid was the focus and players became turned off and distracted. For example, Mark Boucher refused to play until late payments were made into his bank account. I supported Mark and others who were made to wait. Blackberry phones that were distributed at the start by team management for the players to keep were now apparently only "on loan".

Brijesh Patel, a former Indian batsman, replaced Charu Sharma as the chief executive. He didn't do anything to help the situation and couldn't even improve our practice facilities at Chinnaswamy Stadium, where he was stadium boss. Bizarrely, Patel had only recently opposed Mallya in a Karnataka cricket election. Soon our planning and selection meetings comprised of Patel, Thomas, Vardhan, Dravid, Prasad and me. It was bordering on madness.

We kept losing and Mallya kept screaming. In a wild moment during the Turkish Grand Prix in Istanbul – he also owned a Formula One team – he publicly attacked his own captain, Indian icon Rahul Dravid, for picking the wrong team at the auction. He blamed Rahul for picking old mates. It was whipped up by the Indian media. The skipper was livid and beaten. We all were. Mallya had worn us out.

The next extraordinary move came within days. Someone from UB Group headquarters sent an office boy to see me. Young Jacob handed me my three-year contract (it had been extended upon my arrival from one to three years on their insistence) and asked me to re-sign it back to one year. I laughed and sought out Thomas to get to the bottom of it all. He denied any knowledge and life carried on in its normal bizarre way. Two others on the management team were treated to the same manoeuvre – young Jacob called on them, too.

At the very end we enjoyed an astonishing win against Chennai, coming back from the dead. It eased the pain, but in truth we'd already suffered cardiac arrest.

I recruited a new coach for the Royal Challengers just before I departed. Hard-nosed South African Ray Jennings was appointed, chosen to ensure the South African players were re-focused and local players brought into line. The big hurdle for Jennings would be to keep the United Spirits Group big-wigs from continuing to interfere with the cricket.

We went home to different parts of the world. Upon reaching Auckland, I received a termination notice, via email, from Amrit Thomas. I jumped at the chance for a release and to resume normality in my life.

In a smart move, Rahul Dravid stepped aside as captain and retained his dignity. It was about the only decent move by anyone during the two months of the Royal Challengers' existence.

The inaugural IPL final was a ratings success, with the least fancied side at the start, the Rajasthan Royals, led by the clever and resourceful Shane Warne, taking the glory and the title. Ratings went through the roof and the frenzy surrounding the tournament was undeniable.

A year later, the next IPL tournament was staged in South Africa because of terrorist concerns. The Royal Challengers' fortunes rocketed. Under new captain Anil Kumble and coach Ray Jennings, the team reversed their results and faced off in a thrilling final against the Deccan Chargers, who were last in the first year. Deccan won by six runs.

Dravid, Kallis, Kumble, Steyn and Boucher all played significant roles as they adjusted with fresh enthusiasm and vigour. No doubt my absence was helpful, too.

The first year was a nightmare, but all involved learned a better way forward. Under new management, the Challengers finally got on track.

The first two years of the IPL were a box office sensation and showed that to make money luring television, sponsorships and crowds, a Twenty20 league was the way. Cricket Max in New Zealand sowed the seed, England and South Africa took it to a true level of exposure and then India gave it the almighty boost to the moon and back. Before long, leagues were springing up everywhere.

Allen Stanford, the crooked billionaire from Texas, decided to spend good folks' lifelong investments on a West Indian league, involving England in a $20 million match. Not surprisingly, that all went pear-shaped when Stanford was caught with his $16 billion ponzi scheme and was sentenced to 110 years in prison. That disaster didn't deter the rest of the world from joining the fun – The Big Bash in Australia, the HRV Cup in New Zealand, the SPL in Sri Lanka and the BPL in Bangladesh made grand appearances on their domestic scenes, raking in television, sponsorship and gate receipts revenue.

Following on from the entrepreneurial work Lalit Modi did setting up the IPL was the creation of a joint venture between India, South Africa and Australia: the Champions League (not to be confused with the ICC's Champions Trophy, the 50-over knockout tournament played every four years).

The competing teams are the winners of all the domestic T20 tournaments, and come together every September in either South Africa or India. ESPN Star picked up the television rights for 10 years for $1 billion. The great news for the domestic teams (and their boards) that qualify for the tournament is they all enjoy a financial boom.

As an event, the Champions League hasn't really captured the public's imagination, because the net is cast too wide and there are too many unknown teams and players involved.

Modi pulled off a miracle with his Champions League television deal, but soon his time was up. Before long he had not only lost a high-profile libel case with Chris Cairns, but had been kicked off the Indian Cricket Board, and out of the IPL and the Champions League.

After five years, the frenzy around the IPL had died down, but more and more players were queuing up for the chance to earn some of the riches on offer. No-one could blame them, but I did sometimes wonder just what Nate Smith and I started.

CHAPTER 6

Technology Wars: Decision Review System

The technology issue has been botched. The problem is a lack of clarity over what it's meant to be used for and it won't go away either.

From day one, when the ICC decided to use technology to review umpiring, we have witnessed many wars – between boards, between technology providers, between players and umpires and between the ICC and its fans. The infamous Decision Review System (DRS) is a disaster on the main level, a necessary evil on others.

Technology is growing rapidly. The technology in television, and specifically cricket, is consistently improving. It's becoming faster, more accurate, clearer to see, innovative and fresh. But it is expensive. The companies that invest the money do so at great risk.

The need for technology in assisting the officiating became evident when too often the headlines were dominated by umpiring howlers that were perceived to have determined the outcome of matches. Under pressure, umpires were being exposed to the difficulties of working all around the world in a tough professional environment.

When the ICC decided to create an elite panel of neutral umpires, it took on a difficult task. It was assuming that those 12 chosen each year would be able to withstand the travel, the time away from home, the pressures, their age, their health, their confidence and their human frailty.

Umpires are honest, hard-working people by and large. There have been some strange ones, some wacky ones, some corrupt ones and some criminal ones, but overall they umpire for the love of the game. They used to umpire at home, with little travel and acclimatisation required. Once they were appointed to travel the world, it became clear that the umpiring gig was indeed tough.

In many ways it was a sad day when neutral umpires became the norm in international cricket. It meant that Peter Willey and Simon Taufel and Aleem Dar couldn't ever umpire in their own country. It finished Willey's career because he didn't want to travel the world, so one of the greatest umpires was lost. Not to have Dickie Bird standing at Lord's any more didn't seem right. Because of a few isolated nasty incidents, we succumbed to posting neutral umpires to all test matches. Perhaps Mike Gatting poking Shakoor Rana in the chest in a foul-mouthed exchange in 1987 was the catalyst for change. But that incident was by far the exception to the rule.

Nevertheless change took place and the game lost a part of its soul. Becoming an elite umpire meant you were the best of the best, were paid accordingly, were required to be anywhere at any time and expected to make very few mistakes. It all took its toll over time. Umpires showed their age, or their lack of fitness, or their inability to cope. Only the real top guns survived the daily scrutiny. Only Simon Taufel and Aleem Dar from the dozens used today have truly stood out. Before that, David Shepherd and Steve Bucknor were the best of their time. Before that it was Dickie Bird and Peter Willey. In any given period there really are only a few who excel. There will be others who rise, perhaps younger ones, but there is an attrition rate.

Since technology such as ball-tracking became a permanent part of television broadcasts, starting with Channel 4 in 2001, the cry to use what the fans see, but the umpires don't and should see, has grown louder.

There are various types of cameras, and technology is used at different frames per second – the speeds depending on the budget of the production. The cameras are positioned all around the ground, the more the merrier, again depending on budget. Sky New Zealand has up to 24 cameras, including stump cam, but Australia's Channel 9 has almost double that.

NORMAL CAMERAS. The live action is shot from high up behind the bowler and is captured by a standard 25 to 100 times zoom lens (at 25 frames per second).

SUPER SLOW MOTION replays use special Super Slow cameras (and operate at between 125 and 250 frames per second). The super slow motion cameras have been excellent at showing close-up replays of any edges or action around the batsman that may lead to an appeal. Hotspot has lately confirmed what the super slow motion replay has already shown. Super slow motion replays have also been used to pick up low catches, but the 2D image makes action extremely close to the ground difficult to be emphatic about.

ULTRA SLOW MOTION is a fast-developing technology that has become a marvel. The ultra slow motion replay using special cameras (at up to 2500 frames per second) is astonishing. In many ways this for me is the essence of television – the ability to produce a picture that reveals all. However, it takes more time to set up and put to air and is used mainly as an art form, not a tool for officiating. Most networks don't have the ultra slow motion cameras because they're too expensive. BSKYB in Britain and Channel 9 have budgets to burn so have used them expertly.

LINE CALLS – run outs and stumpings. From my recollection, they were introduced following the 1992 World Cup. John Wright's final test in early 1993 finished with two run outs. His fate was decided by the third umpire in both innings, using the pan-eye cameras positioned square of the wicket on both sides. Initially those cameras were of poor quality and showed a grainy, fuzzy picture, making it difficult at times to determine the line. Often the real decision would lie in between frames. Lately the quality has become excellent and replays are often used as part of the production, not just to assist umpires.

SPEEDBALL started in the late 1990s and was a police gun, handheld by a manual operator. It therefore had its up and downs, but gave an indication. Australia's speedgun was always 3kmh to 5kmh quicker than ours in New Zealand. There appeared a need across the Tasman at one point to register Brett Lee at more than 160kmh. These days it is collaborated with the other technology to ensure consistent accuracy around the world.

SOUND – SNICKO. Snicko was a brilliant addition to Channel 4's coverage in 1999. Snicko marries the vision from the broadcast super slow motion cameras with the audio from the stump microphones. The audio is represented by an oscillograph that shows peaks and troughs of an audio signal. The graph shows a sharp rise in sound for a snick, indicating the ball has hit the bat, or a wider picture, indicating the ball has hit the pad, body or glove. Once vision and audio are synchronised, it is possible to tell whether the noise corresponded with the ball going past the bat. Snicko doesn't tell you that a batsman has hit the ball, but rather that a noise occurred at the time when the ball went past the bat. Its problem was that it could take up to five minutes to put to air because of the complexity of setting up the graph. Therefore it was very slow when used to assist umpires. Sometimes the nature of the graph spike is unclear as to what the sound actually was. Therefore this was an entertainment tool, not one for assisting umpires or the Decision Review System. Lately the good news is that Snicko is able to be collaborated in real time, so it can be viewed straight away alongside Hotspot.

VIRTUAL MAT/RED ZONE. The virtual mat or Red Zone, as it was called initially by Channel 4 in 1999, is the line or area between the two sets of stumps. This helps to interpret where the ball landed or where the ball struck the batsman in relation to the stumps. The initial problem was getting a steady camera to keep the lines and area perfectly aligned. In New Zealand we often had to position the cameras on scaffold and when a wind blew it played havoc with the alignment. Often we couldn't go to air with the technology. As time has gone on, the cameras have become properly secured, so there is no movement. The virtual mat is super-imposed over the replay of the action down the line of the pitch to show the action of the ball against the mat.

VIRTUAL 3D STADIUM. Animated Research Ltd came up with a virtual stadium and went to air with it in 2002 on Sky in New Zealand. It was an innovation that took the viewer inside the stadium down on to the pitch, into the slips and could display any run scored or any field position movement, as well as every ball's trajectory. It was a useful tool for many reasons and gave a unique look at cricket in 3D for the first time.

BALL-TRACKING – actual and predictive paths. Hawkeye was designed by Dr Paul Hawkins. The ball-tracking predictive path was launched on Channel 4 in 2001. It was groundbreaking. Six cameras set up around the ground would capture the ball and dot the actual path until the moment it hit the batsman or the bat. Using that data, it would then calculate and predict the path towards and through the stumps. My concerns have always been about the bounce of the predictive path. First, when a full toss or half-volley is bowled it offers no bounce data and comes up as the ball going along the ground. Obviously it has to show some bounce, but it doesn't have the data to do so. My biggest worry is around the bounce for spinners. All I ever see is the ball from a spinner predicted to bounce on the normal trajectory we see from a fast bowler. It doesn't appear to account for the slower pace of the ball and therefore the drop or downward turn of the ball. Often we see the ball bounce high over the stumps when it feels as though it should bounce into the stumps. Hawkeye uses between 200 and 250 frames per second. Animated Research Ltd launched its ball-tracking system in mid-2008 and used cameras at 230 frames per second. They have improved steadily and operate for Channel 9 and Sky New Zealand with growing reputations.

HEAT/HOTSPOT. BBG Sports, which invented Snicko, also created Hotspot. This is based on a heat device using infra-red cameras and lenses at 100 frames per second. The infra-red cameras, which were initially made for the military, pick up the heat, including that of the players, the ball and whatever the ball hits, leaving a white mark against a black or grey background, just as you would see in an x-ray. This has proved to be the most accurate and compelling of all the technology. It becomes clear to all what has happened because the mark is there to prove it. Old cameras made the picture a bit grainy and the white mark was difficult to pick out at times, but Hotspot now has the latest cameras reducing motion-blur. That allows for much easier identification of very faint hot spots.

This is all very expensive – all the more reason to receive funding assistance from the ICC.

By 2005 the ICC had plenty of technology to assess from the various broadcasts around the world. The market that was providing these was becoming reliable and credible.

The ICC decided to experiment during the one-off Super Series test, between Australia and a World XI in Sydney in 2005, allowing the umpires to call for the third umpire to use the technology available. The result was constant referral upstairs and a lot of time wasted. The third umpire became not just the busiest but the key man, rather than the appointed umpires out in the middle.

The experiment showed that the game couldn't afford to be slowed up any further than the pace at which it was already being played. But what of the decisions – were they better? At that point the technology was still developing. Hawkeye had established itself as worth a proper trial, but other technologies, such as Snicko, were still works in progress and took a long time to get on air. Hotspot hadn't quite arrived.

Ultimately, the umpires lost the confidence to make their own decisions and decided to check for almost everything, as is normally the case for all run outs and stumpings. It was an experiment that was never tried again.

In 2006 I was asked to join a newly formed committee set up by the MCC, and in particular by former England captain Tony Lewis. The MCC World Committee was an initiative to go beyond just governing the laws the MCC was the guardian of, but to cast an eye over global cricket issues.

The committee included names and faces from all around the globe – Geoff Boycott, Mike Brearley, Alec Stewart, Mike Gatting and Mike Atherton (all former England captains), Barry Richards, Steve Waugh, Courtney Walsh, Rahul Dravid, Anil Kumble, Majid Khan, David Shepherd, Steve Bucknor, David Richardson (from the ICC) and me. Inside the MCC were two sharp brains, John Stephenson, former England opener and the MCC cricket manager, and Fraser Stewart, its research guru. We planned to meet twice a year; mid-year at Lord's and later in the year elsewhere.

I loved the camaraderie and expertise, the debates and social occasions. We had so many items on the agenda that one-day meetings became two-day forums. The list was vast. To name just a dozen:

Spirit of cricket
Anti-corruption
Future tours programme
Short formats like Twenty20 within international structure
World Cup structure
Slow play
ICC governance
Test cricket's future
Technology
Elite umpiring panel
Throwing
Rules and regulations

The issues were well researched and opinions were presented expertly to the group. At the end of the forum a series of statements would be released to the media. We were independent and were highly motivated. Each country was represented, so someone from each country gave updates on each nation's progress or problems. Steve Waugh looked specifically at anti-corruption, Barry Richards and Geoff Boycott focused on the ICC governance and board administration, John Stephenson on day-night test cricket using the pink ball. I spent much of my time on technology, slow play and the test championship concept.

One of the issues high on the agenda was technology. As an executive producer for Sky Television, I had an advantage as to the ins and outs of the television and technology world. I had already covered the topic extensively in my Cowdrey Lecture in 2006, and so was happy to front the committee's technology research team.

My first task was to open up my mind to ball-tracking and the predictive path that Hawkeye had introduced in 2001 on Channel 4. Instinctively I was against the predictive path. I preferred the subjective decision on lbws to match the fact that the ball never actually went on to hit the wicket, so any decision was therefore purely an umpire's opinion.

Hawkeye began predicting the path from the point where the ball would hit the leg or pad and on to where it would potentially hit the stumps. The assertion that the data was accurate to within 5mm seemed wrong at times. I was against the calculated guessing and preferred the umpire's opinion. I love the lbw law in that a decision is made when the stumps have not been hit. In other words it didn't happen.

I spent many an hour discussing the virtues of Hawkeye with Paul Hawkins until finally I felt the accuracy was sufficient to be used, but only as an entertainment tool, not for determining a player's career or a match result.

I then decided to do two things.

First, I would include Hawkeye in our Sky Television coverage in New Zealand and see how it went. Hawkins dropped his price to New Zealand dollars and that meant we were able to offer the viewers the same technology they were witnessing on our network through the Channel 9 and Channel 4 coverage we beamed in from Australia and England. It was a better result for the subscribers, once we could afford it.

It was not a better result for Animated Research Ltd, a company based in Dunedin that had done amazing work designing and executing the virtual tracking of yachts during the America's Cup yachting in New Zealand. It had a cricket 3D engine that we were excited to include in our Sky coverage, but after three years, I reluctantly decided to move on. I never disputed the company's technology, which was spectacular. The problem was the operational side, which was a bit lazy and lacked properly trained back-up.

I also needed to ensure Sky viewers were getting what they were seeing on overseas broadcasts. Hawkeye featured in every broadcast from England, South Africa and Australia. So, when Hawkeye dropped its price and offered ball-tracking on top of 3D imagery, I changed my mind on ball-tracking and went with Hawkeye. I was impressed by Hawkeye's ability to train many operators, initially through courses in English universities, therefore creating plenty of expert back-up for the various events it was involved in around the world, and not just in cricket.

In 2007, in my role fronting the technology issue for the MCC World Committee, I planned a meeting in Dubai with David Richardson, then ICC general manager, and Paul Hawkins. We sat around for a few days discussing the pros and cons of using technology to assist umpires. The main reason for inviting Hawkins was because of his unrivalled success in providing technology for Grand Slam tennis tournaments. In that case his company was dealing only with the actual path or whether the ball was in or out. It was pretty simple, but it was the challenge system that caught Richardson's eye, and mine. Could it apply to cricket?

We agreed that allowing umpires to refer to the new technology when they wanted didn't work. We felt the challenge system was worthy, but disagreed about the number of challenges that should be allowed and even whether ball-tracking was needed.

My view was that the system should be dead simple to start with, particularly because cricket could be so complex. This system was going to be delicate, so it needed the players and umpires to understand exactly why it was there and how to use it. I felt that there should be only one unsuccessful challenge, so that everyone would realise the system was only to be used for the 100 per cent obvious howlers made very rarely by umpires, the sorts of decision that did nobody any good and could change a match and create headlines.

I also said I didn't feel ball-tracking was necessary for the system to start with because lbws were always contentious and were best left to the opinion of the umpires.

Their angle was that the broadcast would show the ball-tracking imagery later anyway, and most likely show up the umpires' decisions, and therefore prompt the question why technology wasn't being used more. I argued that if it was absolutely clear from the outset that the system was for edges, using Hotspot and super slo-mos, as well as actual path line calls using the 3D mat, then those should be acceptable to everyone. But if we offered players three unsuccessful challenges plus ball-tracking, then they would get into the mode of gambling away at least two if not all of them, especially for lbws.

My point was that it was vital we communicate the system in a simple and clear way so everyone would be sure about the use of the system. Players had to understand that the system was for assisting the umpires when something went wrong, not for assisting their ability to gain an advantage or for tactical use. The system would be called upon only if the players absolutely knew that an umpiring mistake had been made and to protect the umpire and the integrity and spirit of the game. Then the players would come to the rescue of the umpire by referring the decision upstairs to technology.

The ICC discussed it further. Then it all got too much and it was forced to take action. In a particularly feisty and unsavoury test, in Sydney in early 2008 between Australia and India, we all saw the game played in poor spirit. It wasn't so much the umpiring as the attitudes of both teams. They were hellbent on giving no quarter at any cost and there were foul-mouthed and abusive outbursts, which led to frayed tempers and umpiring mistakes. The headlines in that series were for all the wrong reasons. Technology was showing up every mistake and the true spirit of cricket was lost.

Something had to give. To try to counter the problems, reduce player animosity and pressure on umpires, and clean up the game, the ICC finally decided to experiment using technology in a test series. It targeted India's tour of Sri Lanka in July and August 2008. The experiment included ball-tracking, but not Hawkeye. Instead, it strangely went with Animated Research Ltd, which just happened to have the rights to that series. Animated Research Ltd was given 48 hours to prove its accuracy, which was ridiculous.

The ICC allowed for three unsuccessful challenges per team per innings, but didn't use the predictive path. Whether the whole thing was properly communicated to the teams, captains and coaches is unclear. But the results of the three-test series were very clear. For India, it was an unmitigated disaster. Overall 48 reviews were called for, 12 of which were successful (but only one successful review by India). The other 36 reviews by both teams were unsuccessful. There were 39 reviews for lbw and only seven were successful. Appeals for caught decisions were the only positive result: 9 reviews, 5 successful. As a result, India have never agreed to use the Decision Review System again. They simply don't trust the technology. They also felt uncomfortable with the challenge system and in particular the number of times you could challenge. To me, India were the only ones who really understood the initial premise: the need to remove howlers only.

India felt put out by the whole experience and as it unfolded over the years they felt nothing really changed. The ICC, however, felt justified throughout and made only minor tweaks. I was in India's camp on this one.

The ball-tracking technology for this first experiment in the Sri Lanka series was in the hands of Ian Taylor and Animated Research Ltd. Immediately after the series he wrote on Cricinfo: "As Virtual Eye CEO, I wouldn't normally enter this debate, but in the interest of balance I make the following observations. We have always maintained that the technology behind both Hawkeye and Virtual Eye has limitations and that those limitations, whilst not critical for the entertainment value in television, would need to be addressed if there was ever a move to use it to 'assist' umpires (officially). Unlike Hawkeye, which had three months to prepare for its measurement test with the MCC, we had just 48 hours prior to the first test. We believe there is a place for technology – but not at the expense of the umpire."

Clearly it was all a rush job and a poor start for everyone, especially the ICC and Animated Research Ltd. Worse, India were so disappointed with the overall experiment, the ball-tracking technology and the challenge system that they became defiant. Instead of acknowledging their mistakes, the ICC ploughed on as if nothing was wrong. Only Ian Taylor, in his words to Cricinfo, had a grasp on the reality of the situation, but the ICC never listened.

Over a year later, in November 2009 in Dunedin, the ICC officially introduced the Decision Review System to test cricket. The series was between New Zealand and Pakistan. I was in the commentary box, but no longer as executive producer, having been sacked in 2008. Taking my place was James Cameron, who immediately replaced Hawkeye with Animated Research Ltd for coverage on Sky.

Animated Research Ltd would be the first official technology provider for test cricket because of the series chosen and it had satisfied the authorities of its accuracy. Animated Research Ltd performed satisfactorily and proved it was a worthy opponent of Hawkeye.

However, I thoroughly disliked watching players challenge lbws when they knew it was a 50-50 call at best. They were tactically gambling a challenge because they could. It went against the whole premise of what it should have been set up to do.

The other aspect I didn't enjoy, because it was so complicated and hard to understand, was the criteria for overturning a decision.

Take this scenario:

- A batsman is hit on the pads and given out. Knowing it's a 50-50 call, that he is a key batsman and that his team has three unsuccessful challenges up their sleeves, he decides to review. The ball-tracking predictive path shows the ball clipping the leg stump by a whisker, so with the benefit going to the umpire not the batsman, the lbw is upheld and the batsman walks off convinced there was doubt.
- With the next ball the new batsman receives the same delivery. He is hit on the pads and this time is given not out. The fielding captain, knowing it's 50:50 and that he has three unsuccessful challenges left, decides to review the not out decision. The predictive path shows the ball just clipping the leg stump, so the review is turned down, the batsman and the umpire getting the benefit.

The batzsman previously given out is watching in the dressing room as he undoes his pads. Doubtless, he's miffed.

- From the next ball there is another shout for lbw. It looks similar to the one before, so the umpire gives it not out. The fielding captain, knowing he has two unsuccessful challenges left, decides that it's worth the gamble to remove this key new batsman, so calls for another review. The predictive path shows the ball hitting leg stump, but a little closer to the middle of the leg stump. In fact, when it's zoomed in really close, it has hit the leg stump right on the little black centre line, only millimetres inside from the where the previous ball struck. But as it is hitting the centre line of the stump and is therefore inside the "zone of certainty", the third umpire must tell the umpire in the middle to reverse his decision and give the batsman out. The umpire in the middle crosses his arms and raises his finger. The batsman and umpire have both been denied the benefit, while the fielding captain is cock-a-hoop because his gamble has paid off big-time.

In three balls you have a snapshot of the ridiculous system the ICC has hung its hat on. No wonder India have a problem with it and no wonder many players thinks it is flawed and are confused about it. Also, it is little wonder the fans think it's madness, because it's confusing, complex and contradictory.

I would scrap the system as it is and instead would put the following in place:

1. One unsuccessful challenge per team per innings. The clear direction to all players is that the only time the system should be used is when an embarrassing mistake his been made and should be overturned for everyone's sake. In other words, the players are protecting the umpire. The system is not for personal or team tactical use. That would be regarded as going against the spirit of the game and the umpires.
2. No predictive path is necessary. The point of the system is merely to remove the howler, which can be decided by Hotspot and Real Time Snicko or super slo mo replays.
3. The technology that should be used is the actual path and the virtual mat. Because that is accurate to 5mm at the very worst, that is sufficient to assist the umpires with line calls pitching outside leg or hitting outside off, just as it does for line calls for stumpings and run outs.

The only problem with implementing this after five years of getting it wrong is that the players have got used to a certain way of using the system.

For example, on January 20, 2013, at the Sydney Cricket Ground, Michael Clarke was given out lbw to a straight ball by Sri Lankan Nuwan Kulasekera. There was no doubt about the decision. Yet Clarke used the one challenge allowed to his team (recently reduced to one for ODIs, which is smart) and found that the decision not only stood but that he looked ridiculous for reviewing. Even worse, 75 runs later,

David Warner and Moises Henriques were both given out lbw after big inside edges on to the pads. No challenge was left for the mistakes to be reversed. Clarke had simply followed the norm of challenging and gambling because that's how it had been done for so long under the test rules of initially three and latterly two challenges per innings.

The ICC has created a culture over several years and the players will find it hard to change, even if the system is appropriately changed and simplified.

Ian Chappell has a strong view that the players' challenge system be scrapped and that the technology be handed back to the umpires. I can understand his desire to move away from the players using the system strategically, but handing it over to the umpires will bring other problems. The players' challenge was meant to cut to the chase, for a group of players to quickly acknowledge an on-field umpiring howler and get it corrected.

Asking the third umpires to check anything they like when they like will cause incredible delays.

Since 2001, with the introduction of Hawkeye, the game has evolved dramatically. Television coverage is outrageously good in the way it tells the story. From an entertainment viewpoint, the fans are well served with what they see in the comfort of their homes. It's compelling viewing.

What isn't so compelling is the lack of spirit in the way the game is being played. Using technology for tactical purposes is outright wrong. Players do it because they can, so shame on the ICC for allowing that.

In February 2013, the MCC World Committee met in Auckland because it coincided with the England tour. During the two-day forum, the committee listened to Ian Taylor from Animated Research Ltd and Virtual Eye, and Warren Brennan from BBG Sports, which owns Hotspot and Snicko. They both gave outstanding presentations – Brennan with video analysis of Hotspot and Taylor with video and with a compelling document on the fundamental flaws of the Decision Review System. Both were honest and frank and offered a detailed summary of the problems that the Decision Review System creates and the solutions needed. I hadn't spoken to Ian or Warren since 2008, but it was music to my ears to hear them talk about what I believed were the issues and solutions. Both were scathing of the non-existent structure and lack of planning within the system, and were appalled with how it was used when compared to other sports they were associated with.

Sitting there hearing all this was the new ICC chief executive, David Richardson. He had been on the committee for several years as the ICC's representative and was directly responsible for the Decision Review System as the ICC general manager. Often during our MCC meetings he would block any new idea that didn't fit with his thinking or the ICC's. As a former lawyer, he was skilled at waiting for the moment to pour cold water and shut down discussion or remove momentum.

I felt that as time went on having an ICC man on the committee was counter-productive, because we were losing our independent thinking and our ability to debate properly and recommend accordingly.

On this occasion, when Taylor and Brennan finished their presentations, Richardson made the comment that he couldn't agree with the argument, indicating he wasn't prepared to even listen to the experts, the ones investing millions of dollars.

More to the point, the committee needed time to discuss things among themselves before Richardson poured scorn on it all. Our job was to make a recommendation to the ICC, not for the ICC to kill it before we had a chance to assess it.

Richardson showed a glimpse of why the ICC too often is an ineffective governing body. It just doesn't want to know. I sat there wondering what more Taylor and Brennan could do or say, or even why they bothered, because they appeared very frustrated.

After they left, I decided my time was up, too. It felt like there was very little point in the World Committee gathering all these fine people if one of its members – Richardson – was going to shoot down almost every idea and presentation put forward. Most of the rest of the members looked resigned. As one member quietly whispered to me: "Now I know why it's called the DRS – the David Richardson System."

I resigned my post and left the room, thanking chairman Mike Brearley for the honour of being on the committee for seven years, but saying that my days were done. For me, heavily involved in chemotherapy treatment, it was time to head home.

Unless the ICC is prepared to listen, the game is never going to progress.

CHAPTER 7

The Game has Changed: Money, Men and Methods

Cricket has evolved over a century and a half. At times it has exploded into life and made massive change. The greatest seismic shift was created in 1977 by Kerry Packer. His actions changed the landscape of cricket forever. It may not have been his idea per se, but it was his courage and money that made it all happen. The idea, it is said, was conjured up by a couple of television comedians and a fiery fast bowler in Australia.

John Cornal and Paul Hogan were the comedians, Dennis Lillee the cricketer. The subject of the conversation was that Lillee, despite being the best fast bowler in the world, was being paid a miserly $8000 a season to be in peak form. Cornal and Hogan were disgusted by the revelation and came up with the notion of staging a carnival match involving the world's best at the end of the season and getting Channel 9 to televise it. The gate receipt money would go to the players.

Kerry Packer was approached and he was eager to get cricket on his network. He took the one-game idea and enlarged it, secretly signing up 60 of the world's top players for a whole season. It ran foul of authorities around the world, so he went to the High Court to battle the ICC and won, launching World Series Cricket in the summer of 1977-78 to small crowds and a ballooning budget. A year later, 50,000 spectators crammed the Sydney Cricket Ground for a day-night match. Cricket had changed forever.

After that tumultuous two-year period and through the roaring 80s, cricket bloomed into a game of two magnificent forms – the 50-over one-day game and test cricket. The governing bodies' coffers filled and the players felt respected and well remunerated. The game thrived.

Many other ideas for shorter forms were trialled on a low-key basis through those glorious times, but it wasn't until New Zealand's Sky TV chief executive, Nate Smith, spoke about a three-hour time frame that the game took on another significant change.

It's a weird feeling knowing exactly when and where that conversation took place, 1pm, September 25, 1995, in Nate Smith's office. I took those words and designed Cricket Max, took it back to Smith a month later and through his courage and Sky's money, we launched the three-hour game. It was Max that showed that three-hour night-time matches, after work or from 7.30pm under lights, were the future.

In 1998 the ECB showed intense interest in what we were doing, agreed for England to play New Zealand in three Max internationals Down Under and then began designing and marketing its own game – Twenty20.

Twenty20 was simple, a straight derivative of the 50-over game. It took off in 2003 and is still gaining momentum. In April 2008, when the Board of Control for Cricket in India and Lalit Modi launched the IPL to a packed stadium at Bangalore, that was when the game took another permanent twist. The IPL became all about money, private enterprise and ego. No-one could ignore the obscene cash on offer – no-one. The IPL and its T20 format took cricket into a new stratosphere.

By 2013, the salary cap for each franchise was up to $US12.5 million. Players who had never featured for their country in the longer forms became massively rich. The ability to hit 25 in 15 balls was more valuable than any other cricket skill. It was worth $US2 million for six weeks' work! It was outrageous. The employment term "freelance cricketer" became the most sought-after vocation.

The motivation to be physically fit for the IPL, to have the big-hitting skills and all-round ability became the imperative. Not just with the players, either. Coaches and specialists in sport science queued up for roles. New techniques were introduced, baseball hitting methods, for example. The "clearing of the hip" method was practised. Six hitting became the first priority at practice. Bats with huge edges were sought after, and even long handles with half-bats were tried. It became an amazing phenomenon. The game in every aspect changed.

Television changed its presentation – cheerleaders were shown every few minutes, music blared in the background, non-stop shouted commentary became the theme. The quiet, old, long game had turned into a loud, new, short frenzy. Money, money and more money drove the show.

The IPL had taken over the way the game would be played. It changed the way the young would view and aspire to the game, and it began to threaten the future of one-day cricket and test cricket alike.

It could be that one of those two forms will drop off for good, although it is hard to see test cricket becoming extinct. T20 will continue to grow and it just may be impossible for boards to ignore the T20 financial boon. The fans may never allow them to either, because they have embraced three-hour cricket, just as Nate Smith said they would. It's all they have time for and the hype has them hooked.

So where to from here? Three formats crammed into the Future Tours Programme schedule, plus all those Twenty20 leagues make it impossible for the struggling nations to improve their ODI and test performances. Something has to give if the full quota of nations is to continue to play test cricket properly. The 50-over Champions Trophy format being scrapped soon is the start of the cull. Will that mean the 50-over World Cup format will be next to go? Will 50 overs become totally irrelevant as T20 takes complete hold?

I will attempt to look into the future and sense where the game needs to head to save it from becoming a different sport, or at least not cricket as we used to know it. The priorities are the values and principles of the game itself, why it was designed so, and what it must retain to hold on to its integrity. The other factor is the fan base that supports and pays for the game to grow. It is all about balance; it must not be about greed and gain.

Test Cricket

The five-day game is unquestionably the pinnacle of cricket played between two nations' best players. It has been so since 1877 and that has never changed. It started back then with England and Australia, and they were joined by South Africa (1889), West Indies (1928), New Zealand (1930), India (1932), Pakistan (1952), Sri Lanka (1982), Zimbabwe (1992) and Bangladesh (2000).

There is no doubt, therefore, that it is an elite event, played regularly by nine teams (Zimbabwe is a 10th, but often does not have test status because its team is not of the required standard) in an ad hoc home and away schedule over five years. There is no championship or winner of test cricket, just a meeting of Commonwealth countries playing for pride and honour. There are test rankings, a table developed over the last decade, to point to form and the best team at any given time, but there is no true meaning to the table apart from pride, media-speak and a cheque for the highest ranked team each year, regardless of who it played the previous 12 months. Added to that, there is no final, or a fair spread of matches.

As of early 2013 the test rankings read: South Africa 1, England 2, Australia 3, Pakistan 4, India 5, Sri Lanka 6, West Indies 7, New Zealand 8 and Bangladesh 9, with Zimbabwe not having played enough tests to qualify.

Pakistan have done extremely well considering they have not played at home for five years. The rest of the top five have all had turns as the No 1-ranked team during this period. Sri Lanka has stagnated in the middle since Muralitharan retired, and the West Indies, New Zealand and Bangladesh have been stationed at the bottom since 2008. All three of these teams are so low on ranking points that it appears inconceivable they could make much ground on the others, at least in the short term.

That is the structure for international cricket, but it is a flawed and meaningless situation. The only time a winner in cricket is crowned is every two years with the world T20 champs and every four years with the 50-over World Cup. Yet every year, in domestic cricket the world over, competitions are staged and champions crowned. Fans love it, and so do the players.

It follows sport's greatest attraction – that each year in competition the opportunity to win is there for teams and players, and for fans to follow. If you lose or come last, you pick yourself up, regroup and come again another year. Of course, there are the marquee world events – the Olympics, the football and rugby World Cups as examples – that are staged every four years with dozens of countries involved, and golf's Ryder Cup between the United States and Europe is played every two years. Most sports, including athletics, cycling and swimming, have world championships. Golf and tennis have four Majors or Grand Slam events each year. But with test cricket, there is no such opportunity anywhere. Instead, the slow, long-winded merry-go-round of nations popping in to compete in a one-on-one test series (normally over two tests, another curiosity, because often the series is drawn) is played out over half a decade, home and away. It's ludicrous. For test cricket to be truly marketed and grow, a competition must be created, ideally annually, at worst every two years.

At present, the ICC plans to start a test championship in 2017 with only the top four teams. They would play only three matches and then do it every four years! Is that a competition? It feels more like a token gesture at best.

One of my projects within the World Committee was to try to provide a solution for test cricket. My answer was simple. No doubt complexities would arise because of the time it takes to play a test or a series. Nevertheless, the solution feels better than the present one, which is a stranglehold by four nations and a disconnection with the fans.

In 2010 I presented the World Committee with the following plan:
- Test cricket would continue to be played under the Future Tours Programme, each test and series offering ranking points, as happens now.
- Ideally the top eight nations would qualify for the test championship, four in the top tier to play against four in the bottom tier. But owing to the Future Tours Programme schedule there would occasionally be the case of two top teams playing each other and two bottom teams playing each other. That would merely create an opportunity for different clashes and a chance for the underdogs to have their day.
- A top-tier team would play a bottom-tier team in a test match or series between November and February most years. The rotation of who plays who and who hosts who would need to be dependent on the Future Tours Programme schedule.
- The winner of any test championship test (or series if both teams wish it) would advance through to the semi-finals. In the case of a draw, the highest-ranked team would advance because of its performance over the previous 12 months, making all tests played meaningful.
- The semi-finals and final would be played in a mandatory two-week window in the Future Tours Programme in England in September each year, the final to be played at Lord's. Each September, the winner of the annual test championship would be crowned.
- England would seem best suited to host the semis and final.

- In summary, each team has a chance to qualify, compete and ultimately attempt to be a champion on an annual basis.

Every player would aspire to play in a final at Lord's. The final would become a marketing event for the world. I couldn't think of a better occasion. Certainly it would create far more interest than the Champions League that is afforded Future Tours Programme inclusion. The Champions League provides invaluable cash for domestic cricket, but it shouldn't be the priority over a marquee event such as the test championship final.

Competitions in sport should be played annually, and they have to be relevant. At the very least it has to be every two years, like the Ryder Cup, but every four years is unacceptable. Surely staging a minimum of seven tests over 12 months can't be that hard to pull off. By doing so, test cricket would have significant meaning throughout the year with a climax every September.

World Cups and Limited Overs formats

The World Cup is currently played using the 50-over format. It is the right duration to determine the best one-day team in the world. The World Cups since 1975 have been outstanding by and large, with the 1992 tournament probably the best, simply because its structure meant it was finished in five weeks and all teams played each other at least once. That it has never been attempted again is disappointing, but for every World Cup since, the ICC has come up with something new. Four years before tournaments is a long time and people like to interfere, so unnecessary changes were made to a simple and successful formula. The main change has been the desire to bring in a multitude of associate teams to clog up the works. I say that with respect; they fight like tigers when given the chance, but 99 per cent of the time they are simply not able to compete.

Introducing 16 and then 14 teams in 2007 and 2011 respectively was too much and meant the tournament lasted nearly 50 days – a bore for all concerned. The World Cup is not the place to include all of Zimbabwe, Namibia, Netherlands, Ireland, Canada, Kenya and others. Surely the tournament among associates or non-test playing nations could be played before the main event with the winner going through to join the test-playing nations. Then with 10 teams, they could play each country once, playing every three or four days, and finish with two semi-finals and a final. It would be a 40-day event.

The Twenty20 world championship is the place to include the best associate nations and involve 16 teams. The next 50-over World Cup, in 2015, is to be staged in Australia and New Zealand. The number of teams will be 14, so it will be a long, drawn-out tournament once again.

After that tournament the ICC can present to the television market a new proposal because the contract will be up for renewal. The question is: will it present 50 overs or will it be fewer, and how many teams? There is talk that in 2019 only 10 teams, eight top-ranked and two qualifiers, will compete, so that is encouraging. But will pressure mount to change it back again?

It's a tough decision because the one-dayers are helpful to television companies in generating advertising over seven hours, compared with the Twenty20 format which is only 40 per cent as long. However, the fans seem less and less compelled to turn up and watch seven hours, such is the time pressure in society nowadays.

That's where T20 is pulling the punters. Is there a need for both a T20 world champs and a 50-over World Cup? Not really, just as there is no need, outside World Cup years, to play three formats in one tour.

Solution

If T20 went back to just being played domestically, then 50 overs would survive on the international calendar, alongside test cricket. Give the fans a choice between a T20 match or an ODI and most fans would choose T20, so don't give them that choice. Instead let them enjoy T20 in domestic competitions that help boost the local landscape. International cricket doesn't need T20. That is the ICC dilemma. But no doubt it will want to have its cake and eat it, too.

Maybe the 50-over game could be shortened a little, to 40 overs per innings. That would eliminate the slow period in the middle. In each World Cup the format should return to 50 overs to make the event even more marquee and important. Playing 50 overs in a World Cup after a lead-up of 40-over matches would not make any difference. The

40-over format would appeal better to the fans, the 50-over World Cup format would appeal to the event itself. That is where subtle changes and compromises are important to restoring balance. It's pointless to keep tweaking the rules within a 50-over game to make it more palatable when a simple reduction in overs is the solution.

So this is my vision:

1. Tests to continue with a knockout championship scheduled each year or at least every two years, quarter-finals between November and February, semi-finals and final in England the following September.
2. ODIs to reduce to 40 overs, but World Cup matches to be played over 50 overs.
3. T20 to be removed from international cricket altogether, becoming a vital component of domestic schedules.

But that's not all. Let's get less serious and have some fun talking about Max60.

Max60: Fourth Generation Cricket

By the year 2050 cricket will have evolved even further. Time will have reduced the duration cricket is played even more. Twenty20 will be deemed too long, too boring, too old hat. So why not get the creative juices flowing and let's think about how that evolution might look. It's time to bring out the crystal ball.

Let's work with the premise that most sport is played within a 60 to 90-minute time frame. Society is used to watching football, rugby, league, tennis (best of three sets), hockey, netball etc over this time frame. It is a proven duration that can be fitted into a sports fan's day or schedule. So given that, consider this radical idea I have conjured up.

It's 2050 remember. The name of the new game I have designed is Max60. Here it is:

Max60 is played in 90 minutes, maximum. It is 11 per team, played as 60 balls (not overs) per team. It takes a maximum of 40 minutes to complete each innings, with five minutes between innings.

The 60 balls are bowled consecutively from one end. In a 90-minute Max60 game there is no need for two ends and using just one end saves a huge amount of wasted time while the field changes over. If televised, TV cameras can be set up for one end and save on unnecessary costs.

To deliver the 60 balls there are a minimum of four bowlers, of whom two may bowl up to 18 balls. No other bowlers can deliver more than 12 balls, but a team can use as many bowlers as it wants.

A bowler can bowl either a minimum three-ball spell or a maximum six-ball spell. The two best bowlers are able to bowl 60 per cent of the innings.

A batsman is not limited in the number of consecutive balls he can face. This enables the best batsmen to manipulate the strike.

During the 60-ball innings, the batting side has eight batsmen and eight wickets to lose. The last batsman may bat on until dismissed, with the previous dismissed batsman as the runner. That means the three worst batsmen are never seen.

In summary, a minimum of four bowlers and a maximum of eight batsmen are used. That means there must be at least one all-rounder, a player who must bat and bowl.

Field restrictions are set at three fieldsmen outside the ring for the first 20 balls, four out for the next 20 balls and five out for the final 20 balls.

The rules allow Max60 to move quickly and to be ultra entertaining. It's that simple.

So that's my attempt at crystal ball gazing. A game that lasts only 90 minutes! It's time I got serious again and talked about the integrity and true spirit of cricket.

CHAPTER 8

Spirit of Cricket: Cowdrey and Murali

In 2006 I was honoured to give the Cowdrey Lecture at Lord's. The lecture is an annual event on behalf of the Marylebone Cricket Club that honours Sir Colin Cowdrey. Before he died, Cowdrey, along with Ted Dexter, moved to regenerate cricket's true spirit – sportsmanship, integrity and honesty.

That was done as the preamble to the 2000 Code of the Laws of Cricket. It read: "Cricket is a game that owes much of its unique appeal to the fact that it should be played not only within its Laws but also within the Spirit of the Game. Any action which is seen to abuse this spirit causes injury to the game itself. The major responsibility for ensuring the spirit of fair play rests with the captains."

The following year the inaugural lecture was delivered by Richie Benaud, and in subsequent years by Barry Richards, Sunil Gavaskar, Clive Lloyd, Geoff Boycott, myself, Christopher Martin-Jenkins, Desmond Tutu, Adam Gilchrist, Imran Khan, Kumar Sangakkara and Tony Greig.

I decided to use my Cowdrey lecture to focus on technology mainly, which I have already dealt with extensively in this book. I spoke of Twenty20 cricket and the beginnings of Cricket Max. I finished by speaking about the Spirit of Cricket, the mistakes I had made and how the game needed to always show genuine integrity. I also spoke of chucking and my zero tolerance for it.

It was an exhausting 55 minutes, set inside a hot marquee on the Nursery Ground. I had the flu and a high temperature and it drained me totally. I was drenched in sweat and struggled to retain my balance and composure to complete the lecture, but such was the honour and privilege, the focus was there and the task was completed without any great hitch.

It was one of the highlights of my life.

Following the Cowdrey Lecture, the media caught on to the comments I had made about chucking and in particular about "a certain Sri Lankan bowler who bowled me first ball in 1992". They obviously checked Wisden and saw that bowler was indeed Muttiah Muralitharan.

Born in Kandy in 1972, Murali made his test debut against Australia 20 years later in Colombo. Craig McDermott was his first test wicket. In the second innings he snared Tom Moody and Mark Waugh. He took another wicket in the second test. Four months later he bowled to me in the first innings of the second test in Colombo.

In late 1992, as he skipped in to bowl the first ball I had ever faced from him, I reminded myself that he was labelled an off-spinner. As he whirled his arm over the ball came towards me looking like a leg-spin delivery. I shaped to cover off stump and the ball spun past me and hit leg stump. He had bowled off-spin, but it was nothing like I had ever seen. In the second innings he bowled the same ball, but my constant affirmation "off-spin, off-spin" ensured I didn't make the same mistake again. I scored a fast hundred and as I did against many off-spinners, I murdered him through the leg side, until he found an inside edge and had me caught at short leg from a tired prod.

Throughout the innings I watched him closely from the non-striker's end. I was convinced he was bowling illegally. So was everyone else I asked. I never faced him again, but I watched intensely as his future unfolded.

On Boxing Day 1995, I watched on television as umpire Darrell Hair "called" him seven times for chucking, from the bowler's end as well as from square leg. It looked as if his time was finally up. As with Ian Meckiff, Geoff Griffin, Charlie Griffith, Tony Lock and many more, time caught up with those who bowled the ball with a bent arm and straightened it upon release.

"Chuckers", as they became known, were removed from the game or, as in Lock's case, they made drastic improvements to continue. It was always a controversial and sad part of the game, but for the game's integrity, it became necessary.

The Sri Lankans were understandably livid with Hair, especially on the grand stage of the Melbourne Cricket Ground and the Boxing Day test. It was a tough pill for them to swallow. But it was no surprise to many,

Muttiah Muralitharan is a lovely bloke and was one of the greatest wicket-takers in cricket history. He was also fortunate that some of the laws of cricket were changed to accommodate him. *Photo, Fairfax*

and Hair was privately applauded for having the courage to do so amid intense media scrutiny. Many felt for Murali, a colourful and loveable personality, who played the game with a smile and a fierce nationalistic determination. He was liked everywhere, but everyone, with the exclusion of his teammates, thought he was exploiting the rules to an unfair advantage.

With due respect, off-spinners were often referred to as the poor man's spinner, a reference to the ball spinning into the many right-handers who played. There was no doubt that the off-spinner's role against left-handers was invaluable, but to the right-hander, the off-spinner became a chance to attack and score freely. I had noticed that with Viv Richards, Gordon Greenidge, Greg Chappell and Sunil Gavaskar, to name just a few. Off-spinners, unless they had a fabulous arm ball or top-spinner or drifted the ball away skilfully, were too predictable turning into the pads.

Murali, it was felt privately by many, changed all that with his perceived illegal fast action, generating incredible pace and enormous turn and rip off the pitch. Even so, in the early days he bowled only the off-spinner and his arm ball was lousy. So unless he ripped the ball down, he was nothing to unduly worry about once you got used to his unique style. In his first

23 tests, from 1992 to 1995, he captured a normal good off-spinner's return of 81 wickets at 34, on par with off-spinners of the modern era like John Bracewell, John Emburey and Tim May. Jim Laker, Hugh Tayfield and Erapalli Prasanna from previous eras had better records.

Then Saqlain Mushtaq came along.

Saqlain made his debut for Pakistan in 1995 and immediately began to make an impact. It wasn't his off-spinners that were the cause of concern for batsmen, although he was a fine exponent of this stock delivery, but it was his new variation called the "doosra". The doosra spun the other way, like a leg-spin delivery, except it wasn't delivered with the normal leg-spinner's action. The action was a disguise of the off-spin action, but with the ball coming out of the hand with the back of the wrist facing the batsman with the fingers facing skywards, not on a sideways angle as when a leg-spinner is released. The doosra effectively turned the off-spin bowler into two bowlers – an off-spinner and a leg-spinner. It became a mystery and caused havoc among batsmen. Two bowlers in one became the new phenomenon.

The problem with the doosra was that to release the ball out of the hand with the back of the wrist facing the batsman, the arm has to bend and straighten to propel the ball forward. There was no sideways action or sideways release to help that propulsion, so the elbow became the point of providing all the power and purchase on the ball.

Saqlain had a relatively legitimate off-spin action, so his doosra never became a subject of intense scrutiny as it did for Murali. Murali learnt the doosra quickly and soon began tormenting batsmen everywhere.

Following the Hair incident in late 1995, Murali was called twice more by Australian umpire Ross Emerson, first a month after Hair, and second in early 1999. In that period of three years Murali had performed feats of extraordinary proportions. In 1998 at the Oval he mesmerised England in a one-off test, capturing 16-220 – 7-155 and 9-65. The ability to spin the ball both ways was ruling the roost. He became the most feared bowler of his day.

Remember his record prior to the doosra? With the introduction of the doosra he smashed every off-spinner's record by taking 146 wickets in his next 25 tests at a mere 19 per wicket. Further, from 1996-2005, he took 451 wickets at 20.88 in 68 tests at a strike rate of a wicket every 55 balls. It was simply unbelievable.

Despite his success and the consequent huge boost to Sri Lankan cricket, including the deserved winning of the 1996 World Cup, the doosra looked wrong. The ICC had no choice but to investigate. Tests were conducted and it was revealed that during a delivery virtually all bowlers flex and extend their arms naturally to some degree as it rotates around the shoulder.

This testing revealed that the strict Laws of Cricket, which banned any flexing of the arm, were impossible to follow. At this time a set of tiered tolerance thresholds for the amount of allowable elbow extension, or straightening, was implemented: a fast bowler could bend his arm up 10 degrees, a medium-pacer up to 7.5 degrees and a spin bowler up to 5 degrees. But who would keep testing these measurements? It became a flawed rule change because the lab tests did not replicate what happened out in the middle under test match pressure.

After Emerson called Murali the second time and Murali continued to torment batsmen the world over, the pressure increased, the cries for fairness were deafening.

Then in March 2004, Chris Broad, ICC match referee, reported Murali for chucking his doosra. Broad had clearly had enough and cried foul. He claimed that from his expert position the arm was straightening way beyond the 5 degrees allowed. Murali was told by the ICC and Sri Lankan board to cease bowling his doosra. To his credit he flew to Perth and put himself into the hands of two leading qualified biomechanists, Dr Bruce Elliott of the University of West Australia and Marc Portus from the Australian Institute of Sport Biomechanics.

Under the expert bowling eye of former Australian test player Bruce Yardley, Murali performed two tests, one on April 1, 2004, and the other on April 7. The only issue I had with Yardley overseeing the tests was that he had been called for chucking in 1977. Therefore there was an assumption that maybe he would feel some sympathy for Murali, whom he knew well, having spent some years coaching Sri Lanka and Murali himself. Yardley was local, so that was handy, but it was too important an issue and test to have any perceived conflicts of interest.

Murali should have had a total outsider to assess the test from a player's point of view. Perhaps Bishan Bedi or Michael Holding, two of Murali's fiercest critics, could have been invited to attend. If they gave their approval, the world would have to take notice. Either way, the truth would be there for all to see.

The conclusion of those tests completed by Elliott and Portus was: "In making recommendations regarding Mr Muralitharan the following should be stated. While a full run-up and standard pitch were used, data was collected in a laboratory environment. It is our considered opinion that this is the only way to record accurate and reliable 3D data of elbow movement, particularly for spin bowling. The key to the issue with reference to a spin bowler is the quality of the delivery and the rate of rotation of the upper arm. In our case Mr Muralitharan produced high-quality deliveries with an upper arm action that was similar in rotational speed to that of a fast bowler. The mean time for his upper-arm to move from the horizontal to release in testing session 2 (» 0.072s) was compared with the same movement recorded on video from the recent Sri Lanka v Australia test series. This video was provided by Mr Muralitharan.

"While the positioning of cameras for data from the test series was not ideal and video images were recorded at a slower rate, it was evident that the time for the upper arm to move from the horizontal to release was similar for the test series and the laboratory testing. Mean ball velocity at testing session 2 of 72 km/hr was also at the upper end of the range commonly reported for Mr Muralitharan under test conditions. We therefore contend that the bowling action recorded was similar to that used in a test match.

"A case may be made for Mr Muralitharan's initial elbow extension to be acceptable at 14 degrees, particularly when one considers the speed of his arm rotation is similar to that of a fast bowler and the only scientific data related to fast bowling suggested an increase in the acceptable extension threshold from 10 degrees to 15 degrees. However, the mean extension across six deliveries was outside current ICC guidelines for fast bowlers.

"For this reason a period of technique modification was carried out to reduce the level of elbow movement during the delivery of his doosra. Following this remediation his level of elbow extension reduced to 10 degrees, which is within fast bowling guidelines. We contend that because the speed of his upper arm rotation is as fast and in some cases quicker than fast bowlers, his level of acceptability for elbow extension should also be set at the 10 degrees mark.

"With no spin bowling data base to make a comparison, this would seem both a wise and prudent recommendation. Following the findings from Portus et al, we would also recommend that the ICC consider increasing the fast bowling extension threshold to 15 degrees.

"Finally it is our considered opinion that Mr Muralitharan be permitted to continue bowling his doosra at least until a valid data base is collected on the various spin bowling disciplines. The relatively minor level of elbow extension following remediation over the period from arm horizontal to release is not believed to give Mr Muralitharan an unfair advantage over batsmen or other bowlers."

There are many things to be admired about Murali for subjecting himself to a full investigation. In many ways it was his only way to save his career. He did everything right in this regard. The tests themselves, on the surface, read legitimately. However, my reservation stems from the speed in which he bowled in the lab tests, that being 64km and then 72km on average. These two speeds are not in keeping with the speedball radar data taken on a regular basis during his career. The very slowest he would bowl would be 72kmh, while his average would normally be between 80kmh and 90kmh. By bowling 10km slower surely the degree of intent and physical exertion would be different, less dynamic, less stressful on his bowling arm? My doubts about the lab tests being the same as of a test match fitted with my knowledge of playing in a test match. My doubts that the correct former test player was overseeing the tests were part of that concern.

Following the tests, the ICC announced that the threshold for chucking would be a standard 15-degree rule for all bowlers. Adding to this decision was the research done that stated the 99 per cent of bowlers in the history of the game were chuckers, too. They cited McGrath as straightening his arm 12 degrees. They said that Hadlee, Holding and many more – 130 was apparently the number they tested during live matches – were all guilty of bending to some degree. They concluded that the human eye could detect a kink in the bowling action only if it straightened more than 15 degrees. The news shook the cricket world. Ninety-nine per cent chucked the ball? Amazing, we all muttered.

Then the special committee who listened at length to the presentation of facts – Clive Lloyd, Michael Holding, Angus Fraser, Aravinda de Silva and Ravi Shastri – approved the findings. In doing so Murali was cleared of the doosra and all further investigation. He was a free man. He was not guilty of breaking any cricket laws and so his career was firmly back on track. I began to believe, and then I stopped.

I believed the theory that there was some kink in most bowlers, and I accepted scientifically that 15 degrees was the point at which the naked eye could detect the arm straightening. What I still didn't and couldn't believe was that the doosra fell under the threshold at 14 degrees, or 10 degrees if you believed Murali's second test results in Perth.

To my naked eye, the doosra was not only sending me alarm bells that 15 degrees had been breached and that is why I was able to see it, but that it was on occasions breaking the law by double! I began to collect footage of the doosra out of the Sky TV offices and built up a video tape file of the offenders who bowled the doosra. As I watched the doosra bowled in slow motion, from every conceivable angle, it became more and more clear to me that the doosra was illegal and always would be.

On July 11, 2006, I delivered the Cowdrey Lecture. Though I mentioned chucking, I went into no detail as to why I had zero tolerance. I was wrong not to properly make my point. Maybe I needed more of a forum to express or challenge the biomechanics, but my lecture merely stated that I had had enough, literally accepting nothing regarding the testing or new laws.

I regret even mentioning the issue, but felt obliged. It looked as though I was just anti-Murali. I wasn't; I really admired him. I just was totally against the doosra, whoever bowled it.

In December 2006, Sri Lanka toured New Zealand and played tests in Christchurch and Wellington. New Zealand won the first test comfortably in seaming conditions, yet Murali, as he was accustomed to in every test during this era, picked up his share with match figures of 7-99. Sri Lanka's batsmen, with the exception of Sangakkara, failed miserably. In Wellington, Sangakkara led the way and this time took his team into a commanding position. Late on the second day into a howling 50-knot northerly, Murali bowled a magical spell to wrap up the New Zealand innings, taking 4-31.

I was in the commentary box for the final half-hour with Tony Cozier, the well-respected West Indian. As Murali bowled, we both noticed that while the windy conditions were brutal for him to contend with, it made no difference to his pace or trajectory. Notable too was his use of the doosra. At one point during his 12 overs he was using it 50 per cent of the time. As he continued to defy logic and dismantle the New Zealand batting line-up, Cozier and I questioned the legitimacy of the doosra and whether it had properly passed the test as a legal delivery. Both of us, not just me, agreed that it remained an unanswered issue and needed more research. We made no outrageous statements. Instead we applauded Murali for his spell and wrapped up the day's play.

That evening at the press conference, journalists who had heard the commentary informed Mahela Jayawardene, the Sri Lankan captain, of my comments about Murali's bowling earlier, and in particular about the controversial doosra. Mahela came out firing in defence of his man. To Mahela it simply followed my Cowdrey Lecture and I was continuing my witch-hunt of Murali, with perhaps even a racial undertone as well. I was aghast. But it was common practice for Sri Lankans to feel that way. Then John Reid, the former New Zealand captain and a retired match referee, came out and supported Mahela and Murali and nailed me to the cross.

I never said another word publicly, as it proved there was no point. Murali was cleared and that was that.

Back at Sky TV I added the Basin Reserve footage to the file I had. But what was I to do with it? I wanted it to be explained to me how these pictures showed the doosra being bowled at less than 15 degrees of straightening. I left it alone and waited for the next World Committee meeting.

As chance would have it, I was posted to Dubai the following winter to conduct the technology meeting with David Richardson and Paul Hawkins. While I was there I sought out Richardson to have a look at my video, but he declined. I took it to Doug Cowie, a New Zealander in charge of the elite umpires' panel, but he said I was wasting my time, that the file on the doosra was closed, never to be reopened. I accepted it as a fait accompli.

I threw the tape in the nearest bin as I departed the ICC offices. I was over it, too. I decided to accept Murali for what he was and what he had achieved. He had opened himself up for testing and the authorities in their wisdom had given him full approval, at the same time stating everyone chucked as well. Who was I to be the martyr? It was time for me to play ball.

Part of me felt it wasn't a bad thing for the doosra to be in the game. It was amazing to watch, and it levelled the playing field when batsmen had begun to dominate in the modern game. Bats had become bigger and lighter, grounds had become smaller, pitches had become flatter. Along with the T20 format, it had indeed become a batsman's game.

Part of me felt sorry for those who had been victimised in previous eras, but I soon came to the conclusion that rules evolve. I pulled my head in on the doosra.

Muttiah Muralitharan was a phenomenon. He was great for the game, massive for Sri Lanka. I would be the first to congratulate him for all he achieved. But he was also dead lucky. Good luck to him, too, as he did appear to always play in the right spirit of the game. Without question Murali was a great player. The question was: where would he fit in my top 100 test cricketers of all time?

CHAPTER 9

The Best Movers and Shakers: My Top 100 Exceptional Test Cricketers of All Time

From an early age (Dad thought it was eight) I began to read and revere the cricket bible, the *Wisden Cricketers' Almanack*. They were the thick yellow books that contained every match and every statistic from the previous year and every record before that to the year dot. I could soon recite the top run-scorers in tests, the most hundreds, the highest innings ... you name it I was hooked. I couldn't wait for Dad to buy each year's edition. From that beneficial impromptu education my deep appreciation for the history of the game was born.

To prove my endearing love of the history of cricket and in particular of test cricket, I have gone through the challenging task of selecting, in my opinion, the greatest, or most exceptional, 100 test players of all time. I have split it into two eras for some simplicity: 1877-1961 and 1962-2013 and into four categories: batsmen, bowlers, all-rounders and specialist wicketkeepers.

I was born in 1962, so I guess you could say the first group is of the players I never saw and the second are the ones I did, or theoretically may have seen, such as Sobers, even at a tender age. For those I never saw first-hand, I have relied upon the genius writing of the following incredible authors: Ian Peebles, Jack Fingleton, Neville Cardus, E W Swanton, C R L James, John Arlott, John Woodcock, David Frith, Christopher Martin-Jenkins and, from my homeland, Dick Brittenden, as well as the writing of the great players themselves – Jack Hobbs, Don Bradman, Walter Hammond, Len Hutton, Denis Compton, Colin Cowdrey, Keith Miller, Jim Laker, Richie Benaud and Ashley Mallett, to name just a few. All these sit in my large library of old books collected by Dad and me. To top it off if I needed a quick check on a player's bio I could log on to Cricinfo and find it all at my fingertips.

I've chosen 45 batsmen, 44 bowlers, 16 all-rounders, including five batsmen-wicketkeepers (nine of those all-rounders already qualify in the batting or bowling categories) and four specialist wicketkeepers. Overall there are 43 from the first period, which included just over 500 tests, and 57 covering over another 1550-plus tests from the last 50 or so years. England is represented by 32, Australia 27, West Indies 15, South Africa 10, India 6, Pakistan 5, Sri Lanka 3, New Zealand and Zimbabwe 1 each.

BATSMEN
1877-1961 (20)

1.	Don Bradman	Australia	1928-48
2.	George Headley	West Indies	1930-54
3.	Jack Hobbs	England	1908-30
4.	Wally Hammond	England	1927-47
5.	Herbert Sutcliffe	England	1924-35
6.	Len Hutton	England	1937-55
7.	Everton Weekes	West Indies	1948-58
8.	Denis Compton	England	1937-57
9.	Dudley Nourse	South Africa	1935-51
10.	Peter May	England	1951-61
11.	Victor Trumper	Australia	1899-1912
12.	William (WG) Grace	England	1880-99
13.	Neil Harvey	Australia	1948-63
14.	Bill Ponsford	Australia	1924-34
15.	Stan McCabe	Australia	1930-38
16.	Frank Worrell	West Indies	1948-63
17.	Clyde Walcott	West Indies	1948-60
18.	Ted Dexter	England	1958-68
19.	Ken Barrington	England	1955-68
20.	Colin Cowdrey	England	1954-75

Highly considered:

Stewie Dempster	New Zealand	1930-33
Martin Donnelly	New Zealand	1937-49
Vijay Merchant	India	1933-51
Eddie Paynter	England	1931-39

One or two of these players spanned both eras, Barrington and Cowdrey, for example. Cowdrey played tests until 1975, his last as a 42-year-old against the might of Lillee and Thomson. But to me he was always an old-style vintage and probably at his best in the late 1950s.

The first five are easy.

Don Bradman is the greatest, as his average of 99.94 illustrates. He missed averaging the ton by just four runs when bowled for a duck in his last test innings. The standout for me was simply his ability to move from one innings to another, physically and mentally. He appeared to be an unemotional type, which would have helped him to stay grounded no matter whether he scored a duck (he did score seven – one every 10 innings) or a triple hundred. But consider how many times he scored big (29 centuries in 70 innings). He must have felt exhausted. When you consider there weren't the training methods or health cures of the modern day, what he achieved innings after innings is mesmerising. His talent – footwork, hand-eye, strokeplay etc – is well documented, but it's the inner fortitude that intrigues me the most. Being a non-smoker and fairly much a non-drinker, and therefore quiet socially, would have helped his reserves of energy. Some said he was aloof and distanced, but he was devoted and ambitious to set out his goals and achieve them. When you consider what he did for cricket after retiring, in his selection and administration roles, you get a measure of the man. He was in love with the game and gave it his all. Bradman as a batsman was without peer. Even when Bodyline was designed to reduce his run scoring in 1932-33, he still managed to average in that series about what Hobbs, Hutton, Hammond and Headley averaged in their careers.

Behind Bradman is the "Black Bradman", **George Headley,** from the West Indies. He was of a similar build to Bradman, slight, fast of foot, wiry limbs and a huge appetite for runs. He was undoubtedly the West Indies' finest batsman until Weekes came along to challenge that standing. The thing that stood out for me in his short career of 22 tests and averaging over 60 (scoring 10 centuries at almost Bradman's ratio) was his mental strength. He talked of not sleeping much before a test, instead using his mind to visualise the innings he wanted to play. That he played as he wanted most of the time shows why he is compared to Bradman.

Jack Hobbs is ranked third. He had an average of just under 57 and a ratio of a century every four tests. He happened to score 197 first-class centuries as well. He was the finest opener of all time, his partnership with Herbert Sutcliffe being monumental, and he helped England often get the better of Australia until Bradman came along. Hobbs could bat in any conditions against all types of bowlers. He was superb on uncovered pitches but, like Bradman, appeared to have an unemotional approach, therefore conserving his energies for consistent century-making. Hobbs was nearly 48 when he played his last test innings.

Jack Hobbs, who averaged nearly 57 in tests and scored the small matter of 197 first-class centuries.

Wally Hammond was the superstar for England at No 3 or 4. For a short time he was a team-mate of Hobbs and he was a fierce opponent of Bradman from 1928 until 1947. Hammond made 22 test centuries, averaged 58 and his forte was compiling really massive test scores, 336 against New Zealand at Eden Park in 1933 his best. Hammond, the man, had a certain flair and vulnerability, but nevertheless he was a freak player who was ideally placed at No 4 to dominate attacks the world over.

Wherever Hobbs goes in, **Herbert Sutcliffe** has to follow relatively close behind. I have him at No 5. He averaged 60, a few more than Hobbs, and there is really no separating them. Sutcliffe, from Yorkshire, seldom wore a cap. His slick, perfectly-groomed hair was symbolic of his play – clean, crisp and assured. He never looked hurried or agitated; rather he was cruising along like an ocean liner, heading in only one direction – towards another big hundred. In 54 tests he amassed 16 centuries (an incredible ratio), although he never recorded a really big one – 194 was his highest. He scored a fifty every second innings, a hundred every four and a bit. Also, he featured in 33 century partnerships, 15 with Hobbs.

At 6 is **Len Hutton,** another right-handed opening batsman from Yorkshire. He was steely in mind, but graceful in stroke. Hutton scored 364 against Bradman in 1938 and showed Bradman he, too, could grind the best attacks into the dust. Hutton averaged nearly 57 and sits with Hobbs and Sutcliffe as England's greatest opening batsmen. At times he scored slowly, particularly in the 1950s, when slow batting became too prevalent, but ultimately he proved his mastery in all situations and carved out an exceptional record.

Everton Weekes, left, and Frank Worrell, two of the famous West Indies Ws.

When **Everton Weekes,** a tiny bullet of a man, was in the mood he was unstoppable. On two occasions he scored multiple successive hundreds. His best run was five centuries in a row, a world record (and 90 run out in the next innings). He is the first mentioned of the famous three Ws, because his position in the batting order was above the other two. He rivals Headley, Viv Richards and Brian Lara as the Caribbean's finest No 3 of all time. He averaged nearly 59, scoring 15 centuries in just 48 tests.

Denis Compton was a natural, and a match-winner. With flair and flamboyance, he stole the show and won the hearts of spectators all over the world. He had that air of theatre about him and entertained on every occasion. He scored at a fast clip, always on the lookout for dominance and drama. With his "Brylcreem" and good looks, and his array of fine strokes (some of them unorthodox), he thrilled many. A nasty knee injury from playing soccer slowed him down in the end. Interestingly for me, he batted at No 4, played with bad knees, played 131 test innings and registered 17 hundreds. That's where the similarity ends – he scored a lot more runs overall and averaged 50.

Dudley Nourse proved to be South Africa's best, propping up his team's batting with Bruce Mitchell from the mid-1930s. Nourse dominated attacks either side of World War II, hitting nine hundreds in 32 tests and averaging nearly 54, which was phenomenal. South Africa at that time were less exposed to high-level cricket, yet Nourse had the ability to rise above all and entrench his name in the record books.

Controversially perhaps, I have selected **Peter May,** the elegant Englishman, in the top 10. His record is not as good as some below him, but everyone I talk to about May says he was out of this world. He had all the time in the world to play the ball, he stood tall and graceful, played straight and late, and had superb placing and timing. That he played the finest on-drive of all is a big reason for my decision. His average was nearly 47 in 66 tests. He scored 13 centuries, 285 not out at Edgbaston against the West Indies in a record stand of 411 with Colin Cowdrey his best. He captained England in 41 tests, a record for many years, but retired relatively young and became a successful businessman and later chairman of selectors.

Victor Trumper, though his average was only 39, has to be near the top, even if the stats don't measure up to those in the top 10. He was certainly the best opening batsman in the world in his era, and maybe simply the best batsman. The same goes for **William Gilbert (WG) Grace.** He averaged under 31, but it has to be noted that Grace was 10 years past his prime when he started playing tests and that he carried on at that level until he was 51. They both dominated attacks in an era when wickets and conditions in general weren't as good as

WG Grace, the Grand Old Man of cricket.

those that followed. That they stood out as much as they did, the best batsmen of their time, is justification to put them in the top 15.

Neil Harvey, the sublime left-hander, started in 1948, the year Bradman was finishing. Only 19, he scored a century in his second test, against India, and another in his third, a few months later at Leeds. His footwork was his hallmark and he carried Australia through the 1950s with wonderful strokeplay, scoring 21 centuries in 79 tests. Benaud said he was the finest player of spin he ever saw. Harvey saved his best for South Africa, scoring eight hundreds against them, double anyone else. Astonishingly, he scored them all in just two series – four in South Africa in 1949-50, then four more at home in 1952-53, including 205 at Melbourne, his highest in tests.

Two more fine Australians follow Harvey, but from a different era. **Bill Ponsford** and **Stan McCabe** were dominating figures through the Bradman era, and at any other time each would have been the star batsman. Both were courageous players. Ponsford batted at the top of the order and McCabe played with more freedom in the middle order. Both also played monumental innings. McCabe scored 232 at Nottingham in 1938 in what Bradman described as the greatest innings of all, even beating his (McCabe's) 187 not out in the first Bodyline test of 1932-33. Ponsford's 266 was the more significant part of the world record partnership with Bradman (244) of 452 in 1934 at the Oval. Ponsford and McCabe averaged over 48, but were even better than that.

Naturally **Frank Worrell** isn't far away and he makes the top list comfortably. He led a side not as organised as others, such as Australia and England. Worrell was the man to help change that. His all-round record was outstanding. As a batsman though, he was a maestro. Despite paling slightly beside Weekes and Walcott in the record book, Worrell proved his prowess with the bat on numerous occasions. Twice against England he was involved in triple-century partnerships, scoring 167 in a record third-wicket stand of 338 with Weekes in Port of Spain in 1954, then 197 not out in the record fourth-wicket partnership of 399 with Gary Sobers against England at Bridgetown in 1960. Added to that were his highest innings, 261 against England at Nottingham in 1950 and 237 against India at Kingston in 1953.

Speaking of "Ws", the other West Indian to feature highly is **Clyde Walcott,** the highly skilled batsman-keeper. He was a big and powerful man who dominated the middle order, forming wonderful partnerships with Weekes and Worrell. When Walcott had the taste for runs he really cashed in – he scored three centuries against England in the 1953-54 series, and five hundreds in the series against Australia a year later, with centuries in both innings of a match twice! What a player to have in the middle order when the bowlers are tiring.

A fine English aristocrat is selected at No 18. His name is **Ted Dexter.** He was a hugely successful player through the 1950s and early 1960s, smashing more fifties than he would have preferred, but posting nine centuries all the same, and finishing with more than 4500 runs at 47. Dexter was daring and explosive, a real attraction. He drew crowds with his flair and desire to entertain. He would have been a brilliant one-day player. As it was, he was an electrifying test batsman who thrilled many.

At 19 is the stoic and resilient **Ken Barrington,** the English bulldog. He stuck his jaw out and got stuck in. He averaged an astonishing 58, scoring 20 centuries in just 82 tests. An example of his run-scoring ability, if not his entertainment factor, was the fact that he played the same number of innings as Compton for England (131) and scored an extra 999 runs. His broad bat and slow scoring can't be ignored, but it was his fighting spirit, his never-say-die attitude that secures him a spot among the best ever.

Finally to the Lord himself, **Colin Cowdrey,** who averaged 44, was the first to play 100 tests and did so with grace and dignity. He scored 22 centuries in 20 years of loyal service for Queen and country. Cowdrey was subtle and smooth, graceful and thoughtful. He was indeed a delightful man and a lovely player to watch in his heyday. I had the honour of playing against him at Lord's in 1981. He scored 39 and for a 49-year-old he hadn't lost much of that exquisite touch. I later had the privilege of giving the Cowdrey Lecture, a great honour.

1962-2013 (25)

1.	Garfield Sobers	West Indies	1954-74
2.	Vivian Richards	West Indies	1974-91
3.	Greg Chappell	Australia	1970-84
4.	Sachin Tendulkar	India	1989-2013

5.	Sunil Gavaskar	India	1971-87
6.	Barry Richards	South Africa	1970
7.	Graeme Pollock	South Africa	1963-70
8.	Brian Lara	West Indies	1990-2006
9.	Ricky Ponting	Australia	1995-2012
10.	Jacques Kallis	South Africa	1995-2013
11.	Rahul Dravid	India	1996-2012
12.	Javed Miandad	Pakistan	1976-93
13.	Allan Border	Australia	1978-94
14.	Gordon Greenidge	West Indies	1974-91
15.	David Gower	England	1978-92
16.	Clive Lloyd	West Indies	1966-85
17.	Matthew Hayden	Australia	1994-2009
18.	Kumar Sangakkara	Sri Lanka	2000-13
19.	Virender Sehwag	India	2001-13
20.	Andy Flower	Zimbabwe	1992-2002
21.	Graham Gooch	England	1975-95
22.	Steve Waugh	Australia	1985-2004
23.	Michael Clarke	Australia	2004-13
24.	Mahela Jayawardene	Sri Lanka	1997-2013
25.	Hashim Amla	South Africa	2004-13

Highly considered:

Geoff Boycott	England	1964-82
Ian Chappell	Australia	1964-80
Rohan Kanhai	West Indies	1957-74
Mohammad Yousuf	Pakistan	1998-2010

The era from 1962 is a fascinating period, with fluctuations in the game's evolution. As with the first group, the rankings start to sort themselves out from the very great to the great, to the very, very good. Having said that, I think they are all exceptional batsmen.

The thrill of writing about this modern group is because in most cases, I have seen them up close, either playing against them or, more recently, commentating or writing about them.

First among the modern greats is **Garfield Sobers.** He could've featured below Bradman in the first group, but I like the look of him fronting the modern day list. Sobers is the finest all-rounder of all time in my book and the second-best batsman behind Bradman. That he started as a slow bowler, batting at nine, and moved his way to No 3 within four years shows what a genius he was. His world record score of 365 not out in 1957-58 against Pakistan was an incredible milestone because it broke Hutton's 20-year-old record and wasn't broken for nearly 40 years.

Garry Sobers, a wonderful cricketer and my first real hero.

Most of all, he was my first real live hero. In 1969 the Windies toured New Zealand, the first test being played in Auckland, where I lived. At the tender age of six, Dad took me to my first test match. Dad pointed out Sobers to me in the field and immediately I was transfixed by the look of the man – cool, loose, collar up, long sleeves buttoned down and a smile never far away. I noticed that he was always on the lookout, quietly prowling in the field for more prey.

Joey Carew and Seymour Nurse were lovely to watch in the West Indies first innings, but my focus was on Sobers. Alas, he holed out to Vic Pollard for just 11. In a superb test, New Zealand set the West Indies 348 to win on the last day. Seymour Nurse was in prime form and carried the day with a stylish 168. With 50 to win and Nurse and Basil Butcher in full flow, my Dad and I left knowing the game was over, so I never saw Sobers again. But the memory remained. He was the greatest in my eyes.

Sobers had many attributes, but it his instinctive ability stood out. He didn't predetermine a ball. Instead he saw it early and stroked it late. By doing that he kept options open. His hunger for runs and life went hand in hand. If he had a late night he would invariably play a long innings the next day, to prove his love for life – play hard, work hard.

Second behind Sobers is the best I saw close up, **Vivian Richards,** the Antiguan. He was a colossus. From 1976 to 1984 he played like no other. His walk and swagger to the crease, his taking guard, his look around the field, his stance, his chewing gum, his adjustment of the cap, his eagle eye squint, his reaction to the ball leaving the hand, his stroke, his role play between balls – all priceless theatre. If you were to title this stage show, you would simply call it "Fearless". He never backed down. To watch him was to ride a wave of obvious joy and pleasure. Like when he scored the fastest hundred, in 56 balls, against England at Antigua in 1986.

In Jamaica I bounced him, a good one, too, but he saw it early and never moved a muscle as the ball soared up past his right temple. Instead of looking to see where the ball went, he just kept staring at me and then burst out laughing at my attempt. I was firmly put in my place. At that juncture I conceded he was the Boss, the Smoking Joe of batting. On a sad note, I was the one who replaced him at Somerset in 1987. I wish I hadn't. I would have liked him to finish with his adopted county in positive fashion, which he deserved, along with Joel Garner, but Somerset wouldn't release me, so I had no choice. I adored Viv. He was everything you wished you could be.

Greg Chappell made such an impression on me in my first test series that I became a lifetime devotee of his way of batting. He was fit, focused and fierce in all he did. He had that aura about him – standing tall, confident, believing, knowing, controlling and creating. His style was captivating. His elegant, classical swing of the bat produced the timing and placement that kept you looking at the man, not the ball. Chappell was a master and an artist, and had the focus to sustain it. His 176 at Christchurch in my first series, in 1982, was the best I saw. On a green top against a firing Hadlee he surgically dismantled our attack with timing and precision that left me spellbound. Chappell became my mentor, not just in batting but in life, and remains a close confidant. There is no better mind on the game, or any better teacher and guide in life. In a way, I got lucky being selected to play Australia at 19 – I got to see Greg Chappell bat only inches away.

Next is **Sachin Tendulkar,** the wonder kid who at 16 had so much X-factor and whiz, and the grooved veteran nearing 40, still producing good results with a wiser mind but with a slower body and powers of recovery. His 88 at Napier in 1990 in only his sixth test was eerie – he was just so young. To still be going 23 years later was simply surreal. His achievement in scoring more than 15,000 runs – and more than 50 hundreds – at 54 in nearly 200 tests may never be surpassed. His career will stand out as the longest, and under the most pressure, an incredible journey of carrying the weight of an obsessed nation. His attitude throughout has been impeccable, almost divine. He put all before his own wants, often just happy to play as if still a young boy with his first bat. Those types are rare breeds.

Sunil Gavaskar mastered the greatest bowling attack that ever took the field, the all-conquering West Indies led by Clive Lloyd. From 1976 until 1983, when the West Indies boasted their fearsome array of pacemen, Gavaskar played 21 tests against them and scored nine hundreds. No-one in test history had confronted this attack and survived and, at times dominated, as he did. He became the first to score 10,000 runs and held the world record for most centuries (34). He once told me that the secret to his success was keeping his head still at the moment the ball was delivered, his right eye square and level as he looked at the bowler. He said to hold this position he would take up his stance against a wall pressed against his right ear. He would do that for a minute or two, just before walking out to bat. When he batted he felt that wall was always there keeping him still and level. Sunny was a beautiful player all around the wicket, but his on drives will remain for me the crème de la crème.

Barry Richards caressed the ball to all parts of the field. He had balance and poise, and watched, moved and played late. When I was 10 he visited Auckland to coach at an indoor clinic. In his talk I will never forget two bits of advice – perfect practice makes perfect and look at the gaps in the field, not the fieldsmen in the field. The second morsel is very underused and unappreciated. Too often the eyes find other eyes, but Barry Richards proved he was king at finding gaps. He played only four tests, averaging 72. That figure might hardly have dropped if he had played 40 tests. It was a waste, but once he played for Packer, he showed the world again that there were two Richards who could rule, not just Viv.

Graeme Pollock stood tall and delivered crushing blows. His signature was feet wide apart, minimal footwork but the decisive strike on the ball. He kept it simple and it paid off innings after innings. His reach was a key, so a shift of weight to start and then the body and hands would wipe and stripe the ball everywhere. He was hard to bowl to. His height dealt with the short ball, the reach and lean sorted out the skiddy or wide ball, and his stillness and balance enabled him to easily access both sides of the wicket. If he had a favourite it was his off-side strokes, the flail through covers. He was uncomplicated in mind, which allowed him to go long into an innings as his energy levels remained consistent. He consistently scored 100 runs per test from his 23 matches, averaging 60 per innings with seven hundreds, his highest being 274 against Australia in Durban in 1970. His genius qualities were sorely missed when South Africa disappeared into political isolation when he was just 26.

Brian Lara cut deliveries through gaps that never existed. That was simply because as a left-hander he was hitting the ball later than anyone. The ball, seemingly past him and through to the keeper, would be found bouncing off the pickets at deep backward square on either side. His natural high-cocked backlift was all his own, designed to crack the ball at alarming speed. I first saw Lara in the 1992 World Cup, when he hit Gavin Larsen, our most economical bowler, for three sizzling fours in his first over. It was a young, fearless Lara and his imagination for shot-making was evident. His legacy is of a batsman who when in went long and large; 375 and 400 not out, the highest of all time, both against England at Antigua, 10 years apart. He played a lone hand often, too. His gift was God-given, a wonderful talent who, when in the mood, was simply unstoppable.

Ricky Ponting pulled balls that were drivable. Almost all great Australian batsmen can pull or hook – Bradman, Harvey, Greg Chappell and Allan Border, to name a few. Steve Waugh was an exception. Ricky Ponting was as good as anyone playing the shot, perhaps alongside Bradman. His press off the front foot and body swivel with lightning hands through the stroke was his signature. I never saw him close up, but through a decade starting in 2000, he never stopped dominating attacks all over the world, with perhaps a slight stutter in India. His hunger for hundreds was insatiable. Punter took only calculated risks, and they mostly came off.

Jacques Kallis built innings like Mandela built togetherness. Kallis is a model of ultra consistency. He builds and builds, each and every innings. There are no mood swings, no sharp shifts of gear, no selling his wicket short. His priceless approach was the cornerstone of a rising South African conquest. Of all the batsmen in this chapter he is probably the one you could bank on the most, such was his integrity at the crease. He didn't climb the heights of a Lara innings, but he built the foundations on the same principles as Nelson Mandela – honest endeavour.

Rahul Dravid, the Impregnable Wall, just misses my top 10. He faced more balls in tests than any batsman in history. He was one of my favourites to watch, with his smooth, precise, correct movements. Adding to his technique was his intelligent and enduring attitude to his job and the task in hand. He gave it his all; he left nothing out there.

Javed Miandad was the street fighter. He fought like a cornered tiger with intense, cheeky combativeness and antagonism. I saw far too much of him. His love of New Zealand bowling was an addiction and he overdosed way too often! His fighting, never-say-die, shove-it-up-you attitude was annoying but admirable. He played spin in his sleep. Probably of the batsmen I saw against spin, he was the best. He had that ability to play so late and adjust to what the ball was doing with disdain and genius. His footwork down the wicket was assured and crisp, positive and attacking. He wasn't so great to the fastest on bouncy tracks, but conjured up ways to succeed. Overall he was the one you could rarely knock out.

Rahul Dravid, the complete professional batsman. *Photo, Fairfax*

Allan Border was cricket's Ayres Rock, with his unmovable, unrelenting determination to stand tough. Pugnacious, resilient, courageous – all strong, rock-like qualities. He loved scoring 150. It seemed to be his favourite number, especially against New Zealand. The enduring memory of watching him at close hand on many occasions was that he never looked arrogant. Instead he had a self-effacing side, often shaking his head at his supposed inadequacies, which we never saw, but he must have felt. Of course, he was constantly stirring himself on, and never gave up, always fighting for himself and the team cause. I marvelled at his unrelenting dedication to battle through. Indeed a tough cookie, a top bloke, a tremendous servant for Australia.

Gordon Greenidge was the deadly assassin, a brutal striker of the ball. When he was limping or cruising between the wickets, then it was clear he had brought his A game. He didn't bother with running between wickets much, conserving his energy and power for his deadly destruction of the red ball. He always sent it back with interest and then some. He had a mean streak, which was easily noticeable if you ever brushed slightly with him. He was a rebel with a cause, the cause being remaining the mainstay of Calypso dominance. He didn't like the opposition and it showed with his flashing blade and serious expression.

David Gower was style and class on and off the field.

David Gower was the easiest batsman on the eye, one of those players you never got sick of watching. He was so free and easy, yet still hungry to play vital innings. He often came up against the West Indies, with the greatest fast bowling attack ever, but still created a proud record. He walked out for England 204 times in 117 tests, scoring 8231 runs, including 57 innings past 50, and 18 centuries. He reached the boundary only 11 shy of 1000 times. At Lord's in 1983 I bowled him a bouncer early in his innings. He pulled it straight up and Lance Cairns put down a dolly catch. A hundred runs later I had him given out lbw, to a ball that pitched outside leg stump, a bad decision. As he walked off he smiled wryly and said: "You deserved it, Hogan." Gower is immensely likeable. I loved his style and grace and often the shared wine that followed.

Clive Lloyd was a brilliant batsman and a massively influential leader. Batting is one thing, but when you can do it for as long as Lloyd while he was also the captain (from 1974-85), you have special qualities that can't be ignored. He was a pivotal player in the rise of West Indian cricket and led by example. He started well on debut in 1966 with 82 and 78 not out in a fine victory over India in Mumbai. From there he continued to amass runs regularly, completing 19 hundreds and 39 fifties. Lloyd presided over the era of West Indian dominance, and when they needed his power with the bat, the Big Cat strolled in and delivered.

Matt Hayden had the presence of a large wide wall that could not be passed. He drove as confidently against the new ball as any before or since. Often the fast bowler would be in danger of permanent injury when the ball was drilled straight back down the ground. If there was an adjustment to the length he would punch-pull square. He had the mode of a Pollock, the straightness of a Chappell, the power of a Richards. Hey, he scored 30 test hundreds, after all.

Kumar Sangakkara is the Speaker of the House, a fabulous spokesman for batting excellence. As he showed in his Cowdrey Lecture, he is a spokesman for the game and for batting of the highest order. A complete player, able to play late in swinging conditions, use his feet on turning wickets, accelerate or consolidate. Most importantly he became a hungry century-maker for Sri Lanka, averaging a hundred every six innings. That speaks for itself.

Virender Sehwag is the executioner, with his extraordinary hand-eye ability. Poor bowlers. They often thought they had him. They could see the opening and then they groaned and the door shut, another scythe cut for four. No real footwork, but enough weight shift and plenty of hand-eye genius. Adding to his aggressive style was an insatiable desire to entertain for long periods. Only a small group of batsmen (21) have scored a triple hundred, let alone score two (Bradman, Lara, Gayle and Sehwag), and he also has a 293 to his name! You simply can't deny his care for his performance, despite an apparently nonchalant appearance. This man was indeed gifted, a rare treasure.

Andy Flower was a wonderful thinker and improviser in a losing cause. The England coach previously enjoyed a fabulous career crafting big scores for Zimbabwe. He is easily his country's finest, and it's amazing to consider his performances in comparison with his countrymen. I came across Flower in 1992 and he showed fast footwork, an inquisitive mind and steely resolve. He was at his best against spin and his reverse sweeping became his signature, especially on turning tracks.

Graham Gooch travelled the world taunting bowling attacks. Despite his abysmal start in 1975 against Australia, when he collected a first-up pair, he hung in and forged a remarkable second half to his career. In the 10-year period from 1985-1994 he scored nearly 6000 runs in 68 tests at nearly 50, with 16 centuries, including his famous 333 at Lord's in 1990. In that period he showed he was truly world-class, devastating on his day and against the West Indies a granite rock under extreme pressure.

Steve Waugh was the iceman. He got off to a horror start in his career, exposed too young, but he always held hope and resolve to go with his natural ability. Once established, he set out to remain undefeated every day to make up time, and in doing so was irrepressible. He learnt his game and his limitations and never abandoned his plan. Plus he was tough and icy as. He wore the baggy green with immense pride, more than any other player I saw. He batted with the tail better than any other, instilling belief that they, too, could prosper by occupying the crease.

Michael Clarke is a super player with magnificent footwork and a magnificent attitude to batting. His Superman year in 2012 was flawless – he broke the Australian record for most runs in a calendar year, rising to the No 1 world ranking along the way. He kept scaling the greatest heights and in doing so pulled Australia through a difficult period. His footwork to spin bowling is a throwback to the good old days. He's a favourite to watch.

Mahela Jayawardene is a sweet timer and a classical mover, an opera singer at the crease. The Sri Lankan is a joy to watch. His every move is subtle and succinct. His decisions are clever and accomplished. His longevity is a thing of beauty, as the graceful glide continues, as the runs accumulate. He will certainly go down as Sri Lanka's greatest right-hander.

Hashim Amla has a spiritual element to his batting. His strokes are so easy on the eye, his demeanour so calm. His style is so wristy and fluent, his appetite to be admired. In all forms of the game he has shown why he is a permanent fixture at the top of the rankings and one of the South African mainstays. It is never easy deciding on the final player in such a group – just look at the impressive list in the highly considered category. But Amla has things about him that can't be ignored: his record, his nerve under pressure, his ability in all conditions against all bowlers, his demeanour, his spirit, his camaraderie, and his style. He sneaks in, but I feel really happy with that choice.

BOWLERS (44)
1877-1961 (20)
The bowlers who dominated in the first 84 years of test cricket were a remarkably diverse and skilled bunch who shaped their teams' fortunes.

1.	Sydney Barnes	England	1901-14
2.	Bill O'Reilly	Australia	1932-46
3.	Clarrie Grimmett	Australia	1925-36
4.	Fred Trueman	England	1952-65
5.	George Lohmann	England	1886-96
6.	Jim Laker	England	1948-59
7.	Alan Davidson	Australia	1953-63
8.	Ray Lindwall	Australia	1946-60
9.	Keith Miller	Australia	1946-56
10.	Fred Spofforth	Australia	1877-87
11.	Charlie Turner	Australia	1887-95
12.	Hugh Trumble	Australia	1890-1904
13.	Alec Bedser	England	1946-55
14.	Maurice Tate	England	1924-35
15.	Hedley Verity	England	1931-39
16.	Brian Statham	England	1951-65
17.	Frank Tyson	England	1954-59
18.	Harold Larwood	England	1926-33
19.	Fazal Mahmood	Pakistan	1952-62
20.	Richie Benaud	Australia	1952-64

Highly considered:

Colin Blythe	England	1901-10
Jack Cowie	New Zealand	1937-49
Hugh Tayfield	South Africa	1949-60

Sydney Barnes, the deadly medium-pacer from early in the 20th century.

Though they played relatively few tests, there is no doubt that the top pair are **Sydney Barnes** from England and **Bill O'Reilly** from Australia. Each played only 27 tests. They were very different, but both were totally destructive.

Barnes, a right-arm medium-pacer from Staffordshire, captured 187 wickets in 27 matches at an unbelievable average of 16.43. Most impressive of all, he took 24 five-wicket bags and seven 10-wicket match hauls in those 27 tests. His best figures were 9-103 and 8-56 at Johannesburg in 1913-14, the series in which he set the record for most wickets (49) in a series. The year before, he demolished South Africa in England, taking 8-29 at the Oval.

O'Reilly, a tall leg-spinner from New South Wales, has less impressive statistics than Barnes, but was regarded by Don Bradman as the finest bowler he faced. In his 27 tests he took 144 wickets at 22 runs apiece, securing nine five-wicket bags and three 10-wicket match hauls. The Australian was a dominant and much-admired bowler. He was a hard-nosed competitor who gave nothing away. His strength, apart from his mental toughness, was outstanding accuracy and the bounce he obtained. Not a big turner of the ball, he pinned batsmen to the crease and denied any opportunity to advance or attack with conviction. He was to Australia's bowling attack what Bradman was to the batting.

New Zealand-born **Clarrie Grimmett** is next. This tiny giant of a man, with the magical wrists and steely character, was a freak from the minute he debuted for his adopted country, Australia. He was 33 when he played his first test, in Sydney in 1925. From the beginning, he taunted England, capturing 11 wickets in the match, including Hobbs. He and Tiger O'Reilly later formed a famous partnership. In his final test, Grimmett took 13 wickets at Durban in 1936. He was controversially dropped later that year and never played test cricket again. He ended with 216 wickets in 37 tests, six wickets per test, a phenomenal rate.

"Fiery" **Fred Trueman** was a wonderful personality and character. He was larger than life and his forte was bowling quick, terrorising his opponents and keeping the English fighting spirit alive. He had a beautiful action, delivering genuine fast outswing and some lethal bouncers, and had the stamina to sustain the pressure for long periods. Trueman became the first man to reach 300 test wickets, and finished with 307 at 21, including 8-31 in his third test, against India in 1952. His strike rate was outstanding – a wicket every 49 balls, better than Lillee and just behind Marshall. Trueman became an icon for Yorkshire and England.

Next is **George Lohmann,** the medium-pace bowler from England. He played from 1886-96 and his record is the best of all: 18 tests, 112 wickets, average 10! In those tests he took nine five-wicket bags and five times took 10 wickets in a match, with incredible best figures of 9-28 and 8-7 against South Africa in Johannesburg and Port Elizabeth respectively in 1895-96. He took 35 wickets at 5.8 in the series, as well as 8-35 in Sydney a year later. Just to remind the Aussies who was boss, he returned in 1891-92 and took 8-58, again at Sydney, but more expensive!

Jim Laker will forever be remembered as the only man to take 19 wickets in a test match (only Sydney Barnes of the rest has reached even 17.) It was 1956 at Old Trafford that he spun his off-spin magic right through the Australians with 9-37 and 10-53, and match figures of 19-90. Born in Bradford, Yorkshire, he settled further south, playing for Surrey. Once in the England team, he was generally the first-choice spinner, with Tony Lock in support. He played 46 tests and took 193 wickets at a superb 21.24 and the incredible economy rate of just two runs per over. His strike rate of 62 balls per wicket is only just behind Warne and Murali.

Three Australians line up next – **Alan Davidson, Ray Lindwall** and **Keith Miller.** All played together from 1953, when Davidson joined the famous new ball duo, until Miller retired in 1956 after 55 tests and 170 wickets at 22.97. Lindwall played on until 1960, by which time he'd played 61 tests and taken 228 wickets at 23. Davidson's career didn't last as long – 44 tests, but his record was superior – 186 wickets at 20. All three can be counted among the greatest to wear the baggy green cap – Lindwall and Miller as a feared partnership, Davidson as their finest left-arm swing bowler.

The next three are also Australians, but from a generation or three earlier – Fred Spofforth, Charles Turner and Hugh Trumble. **Fred Spofforth**, "The Demon", from Balmain played just 18 tests from 1877-87, secured the first hat-trick in tests and the second-best bowling figures ever by an Australian – 14-90 against England at the Oval in 1882. The fearsome fast bowler retired early owing to business interests. **Charles Turner,** the right-arm medium-pacer from Bathurst, played only 17 tests from 1887-1895, taking over from Spofforth and producing his own devastation. He took 101 wickets at just 16.63. Those playing with him considered him without superior. **Hugh Trumble** was an off-break bowler from Melbourne, and played 32 tests from 1890-1904, capturing 141 wickets at 21. His forte was on wet wickets, especially in Melbourne, where he snatched two test hat-tricks, the first to do so.

Fred Spofforth, "The Demon", and the Dennis Lillee of his day.

The next six are all outstanding English bowlers – Alec Bedser, Maurice Tate, Hedley Verity, Brian Statham, Frank Tyson and Harold Larwood.

Bradman rated **Alec Bedser** as the finest swing bowler he faced and when the greatest batsman rates you there is no higher praise. Bedser took 236 test wickets though he started late, at 28, after World War II. Bedser quickly made up for lost time with 11-wicket hauls in his first two tests, against India in 1946. His best series was his 39-wicket haul in the Ashes series in 1953, when he almost single-handedly carried England's attack.

Maurice Tate is a whisker behind Bedser, owing to Bradman's vote, but Tate was rated by many, too, in particular CB Fry and Jack Hobbs, who both said he was the greatest they had seen. His greatest legacy was the length he bowled at a brisk pace, the ball spitting off the pitch. Herbert Strudwick, the finest keeper in his day, said Tate and Barnes were the best he kept to. Tate loved Australia, a difficult place to perform. His tireless line and length captured the hearts of his fiercest foe. In 10 tests Down Under he took 55 wickets, including five five-wicket hauls and his best test match tally of 11-228. Overall, he took 155 wickets at 26, an economy below two runs an over.

Hedley Verity, the wily left-arm spinner from Leeds, broke the record for the most wickets taken in one day – 14. He finished the test, against Australia at Lord's in 1934, with 15-104. He debuted in 1931 and by the time he retired to join the war in 1939 he had 144 wickets at 24. He achieved 100 wickets in the shortest period of any Englishman.

Brian Statham will forever be known as Trueman's foil, yet they played just half of Statham's 70 tests together. In truth, Statham could stand alone, such was his accuracy. He had an "If they miss I hit" mentality, and kept close to Trueman in wickets taken, ending with 252 at a superb average of 24.8. His finest hour was at Lord's in 1955 against South Africa, when he returned the phenomenal figures of 29-12-39-7. Statham was the glue that made Trueman and Frank Tyson stick.

Frank Tyson was a freak tearaway quick, lightning quick. Once he cut the length of his run-up in Australia in 1954-55, he was a different bowler. His final career figures were 76 wickets at just 18 apiece. His career was short but anyone who faced him had long memories. Richie Benaud claimed he was the fastest bowler he ever saw. Tyson's 7-27 at Melbourne in 1955 was testimony to his pace and hostility.

In the same category, if not the same era, is **Harold Larwood** from Notts. His legacy is controversial, but Larwood was an honest team man who bowled extremely fast. He started for England in 1926, but it was the 1932-33 Bodyline series in which he showed the world, and especially Bradman, that he was a special case. In that series he tormented the Australians and earned England and his captain Douglas Jardine the Ashes. That he never played again was the cruelest punishment for a man who simply followed instructions. He stopped Bradman, a feat no other bowler achieved. His test record of 78 wickets in 21 tests at 28 each does no justice to the man who grew up in the coal mines.

Fazal Mahmood was Pakistan's first great bowler. All their early victories were indebted to his genius, especially bowling on matting wickets. His finest moment came early, in 1952 at Lucknow, in Pakistan's second test, when he took 7-42 in the second innings, 12 for the match, and India were beaten by an innings. On Pakistan's first tour of England, in 1954, he took 12 wickets at The Oval to level the series. England were 109-2, chasing only 168, but lost their last eight wickets for 34, with Fazal to the fore. When Pakistan won their maiden test against Australia, in Karachi, he took 13-114, his best match figures. Overall, he captured 139 wickets at 24, in 34 tests, returning an outstanding 13 five-wicket innings and four 10-wicket match hauls.

The final spot goes to **Richie Benaud,** the outstanding leg-spinning all-rounder and leader from New South Wales. Benaud became famous for many things in cricket, his leadership and commentary the standouts, but it was as a classic leg-spinner he initially made his name. He saved his best for the Ashes. In 1958-59 he took 31 wickets at only 18 apiece. His career highlight was at Old Trafford in 1961 when the series was in the balance, with England 150-1 chasing 256. Benaud bowled his heart out, capturing 6-70 and sealed the urn for Australia.

1962-2013 (24)

1.	Shane Warne	Australia	1992-2007
2.	Malcolm Marshall	West Indies	1978-91
3.	Dennis Lillee	Australia	1971-84
4.	Wasim Akram	Pakistan	1984-2002
5.	Richard Hadlee	New Zealand	1973-90
6.	Muttiah Muralitharan	Sri Lanka	1992-2010
7.	Imran Khan	Pakistan	1971-92
8.	Curtly Ambrose	West Indies	1988-2000
9.	Glenn McGrath	Australia	1993-2007
10.	Michael Holding	West Indies	1975-87
11.	Waqar Younis	Pakistan	1989-2003

12.	Mike Procter	South Africa	1967-70
13.	Allan Donald	South Africa	1992-2002
14.	Joel Garner	West Indies	1977-87
15.	Andy Roberts	West Indies	1974-83
16.	Dale Steyn	South Africa	2004-13
17.	Wes Hall	West Indies	1958-69
18.	John Snow	England	1965-76
19.	Courtney Walsh	West Indies	1984-2001
20.	Bob Willis	England	1971-84
21.	Anil Kumble	India	1990-2008
22.	Shaun Pollock	South Africa	1995-2008
23.	Derek Underwood	England	1966-82
24.	Jeff Thomson	Australia	1972-85

Highly considered:

Bishan Bedi	India	1966-79
Ian Botham	England	1977-92
Kapil Dev	India	1978-94
Lance Gibbs	West Indies	1958-76
Vernon Philander	South Africa	2011-13

Topping the modern list is **Shane Warne,** the leg-spinner extraordinaire from Victoria. It's not just the masses of wickets he took, it's the domination and the legacy he created. Leg-spin bowling is arguably the most difficult art of all. He started badly, 1-150 in Sydney against India, but from there he stepped up and mesmerised most. Only the Indians had a clue against his accuracy, brilliant variations, mental fortitude and wonderful cricket brain. Warne bowled an astonishing 40,705 balls in test cricket over 145 matches, securing 708 wickets, including 37 five-wicket bags and 10 ten-wicket match hauls. They are incredible stats. I played four tests against him, but he didn't bowl much to me and when he did I looked to sweep, pull or cut, such was the prodigious spin he would get with his stock leg-spinners. Then he bowled me a wrong-un and that was that. A few weeks later he cleaned out Mike Gatting and the rest is indeed history as he went on to become arguably the finest bowler of all time.

Not too far behind the blond Aussie is the bristling Barbadian, **Malcolm Marshall.** He ran in on an angle and delivered open-chested, bursting with energy and strategy. He intimidated all he bowled to, such was his unrelenting approach. He just kept charging in. He did so to enormous effect, capturing 376 wickets at 20 with a resounding strike rate of only 46 balls per wicket. He joined the mighty Windies fast bowling battery in 1978, and became the leader through the 1980s with his late swing, skiddy bounce and relentless attack. In particular, he preyed on English scalps, taking 7-56 in 1984 and beating that with 7-22 four years later. The over-riding factor behind his success was his ability to outthink any opposition on any surface. There was far more brain than brawn in his art. He had an unnerving act of screaming his displeasure at you when the plan wasn't working – he once told Ian Smith he was going to kill him in Barbados, the next venue. He didn't quite manage that, but put him in hospital anyway.

Dennis Lillee, a terror on the field, friendly and approachable off it.

Dennis Lillee was the modern-day Demon Spofforth – tall, dark, moustachioed and deadly. His career worked in three parts – the tearaway before a severe back injury, the refined, complete fast bowler, and then at the end, the master for all occasions. He tore in to begin with, chains, sleeves and hair flying madly as he raced towards his target. The jump, the fierce power of the wrist snap and the long intimidating follow-through, all made him Dennis the Menace. His back injury taught him to refine and hone the art of fast bowling and of preparation and recovery. His fine finish showed he could master any conditions, subtly changing pace and position, pacing himself and always meeting the team's needs. I faced him in my first series. He had me caught at short leg, but given not out. I walked anyway. The next day he gave me firm advice: "Don't ever **** walk again." Always the mentor and most approachable, Dennis helped many cricketers during and after his career.

I played in **Wasim Akram's** first first-class match and first test series. He took seven wickets on first-class debut and 10 wickets in his second test. After that he never stopped taking wickets. What a natural. Off an economical run with a fast arm action he transformed swing bowling, including reverse swing, like no other, dragging his mate, Waqar, with him. No doubt he learnt from Imran initially, but he seemed to take the advice to another level. I watched him from the slips at Scarborough one day and he took seven wickets in five overs, hitting the base of the stumps six times with fast swinging yorkers. He forced me to wear a grill on my helmet for the first time when he bowled two bouncers in two balls. The balls moved in different directions, and both grazed my mouth. Relieved to make it to stumps unscathed, I used the rest day to get used to a grill and stayed with it after that, so inadvertently he saved my teeth!

Richard Hadlee is the bowler I know the best, of course. He was calculating, articulate and spectacular in his overall approach to his craft. That he maintained such a high standard until he was nearly 40 was mind-boggling. He actually got better and better. For eight straight years through the 1980s he was the world's No 1 bowler, ahead of Marshall, Imran and Holding. His bowling action was freakish, especially once he cut his run-up to 14 paces. It grooved a smooth ride in and an efficient, slick wrist release. He was quicker than he looked, often pinning the underprepared. But he didn't waste his energy. Rather, he sought out either edge of the bat. He moved it just enough, focusing on the base of off stump, on rhythm, on building pressure. One of my proudest achievements was never to be dismissed by this machine in eight first-class matches. But when he played tests he was a different beast, a genius who always triumphed.

Muttiah Muralitharan sits at No 6 on the list, the second best spinner of his time behind Warne and in the top five spinners ever, along with Warne, O'Reilly, Grimmett and Laker. Murali became the greatest Sri Lankan cricketer, with 800 wickets in 133 tests, capturing an unbelievable 67 five-wicket bags, the most by far. He is a wonderful man and has done a vast amount for the goodwill of the game with his smile, endearing character and joyous spirit. He was lucky that a change in cricket's laws suited his bowling action and he made the most of that luck.

Imran Khan refused to play New Zealand in my first series as captain, in Pakistan in 1991. Just as well. Wasim and Waqar were plenty of trouble anyway. So I faced Imran only in New Zealand in 1988, when his shoulder was niggling him. He was accurate but not quick, swung it but not as he had in his prime. Until that year he was devastating wherever he went around the world, relying on his late swing, pace and bounce. He was a beautiful sight when charging in, leaping high and wide of the crease, slinging the ball down with so much spit and venom. A class act, he was arguably Pakistan's best player ever.

Curtly Ambrose was another I briefly encountered – at the 1992 World Cup on a slow pitch. He was frustrated, and I sensed his demeanour at close hand, his hatred of batsman. Nothing that day was assisting him and we cruised to a comfortable win. But whenever I saw him in the highlights or in New Zealand two years later (when I was injured) he was mean, mean, mean. Pace and bounce were his weapons, but his accuracy, too, was unrelenting and awkward. It looked from a distance that there was nowhere for the batsmen to hide or find any freedom. He found out at least 405 of them in his fine career. And he removed them cheaply, at 20 apiece, and quickly, every 54 balls. It didn't help, either, that Courtney Walsh was doing the same at the other end.

I was privileged to face **Glenn McGrath** in his first test, in Perth in 1993. He reminded me immediately of a young Hadlee, close to the stumps, tall action, unnerving accuracy and movement. He soon developed into the one and only McGrath, one of Australia's finest. His bounce was greater than Hadlee's, his length not as full. He spearheaded a major period of domination for Australia and fittingly retired in the same test as his long-time partner, Shane Warne. McGrath was lethal when there was a hint of grass or juice in the wicket, but he also developed a clever reverse swing when the ball was old and soft. He became a complete package as a bowler, in all conditions, capturing 563 wickets at just 21, striking at 52 balls with 29 five-wicket hauls.

Whispering Death perfectly sums up the theme of **Michael Holding.** From 40 yards out he would set off on his long loping run-up, cruising along with sublime balance and grace. Then at the bowling crease he would climb into the air, turn his shoulders, and unleash hell. He made life miserable for Tony Greig's 1976 England team, repeatedly crashing yorkers into the base of their stumps. Holding intimidated me like no other apart from Jeff Thomson. As he ran in, your heartbeat climbed a few notches, and as he approached the crease it was pumping stupendously. He bowled to me in Barbados for an hour, bringing me forward and then forcing me back, forward and back. In the end I took four rib cage deliveries and as I jumped to play each one, I landed closer and closer to my stumps. Finally, the torment ended when, in knocking down another bouncy bodyline ball, I took out my off stump halfway up with my back foot, out hit wicket. He had an uncanny knack of making you dread the moment when he started that lovely smooth run-up.

Waqar Younis enjoyed following Imran and Wasim. However, he proved he wasn't a follower, but a leader in his own right with 373 wickets at the extraordinary strike rate of a wicket every 43 balls. He never had the height of those two legends he learnt from, but he certainly had amazing stamina and sustainability to go with his accuracy. I faced him often in 1990 in Pakistan, and he kept on running in, over after over, often 10-over spells or more. He was quick, too, early in his career, up there with Marshall and Donald, but not quite Thomson and Holding. He bowled relentlessly at the stumps and my method was no backlift, just a short jab at the ball to keep it out. I was happy to be patient and wait, but you had to wait a long time before he called for his sweater. Seeing him off was always a notable achievement.

At 12 is **Mike Procter,** the South African who, like many of his countrymen, was denied a true test career. He did have seven tests and excelled. In the English county game and the South African Currie Cup he expressed himself to the maximum and showed why he was such a feared bowler. His seven tests against Australia in South Africa reaped 41 scalps at just 15 runs each! It's not much to go by, but as with Barry Richards, you just know talking to everyone he played against that he was freakishly good. His wrong-footed action and booming fast in-swingers were his signature.

Joel Garner and **Andy Roberts** went hand in hand. They were the ideal opening pair, Garner with height and bounce, Roberts with pace, skid and movement. I faced Garner in seven tests and had some joy, but mainly pain. Twice he sent me to hospital with suspected broken bones, one a rib, the other a finger. He could get the ball into the batsmen's ribs at will and was hard to counter. I applied the theory of wearing him down and seeing him off, but of course that just meant one of his mates replaced him. His record was impressive: 58 tests, 259 wickets at only 21 each.

I encountered Roberts in a nasty incident at Taunton in a county match between Somerset and Leicestershire in 1984. He was at the end of his career, cruising in off 14 paces, bowling well-controlled out-swingers and the odd bouncer. He had it on a string that day and cleaned out our top five easily enough. I managed to stay down the other end, another of my theories about how to deal with the Windies quicks, until it was clear I needed to counter-attack before the innings folded. So I left the out-swingers outside off stump and he tried his two-bouncer attack. That went okay, and on the third ball, when he pitched up, I lifted him over his head for six. So he reverted to more drastic means, the bean ball approach. Luckily I got a warning from Peter Willey in the gully as to what was coming and managed to steer clear of the head-high beamers. I don't think he liked New Zealanders, perhaps because of a certain New Zealand umpire – Fred Goodall. Seeing the whites of Roberts' eyes is my enduring memory.

Allan Donald and **Dale Steyn** have been South Africa's finest fast men. They played in back-to-back eras, but that only helped sustain their high ranking, leading the attack for long periods. Donald captured 330 wickets in 72 tests at 22 apiece and Steyn is fast approaching that at the same price, but with a slightly better strike rate. They relied on blistering speed, coupled with movement away, Donald more off the seam and Steyn more through the air. I faced Donald once in county cricket when he was a rookie in 1987 and then at the end of my career at Eden Park in 1995. He would have played a lot more if it wasn't for South Africa's absence from international cricket until 1992. By 1995, he had become a refined bowler and he carried that sophistication through to 2002, when he hung up his well-worn boots. Steyn has carried on the mantle flawlessly. His stamina, skill and fiery disposition make him the greatest threat in world cricket.

Wes Hall was the forerunner of the great West Indian fast bowling factory that came later. He set a menacing tone from the moment he began his long, lithe run. Immensely popular with team-mates, but feared the world over, he captured 192 wickets at 26 at the excellent strike rate of a wicket every 54 balls. He was the central figure in the first tied test, in Brisbane in 1961, taking 9-203. His last test, in Auckland, was the first I ever watched, as a six-year-old with my dad. Hall took only one wicket, Glenn Turner for a duck on debut, but I've never forgotten his presence.

Courtney Walsh was a nightmare for me. He often took my wicket when I thought I had done well to get away from Marshall, Garner and Holding. He knew his role well and kept probing on a length, his greatest strength. He had pace but wasn't lethal, and he had bounce, but again it wasn't lethal. What was lethal was his battery for bowling. He was a cricket Energizer Man. He often did the dirty work, into the wind, or the long spell until the next new ball. When the big guns retired and it was just Walsh and Ambrose, he stepped up manfully. Over his long career of 132 tests, he bowled more than 30,000 balls off a long run, taking 519 victims at under 25, proving his stature as one of the giants of the game. I was always a massive fan of this loveable rogue.

Courtney Walsh, left, Brian Lara, rear, and Curtly Ambrose, three legends of West Indies cricket, celebrate a victory at the Basin Reserve.
Photo: Fairfax

Ian Chappell rates **John Snow** as the best fast bowler he faced, and Chappell was no mug against pace. Snow carried England for many years and had a mean streak to boot. He appeared to saunter in and then unleash.

That's what seemed to surprise many batsmen. He got the ball to kick off a length and his line was immaculate because of his efficient, tight action. Snow secured 202 wickets at 26 from 49 tests.

Bob Willis was another menace to me, knocking me over too many times. Mind you, I was pretty young when he took my off stump at the Oval in 1983, one of the best balls I ever faced, pitching middle and hitting off at speed. I punched a three off his bowling to register my first ton a year later and he showed a nice gesture when he veered off his normal trance-like march back to his mark to shake my hand. It was a cool feeling. When he bowled at you, you felt a bit trapped by his large presence and short-of-a-length attack. A nice quiet man, he was sometimes under-rated in my opinion, which after he took 325 wickets at 25 sounds rather strange. I rated him easily the best England bowler I faced.

I was **Anil Kumble's** 100th test victim at Bangalore in 1995, caught off the arm at slip. I say that because he often got steeple bounce – it was a damn shame that the local umpire missed where it struck me! Anyway, he went on to take another 500 wickets, including a Laker-like 10-wicket innings haul, 10-74 against Pakistan. Kumble was an unusual leg-spinner, relying on bounce and accuracy, a sort of modern-day Tiger O'Reilly, praise indeed. He bowled more than 40,000 deliveries in tests, all with a super attitude. Kumble was a real gentleman and an Indian gem.

Shaun Pollock was the straightest bowler in world cricket during his time. He had accuracy, an ability to move the ball both ways, and was a perfect foil for Allan Donald. His endearing quality was his consistency in attitude and performance, resulting in a top-notch record of 421 test wickets at 23 runs apiece. He also possessed stamina and courage, as he proved in the searing heat of Adelaide in 1998 when, on a superb batting track, he toiled over after over to take his best test haul of 7-87 in 41 energy-sapping overs.

I faced **Derek Underwood** late in his career, early in mine, while in county cricket. He had Knott behind the stumps and I fancy that combination for Kent and England was a huge boost to his career. He was renowned for being deadly on uncovered wickets, because he was quicker than most left-arm slow bowlers. He angled in with a flattish flight, never allowing batsmen to move out to him often, preferring to pin them to the crease. He was unusual in that way, but highly effective, as proven by his 297 wickets at 26 apiece.

Finally, **Jeff Thomson,** my head-banging nemesis, completes the modern bowlers list. Thommo bowled at me in my first test, at the Basin, just before lunch on day five (first four days rained out) with a brand new ball. He came out of the Norwood Room's dark windows and flung the ball at me for five overs. He hit me in the head three times, knocking my chinless strapped helmet off in the process. He pitched up twice. The first one I jabbed down and got four because no-one was fielding in front of the wicket. The second one I hit to mid-on and called for an easy single. Geoff Howarth, at the non-striker's end, was sitting on his bat enjoying the view. He woke up late and sent me back so Thommo, having gathered the ball himself, raced me to the striker's end and he took the bails off to run me out. My first test innings was definitely no stroll in the park! Hey, he scared the daylights out of hundreds of others, too.

ALL-ROUNDERS (16)

1877-1961 (4)

It is not surprising that with the advent of the one-day game, all-rounders have become more prominent since the 1960s. But there were still plenty of highly skilled all-rounders earlier on. An asterisk denotes that players have already been chosen in a specialist category.

1.	Keith Miller*	Australia	1946-56
2.	Les Ames (w)	England	1929-39
3.	Clyde Walcott (w)*	West Indies	1948-60
4.	Wilfred Rhodes	England	1899-1930

Highly considered:

Jack Gregory	Australia	1920-28
Vinoo Mankad	India	1946-59
Monty Noble	Australia	1898-1909
John Reid	New Zealand	1949-65

(w) Wicketkeeper

Keith Miller, left, one of the greatest all-rounders of all time, strides out to bat, accompanied by New Zealand's own Martin Donnelly.

The standout all-rounder was **Keith Miller.** His bowling was his trump card, especially in tandem with Ray Lindwall, but he had the ability in the middle order to turn a game. That he could be selected as either a bowler or a batsman is the reason why he is so revered. Few can lay claim to that.

Les Ames was another whose skills meant he could be selected for either of two skills, batting or wicketkeeping in his case. His test average was 40, but he was a better keeper than Walcott and so jumps in behind Miller as a top all-rounder.

Clyde Walcott's batting record has been dealt with, but his keeping was instrumental in allowing the West Indies to squeeze an extra player into their line up. His huge presence, as part of the three Ws, was a major reason for the West Indies becoming such a force during that period.

Wilfred Rhodes is a must. The Yorkshireman was such a personality that he became a legend. He played his first test at 21, batting No 11, and put on 130 for the last wicket with Reginald Foster. Then eight years later he opened with Jack Hobbs and put on 323 against Australia. But his forte was his shrewd left-arm spin. He played 58 tests, his last in 1930 at the age of 52. Rhodes scored more than 2000 runs at over 30 and secured 127 wickets at just 26, his best being 8-68. It should be mentioned that he took 4204 wickets in first-class cricket, by far the record.

1962-2013 (12)

Such has been the development of the game over the last 50 years that we have seen more and more multi-purpose cricketers come to the fore. Again an asterisk denotes that players have already been chosen in a specialist category.

1.	Garry Sobers*	West Indies	1954-74
2.	Jacques Kallis*	South Africa	1995-2013
3.	Adam Gilchrist (w)	Australia	1999-2008
4.	Ian Botham	England	1977-92
5.	Imran Khan*	Pakistan	1971-92
6.	Richard Hadlee*	New Zealand	1973-90
7.	Mike Procter*	South Africa	1967-70
8.	Kapil Dev	India	1978-94
9.	Shaun Pollock*	South Africa	1995-2008
10.	Tony Greig	England	1972-77
11.	Andy Flower* (w)	Zimbabwe	1992-2002
12.	Matt Prior (w)	England	2007-13

Highly considered:

Chris Cairns	New Zealand	1989-2004
AB de Villiers (w)	South Africa	2004-13
Mahendra Singh Dhoni (w)	India	2005-13
Alec Stewart (w)	England	1990-2003

(w) Wicketkeeper

Garfield Sobers at No 1 is easy, but **Jacques Kallis** is right on Sobers' coat-tails. Sobers batted superbly, and could bowl pacy left-arm swing, orthodox left-arm spin or chinamen. And he could field anywhere. He's the greatest all-rounder ever.

What an incredible career Kallis has crafted. His batting we have touched on, but his bowling and fielding are also superb. He could for a time have been picked for South Africa as a third seamer, such was his ability to bowl a sustained line and length at pace. Instead, he was the perfect foil as the fourth seamer while churning out century after century.

Adam Gilchrist was a truly great test cricketer. He followed Ian Healy into the Australian test side, no mean feat, and took the world by storm. It was his batting at No 7 that did the most damage. Just when you thought getting through Ponting, Waugh (M) and Waugh (S) was progress, in marched Gilchrist with his high grip and natural swing of the bat. He stroked 17 hundreds, the most by any true keeper, and averaged a mighty 47, showing he could have made the batting category alone if he'd been focused only on batting. His keeping kept improving until he became arguably the greatest keeper-batsman ever.

Next is the one and only **Ian Botham.** He is above others because he developed into a genuine No 6. He scored 14 hundreds, the most by any bowling all-rounder, proving many times what a match-winning maestro he was. His batting was often superb, when he was truly focused, with a correct technique hitting straight and hard. With his bowling, he began with a five-wicket haul on debut against the Aussies in 1977, and swung the ball prodigiously for another decade. He was an audacious bowler, always gambling on the one-on-one duel. He could be quick early on in his career, but settled mainly for swing both ways. I faced his bowling many times and he came out on top of a few occasions. Mostly he was annoying, such as when he ran in to bowl at Lord's in 1983 in my sixth test. I was on 46, my highest score to that time, and as he ran in he gave the Taverners crowd the fingers halfway in, delivered the ball and ripped out my off stump with one that pitched on middle and hit the top of off. I got him a year later, posting my first test century at Wellington, relishing his long hops. But he kept coming back at me and got his revenge at Christchurch a week later. He was just an all-round freak and an entertaining one at that. He was a huge favourite of mine.

Imran Khan, Richard Hadlee and **Mike Procter** have been dealt with in the bowling category because that was their dominant role. But these three had an innate ability to pick up the bat and tear a bowling attack apart. Hadlee was more of a No 7 and a hitter, but Imran and Procter were genuine No 6s and wonderful strokemakers.

Kapil Dev was in a similar class to the four above, but I have placed him down a notch because of his lack of hundreds. He batted with great panache, hit massive sixes and turned many games with a fast cameo. However, it was his bowling over a long period, resulting in him becoming the record-holder for most test wickets, that was his forte. He also captained India to their first World Cup triumph, in 1983. Kapil finished with 434 wickets at 29. It was his against-the-odds performances in India that made him a superstar. For a fast-medium bowler to take

219 wickets at 26 apiece in the unhelpful conditions of India shows why he was world class. His ability to swing and cut the ball both ways, and persevere when nothing was on offer from the pitch, won him admirers everywhere.

Shaun Pollock makes the list because of his long-serving consistency and natural talent. Born with cricket in his blood, he championed South Africa's cause with the new ball and a steady bat for many a year, with the capacity to murder a tired attack, but the technique to counter a second new ball. During his era, South Africa were blessed with many gifted players, but he was the standout bowling all-rounder.

Tony Greig stood tall for England through the 1970s. His pioneering upright stance, helmet wearing and rebellious actions against the Establishment made him one of the strongest personalities to play and endorse the game. He averaged 40 with the bat and had a touch of Sobers about him in that he could revert from seam to spin, depending on the conditions. His finest performance was his match haul of 13-156 at Trinidad in 1974, including 8-86 bowling spin. He packed a lot into a robust travelling life in which he become known the world over.

Tony Greig stood tall during a tough time for England cricket.

Andy Flower need not be recognised here because he qualifies in the batting category, but he was a genuine wicketkeeper, which is often overlooked, and he carried so much weight and responsibility for Zimbabwe that he was exceptional.

Just before this book was closed off, **Matt Prior** confirmed his courage and skill with a match-saving century against New Zealand in Auckland. It confirmed for me his place among my elite 100. By 2013 Prior was closing in on Les Ames' record of eight hundreds for England, and had taken his batting average above 45. Through all that, he remained one of the best keepers in the world.

SPECIALIST WICKETKEEPERS (4)

It's very important to recognise real skill, including that of wicketkeeping, a role accurately described by Ian Smith as being the drummer in the band. Hard-working talent behind the stumps drumming to the beat of the team can make a test side operate successfully. I have selected four standout specialist keepers, three from the 1962-2013 period and one before 1962 to round off my finest top 100. As it happens, they could all also bat.

1.	Ian Healy	Australia	1988-99
2.	Alan Knott	England	1967-81
3.	Godfrey Evans	England	1946-59
4.	Rod Marsh	Australia	1970-84

Highly considered

Mark Boucher	South Africa	1997-2012
Syed Kirmani	India	1976-86
Bert Oldfield	Australia	1920-37
Ian Smith	New Zealand	1980-92
Bert Strudwick	England	1910-26
Bob Taylor	England	1971-84

In my opinion, the finest with the gloves on, standing back or up to the stumps, is **Ian Healy** of Australia. He took the role to a new level with his fitness, fire and flair. He was agile and sure, fast and assured to all types of bowling. His combinations with Warne and McGrath make him the most potent of all. He kept in 119 tests, snaring 395 dismissals.

Who else to back up Healy than **Alan Knott** of England? He lifted the art of wicketkeeping, adding his own nuances and idiosyncrasies and being much admired around the world. His batting was unorthodox and mighty effective.

Godfrey Evans took wicketkeeping into a new age after World War II. His athleticism and longevity as England's Mr Reliable for 14 years and 91 tests make him one of the standout specialist keepers of

Godfrey Evans brought unheard of athleticism to the art of wicketkeeping. Here South African Dudley Nourse watches anxiously as Evans goes off in search of another wonder catch.

all time. He famously stood up to Alec Bedser, encouraging Bedser to bowl a fuller length and become a better bowler. Evans had a strong physique – sturdy, squat and incredibly resilient – a keen eye, wonderful hands, remarkable concentration and sharp reflexes. He led the way for wicketkeepers.

In fourth spot is **Rod Marsh.** It just isn't right not to have another match-winning combination in the top 100 and caught Marsh bowled Lillee (I was one of those for a duck and am secretly proud of it) is present 95 times on test scoresheets. Marsh was predominately a keeper who stood a long way back to Lillee and Thomson and many other Aussie quicks. He had a theatrical way about him, diving through the air, grubby shirt flapping, pulling in fantastic one-handers.

So there it is folks, 100 of the best test players of all time. What a wonderful project it has been, with many hours of deliberation and research and then the final decision. I loved describing their genius and in particular my experience facing many of them up close. Wouldn't it be grand if we were to pick a team from each period and line them up at Lord's for five glorious days in a dream test match?

CHAPTER 10

The Dream Test: At Lord's

This imaginary test match would be cricket's ultimate. In my dream project, I have selected two teams who will face each other – the greatest names to have graced a cricket field.

The 1877-1961 team would be called the Black & Whites, which are the colours we saw them in when we watched on video or in picture form. The 1962-2013 team would be called the Colours, for the vibrant colours we witnessed with the advent of colour television and photography.

THE BLACK & WHITES (1876-1961)

Jack Hobbs	England
Herbert Sutcliffe	England
George Headley	West Indies
Don Bradman (captain)	Australia
Wally Hammond	England
Keith Miller	Australia
Les Ames (wicketkeeper)	England
Alan Davidson	Australia
Fred Trueman	England
Bill O'Reilly	Australia
Sydney Barnes	England
George Lohmann (12th man)	England

THE COLOURS (1962-2013)

Sunil Gavaskar	India
Barry Richards	South Africa
Viv Richards	West Indies
Sachin Tendulkar	India
Greg Chappell	Australia
Garry Sobers	West Indies
Adam Gilchrist (wicketkeeper)	Australia
Richard Hadlee	New Zealand
Shane Warne (captain)	Australia
Malcolm Marshall	West Indies
Dennis Lillee	Australia
Wasim Akram (12th man)	Pakistan

The Black & Whites are led by Don Bradman, the best player and the shrewdest mind. The Colours are controversially led by Shane Warne. One reason is because there is no standout leader, the other because Warne has a fantastic cricket brain and will serve this fabulous team well.

The match-ups are the key: Hobbs, Sutcliffe and Headley against Lillee and Marshall; Bradman, Hammond, Miller and Ames against Hadlee, Warne and Sobers. On the flipside, Gavaskar, Barry and Viv Richards to face Trueman, Miller and Davidson and Tendulkar, Greg Chappell, Sobers and Gilchrist to face Barnes and O'Reilly, a mouth-watering prospect.

THE UMPIRES

Dickie Bird	England
Simon Taufel	Australia

No Umpire Decision Review System is required.
The umpires are the two best of all time. They come from different eras – Dickie Bird from England, 1973-96, with 66 tests umpired, Simon Taufel from Australia, 2000-12, with 74 tests umpired.

THE MEDIA

TELEVISION TEAM

The media for this test are the finest the world has produced. Television will be anchored by Richie Benaud, the best of the best, from the studio set at the ground. Mark Nicholas will be in the middle interviewing the captains and experts and setting the scene. In the commentary box will be first, and most important, a mixture of outstanding voices, and second, those who can enhance the picture with their experience and entertainment value. Jim Laker, the droll Englishman who commentated many years with Benaud for the BBC, will add dry humour and off-spinning expertise. Tony Greig, an all-rounder and captain, will bring his lively and colourful South African voice. With Greig there, Bill Lawry, is a must. Lawry, the Victorian whose love for what he is witnessing is always abundantly evident. From Asia is Ravi Shastri, a polished broadcaster with great all-round expertise and wisdom. Ian Smith has earned his call up-with his honest fresh Kiwi delivery, punctuated with humour and insight. Finally, two outstanding English voices – Geoff Boycott, with his recognisable broad Yorkshire accent, and Michael Atherton, with his Lancastrian pitch. They will provide thought-provoking commentary and expertise on batting.

Richie Benaud (Australia), Mark Nicholas (England), Jim Laker (England), Bill Lawry (Australia), Tony Greig (South Africa), Ravi Shastri (India), Ian Smith (New Zealand), Geoff Boycott (England), Mike Atherton (England).

RADIO TEAM

Radio is represented by the greatest storytellers the cricket world has heard. John Arlott and Alan McGilvray, will anchor the call of play. To provide analysis, humour and the X factor are Jonathan Agnew, Lindsay Hassett, Jeremy Coney and Kerry O'Keeffe. To back up the two main callers are Christopher Martin-Jenkins, Jim Maxwell, Harsha Bogle and Tony Cozier, all four with wonderful voices.

John Arlott (England), Alan McGilvray (Australia), Christopher Martin-Jenkins (England), Jim Maxwell (Australia), Tony Cozier (West Indies), Harsha Bhogle (India), Jonathan Agnew (England), Lindsay Hassett (Australia), Jeremy Coney (New Zealand), Kerry O'Keeffe (Australia).

PRINT TEAM

The writers on this famous test will be the best in the business – Jim Swanton and Neville Cardus offer the English prose, Jack Fingleton delivers the Aussie counter punch and CLR James the West Indian flair. New Zealand has its own Cardus, the thoughtful Dick Brittenden, who covered many of New Zealand's finest moments and tours. Mike Coward, full of humour and wit, knows the 1960s and 1970s of Australian cricket better than anyone. Bringing in the modern perspective are four superb specialist journalists on cricket: Peter Roebuck and Michael Atherton, both former players, and Gideon Haigh and Sambit Bal. Atherton is going to be busy, providing television comments and also writing a summary each day. I'm sure he can handle it.

Jim Swanton (England), Jack Fingleton (Australia), CLR James (West Indies), Neville Cardus (England), Dick Brittenden (New Zealand), Mike Coward (Australia), Peter Roebuck (England), Gideon Haigh (Australia), Mike Atherton (England), Sambit Bal (India).

THE DREAM TEST AT LORD'S

The squads arrive at Lord's fit and raring to go. Don Bradman announces Alan Davidson will play instead of George Lohmann, because he feels the left-arm variety on the slope at Lord's will be important and Davidson bolsters the batting at No 8. Bradman also notes that Headley will bat ahead of him at three, allowing Headley to play in his favourite position. Warne confirms his team, with Wasim Akram missing out to Richard Hadlee. Garry Sobers' left-arm swing provides suitable variety, but it is a huge call to exclude Akram, who is regarded as the finest left-arm pace bowler of all. Hadlee, however provides a slightly better batting record at No 8. (Truth be known, I couldn't not have a New Zealander play in my own dream test.)

Bradman wins the toss and decides to bat on a hard, bouncy pitch under clear skies.

Day One

Hobbs and Sutcliffe get in slowly, the pitch playing well. Lillee and Marshall are wayward to start, but begin finding their radar. In the 10th over Sutcliffe is bowled by a devastating off-cutter from Marshall for 10,

George Headley: batting one above Bradman for the Black & Whites.

the score 32-1. Hobbs is joined by Headley, who is in a frisky, positive mood. All the bowlers are tried by Warne, but the pitch is playing evenly with little movement under perfect overhead conditions.

At lunch the Black & Whites are 94-1, Headley 44, Hobbs 38. After lunch Headley plays freely, but attacks once too often, skips out to Warne and is stumped by Gilchrist for 60, with the score at 126. Hobbs then goes for 57, caught by Gilchrist down the leg side off a persistent Hadlee, and its 148-3. Bradman and Hammond bat well together and score nicely until tea, adding 50 at a run a ball. At tea it's 198-3, Bradman 41, Hammond 20.

After the tea break Bradman races along, with Hammond happy to feed his skipper the strike. Bradman is looking to dominate and calls Hammond for a sharp single, only for Viv Richards to pounce from behind square and throw down the stumps from side on. Hammond is run out for 35. 238-4.

The Colours take the second new ball and immediately Miller is beaten by Marshall and trapped lbw for 8. Lillee builds up his pace to more than 150kmh for the first time in the day and removes Ames, fending a brute of a ball, caught at gully by Barry Richards for 8. 256-6. Bradman has been tested by Marshall around the wicket in the final overs of the day and takes a few in the ribs. He appears in discomfort but survives. Bradman and Davidson nervously see out the first day with the stumps score 275-6, Bradman 92, Davidson 5.

Day Two

On an overcast second day, Lillee opens up with great hostility and control and bowls Davidson without addition to the score. Next ball

Trueman pushes forward and is given out lbw, although the ball appears a touch high. Dickie Bird has no hesitation in raising the finger to send the Yorkshireman on his way. The Black & Whites are stumbling at 275-8 after 91 overs. Bradman, sensing a need to counter-attack, gives himself room and cuts Marshall twice over the slips for four to bring up a resourceful century. The Lord's crowd rises to the batting genius from Bowral.

Lillee is on a hat-trick and charges in to O'Reilly. Again a big shout for lbw, but this time Dickie Bird turns down the raucous appeal and Lillee, full of emotion, flicks sweat from his brow in frustrated fashion. Marshall goes around the wicket to Bradman and delivers two vicious bouncers, both just missing Bradman as he ducks for cover, losing his cap in the process the second time. Bradman steals a quick single off the final ball.

Next it's Lillee to Bradman. Twice Bradman is beaten outside the off stump with rising balls, but Bradman moves into line for a shorter delivery and flicks Lillee with a masterly pull stroke through square for four. Bradman again steals a single off the last ball. Marshall bowls an impeccable maiden over. Then Lillee dismisses O'Reilly, who swings agriculturally to leg and lofts the ball to Gavaskar.

The batsmen cross. Bradman sees out the over with another mighty pull to leg to take his score to 111, with Barnes last man in, to face a rampaging Marshall. It's a no-contest as the Barbadian rips one through Barnes' defences to finish with three well-deserved wickets. Bradman leads the players off to a standing ovation.

BLACK & WHITES
First innings

Hobbs ct Gilchrist b Hadlee	57
Sutcliffe b Marshall	10
Headley st Gilchrist b Warne	60
Bradman not out	111
Hammond run out	35
Miller ct B Richards b Lillee	8
Ames lbw Marshall	8

Davidson b Lillee	5
Trueman lbw Lillee	0
O'Reilly ct Gavaskar b Lillee	2
Barnes b Marshall	0
Extras (1lb, 1nb)	2
Total (99.1 overs)	298

Lillee 22-3-65-4
Marshall 24.1-4-78-3
Hadlee 19-5-58-1
Warne 22-6-59-1
Sobers 12-1-36-0

Gavaskar takes the first over from Trueman and is trapped in front for 0, second ball. Viv Richards takes an eternity to arrive at the crease and holds up Trueman twice before settling in. The first ball flies past his cap into Ames' gloves. The next ball is the same, but Richards is ready and swings it hard into the Taverners for six. The crowd goes wild. Trueman, not to be outdone, gives Richards an earful and finishes the over with two superb out-swingers, the second beating the bat by a whisker. It's game on!

Barry Richards faces Miller from the Nursery End and looks comfortable, chipping two twos, one through mid-wicket, the other past the bowler. Trueman steams in again and Richards this time steps forward and whacks the Yorkshireman back over his head for a one-bounce four and then trots all the way past Trueman to pat the pitch. Superb theatre. Davidson is tried, but the score rises quickly as both Richards play their strokes sublimely, Viv with brutal force, Barry with exquisite timing and placement. They reach lunch with no further trouble. 58-1, both batsmen on 28.

After lunch, Barnes and O'Reilly settle in for a long spell, taking the pace off the ball, giving little away. Both Richards look a touch rattled, especially Viv. The pressure builds and before long Viv is caught on the deep square leg boundary trying to put O'Reilly into the Taverners again. His innings of 46 includes two sixes and seven fours. Tendulkar strides in and immediately gets off the mark with a punched straight four off Barnes. However, his bad luck at Lord's continues and he plays a fraction early and chips to short mid-wicket, where Bradman has positioned himself to take a smart catch low down.

Greg Chappell and Barry Richards continue, looking poised and in control. Richards brings up his 50 with a deft fine sweep for four off O'Reilly. Barnes is replaced by Trueman at the Nursery End, but Trueman can't find his rhythm, preferring to bowl from the Pavilion End. O'Reilly is enjoying the slope into the right-handers' pads and the runs dry up. Miller comes on for Trueman and looks relaxed and on song. Tea arrives with the game in the balance. Richards is 68, Chappell 27, and it's 147-3 off 47 overs. O'Reilly bowled unchanged after lunch, returning 1-32 off 17 superb overs.

Bradman starts after tea with Barnes and Davidson, Barnes using cutters and unerring accuracy, Davidson swinging the ball slightly, from left-arm over the wicket. Bradman sets a defensive field and tries to shut down the two tall right-handers. Only 23 runs come in the first hour as the score moves to 170-3, Richards 80, Chappell 38. After drinks Bradman tries O'Reilly for Davidson from the Nursery End. Barry Richards attempts another sweep, but is caught in front as umpire Taufel decisively raises his finger. In comes Garry Sobers, who is in no mood to be bogged down. Using his feet he begins getting to O'Reilly on the half-volley and eases into double figures. At the other end Miller has resumed from the Pavilion End and begins working over Chappell with a series of bumpers. Chappell reaches his half-century with a fine hook, but in attempting a repeat, is caught in the deep by Davidson, who makes good ground to pull in a vital wicket. It's 199-5, honours even.

In the final hour Sobers and Gilchrist, two fine left-handers, have the measure of O'Reilly and Miller, so Bradman goes back to Barnes and Davidson to shut up shop again. The ploy almost works, but Sobers is inspired and as the heat takes its toll on the bowlers he peels off six beautiful boundaries in the last five overs to give the Colours control at stumps. 250-5 off 77 overs, Sobers 45 not out and Gilchrist 15.

Day Three

It's the Saturday of the Lord's test and the capacity crowd anticipates another fine duel. The new ball is three overs away, so Sobers and

Gilchrist attack O'Reilly and Barnes, scoring 22 runs in quick time. Sobers brings up a superb 50. Bradman grabs the new ball and marches up to Trueman with a few stern words of advice. Trueman, who struggled yesterday, looks focused and ready, especially from the Pavilion End. First, he rips one past Sobers, who shrugs it off with a laugh and a look to deep square leg. The next ball is a bit slower and swings and Sobers swings himself off his feet, missing the moving ball. Trueman is all fire as he tosses his hair back before letting Sobers have a verbal spray.

The scene has been set, with Miller picking up on Bradman's mood. After a few customary looseners, Miller cuts one back on Gilchrist and cleans out middle stump. 272-6. Miller is in perfect rhythm as Hadlee faces up, and the New Zealander has no answer to a rip-snorting bouncer that takes his glove and is easily caught by Hammond at second slip. 272-7.

Somehow Warne survives the hat-trick, but not the next ball as a yorker swings in and sends leg stump flying nearly back to Ames. 272-8. What an over by Keith Miller! Sobers, at the non striker's end, is full of admiration for the Australian, but knows he needs to take charge of an innings rapidly disintegrating. Sobers, however, has an angry Fred to deal with. There is no respite from the two fast men. Sobers, stuck on 62, watches helplessly as Miller sends Marshall back for 2, a leg-cutter caught by Ames at the wicket. 280-9. Trueman had started the innings removing Gavaskar for a duck and now completes it by demolishing Lillee's stumps, also for a duck. The Colours are all out for 280 in 83 overs, and trail by 18.

COLOURS
First innings

Gavaskar lbw Trueman	0
B Richards lbw O'Reilly	80
V Richards c Miller b O'Reilly	46
Tendulkar c Bradman b Barnes	4
Chappell c Davidson b Miller	50
Sobers not out	62
Gilchrist b Miller	22

Hadlee c Hammond b Miller	0
Warne b Miller	0
Marshall c Ames b Miller	2
Lillee b Trueman	0
Extras (7lb, 3b, 3nb, 1w)	14
Total (83 overs)	280

Trueman 12.1-1-67-2
Miller 18-4-59-5
Davidson 13-3-42-0
Barnes 14-4-39-1
O'Reilly 26-7-59-2

It's high noon on Saturday and there is nothing to separate the teams so far. Hobbs and Sutcliffe begin the second innings and look at home on a perfect batting pitch. They bat 22 overs before lunch and post a steady if not remarkable 60-0. Sutcliffe, in particular, is in fine form and has dominated the partnership, scoring 38, with Hobbs on 20.

After lunch, Warne tries all his frontline bowlers, but to no avail. Sutcliffe brings up his half-century by lofting Warne down the ground. Eventually Warne tries Greg Chappell with his medium-paced out-swingers. It's a genius call – Hobbs plays loosely into the off side and steers a catch to second slip, where Sobers takes a blinder, low to his right.

Warne, buoyed by his own tactics, starts to get significant turn out of the rough and Headley, in the next over, tries a dab sweep and is bowled around his legs for one. 95-2. Sutcliffe continues serenely, moving to 70 as the 100 is reached. Bradman is fidgety and looks to stamp his mark on Warne, but before settling he tries to pull a flat, skidding flipper and is bowled off an inside edge for a duck, having faced nine balls. 104-3. Hammond and Sutcliffe have batted together many times and have a brief chat. They dig in. Warne attacks with close men around the bat, and the atmosphere is electric. Lbw shouts are turned down by Bird as Warne starts getting frustrated. Sutcliffe and Hammond slowly pick up the rate as Warne and Sobers, bowling left-arm chinamen, offer scoring opportunities on both sides of the wicket. On 98 Sutcliffe late cuts Warne for two and brings the Lord's crowd to their feet. It's been a sweet Saturday for Sutcliffe. By tea he is in total control as he strides off for a well-deserved cuppa. The Black & Whites lead by 166 and their score is sitting pretty at 159-3, Sutcliffe on 100, Hammond 22.

After tea, Warne brings back Lillee from the Pavilion End. With a fresh shirt and headband Lillee steams in. He senses it's crunch time. Hammond looks almost bored as he strokes Lillee through the covers for four to begin the session. This fires up Lillee more, but Hammond, sensing a bouncer, stays back and, using the pace, clips the short ball through point. The third ball is straight and fast. Hammond is again waiting on the back foot, and is caught in front as Lillee explodes into the air with an emotional appeal. Simon Taufel, who has had a quiet match so far, slowly raises the finger for Hammond to go, lbw Lillee for 30.

Ames is promoted to see off Lillee and joins Sutcliffe in mid-pitch and discusses tactics, making Lillee wait. He charges in again and beats Ames comprehensively. Ames eases the next ball into the covers and gets off the mark. In comes Lillee again. This time it's Sutcliffe, not having faced a ball since tea. He fishes at an outswinger, and gets an edge to the slips. Alongside Gilchrist are Chappell, Sobers and Viv Richards, with Barry Richards in the gully, a formidable cordon. The ball flies towards Chappell, but Sobers sensing the ball dying a little off the soft hands of Sutcliffe, dives forward and to his left and grabs the catch of the century. Sutcliffe is gone, and Lillee is on fire. 175-5.

Ames is joined by the cool, suave-looking Miller. Warne calls up Hadlee to the Nursery End. Hadlee is ready, too. He finds a length with his first ball and Ames scoops it to Tendulkar, lurking in the covers. Ames, head down, walks off having not fired with the bat in the match. 175-6. Hadlee waits while Davidson takes guard: two great all-rounders going head to head. An accurate bouncer hits Davidson on the shoulder. The crowd loves the confrontation as Hadlee nods his approval. Miller wanders down to take the sting out of the situation and offers some assurance to his Aussie team-mate. Davidson swings at Hadlee and the ball sails over the slips for four. Then again, this time over gully as Hadlee rues his luck. Hadlee goes around the wicket and Davidson has no room to swing and instead plays defensively. Another fine over of drama finishes.

Slowly Miller and Davidson rescue the situation and Warne brings on Marshall to rest Hadlee. But the West Indian can get little out of the pitch. After an hour, Warne replaces Lillee, who is tiring fast. The lead creeps past 240.

Warne wants one more breakthrough so he can use the new ball on the fourth morning against the tail. Miller is 33, Davidson 30, six overs left. Warne will bowl three and Hadlee is back for one last attack.

The left-hand/right-hand combination of Miller and Davidson is proving vital to upsetting the lines and fields of Warne's men. Warne goes around the wicket to Davidson and bowls wide into Lillee's footmarks. He finds a length and the ball begins to jump. One ball kicks up and hits the shoulder of Davidson's, ballooning on the on side behind square. From nowhere, Sobers, at leg gully, springs into the air and pulls in a one-handed screamer. 231-7, a lead of 249.

The Colours sense blood. Hadlee bounces Trueman twice. Miller tries to cool Fiery Fred, but next ball from Hadlee hits the mark and Trueman's off stump is sent spiralling. 231-8. The day ends with three more runs added, and the Black & Whites lead by 252.

Day Four

Low cloud and drizzle delay inspection of the ground until after lunch. Bird and Taufel decide that play will start at 3pm, with 42 overs possible in the day. The Black & Whites resume on 234-8, with Miller 37, O'Reilly 1. The new ball is due in four overs.

Warne starts with Lillee and Hadlee, the men who will take the second new ball. He wants his most accurate operators in action from the get-go. Miller looks in good touch from the start and races to 47. It's not the start Warne was after. Hadlee again is accurate, but can't penetrate O'Reilly's defence.

Shane Warne striving for the vital breakthrough. *Photo, Fairfax*

The new ball is taken. The tension is palpable.

Lillee charges in from the Pavilion End, knowing the game is in the balance. Getting in close to umpire Bird, he finds a tight line on Miller's off stump. Two deliveries beat Miller's attacking attempts. The next is the off-cutter down the hill and Miller, not backing off an inch, looks for some joy a third time. The ball seams off the pitch, clips Miller's inside edge and crashes into leg stump. Lillee is in raptures as Miller throws his hair back in disgust and departs for 47. 244-9.

Barnes, last man in, joins O'Reilly. Lillee tries the yorker, but Barnes is up to the task. Hadlee has been immaculate all match, but for the first time loses his length and O'Reilly picks off a couple of vital boundaries on the off side, one a thick edge through the slips. Barnes hangs on as the total creeps up to 264. The last wicket has somehow managed 20.

Marshall replaces Hadlee, and Warne brings himself on at Lillee's end. He lures Barnes with a beautifully tossed leg-spinner. Barnes lashes out and swings early sending the ball over mid-wicket. Viv Richards, lurking with intent, makes haste backwards and tracks the ball out of the clouds and into his secure buckets. The Black & Whites are all out for 264.

BLACK & WHITES
Second innings

Hobbs c Sobers b Chappell	32
Sutcliffe c Sobers b Lillee	100
Headley b Warne	1
Bradman b Warne	0
Hammond lbw Lillee	30
Ames c Tendulkar b Hadlee	1
Miller b Lillee	47
Davidson ct Sobers b Warne	30
Trueman b Hadlee	0
O'Reilly not out	14
Barnes c V Richards b Warne	6
Extras (1lb, 2nb)	3

Total (102 overs)	264

Lillee 23-5-61-3
Marshall 16-2-42-0
Hadlee 24-4-64-2
Warne 28.1-6-71-4
Sobers 5-1-9-0
Chappell 6-2-14-1

The Colours need 283 to win, with 120 overs remaining. Tea has been taken. After the break Gavaskar and Barry Richards take up the challenge. Trueman is again looking for Gavaskar's scalp, but the little master is quickly into line and off the mark. So too is Barry Richards, who punches Trueman twice for twos and a single into the off side to get his innings under way.

Bradman has decided on Davidson for the new ball instead of Miller. The decision works well when Barry Richards walks across a fast in-swinger and is trapped lbw for 5. Gavaskar is busy, however, and is scoring freely on both sides against the new ball bowlers.

Miller replaces Trueman and looks to be bowling well again. Viv Richards is playing to the drama with his swagger but Miller is in no mood for the theatrics and rips one across Richards, who is caught by Sutcliffe at third slip. 36-2 after 12 overs.

Tendulkar joins Gavaskar. It's an all-India affair. Neither has had much joy at Lord's previously, and both talk often, urging each other on.

They put on 50, Gavaskar on 38, Tendulkar 24. Suddenly the skies open up and the players are sent scurrying from the field.

That's the end of play for the day. The Colours need a further 197 with eight wickets in hand.

Day Five

The fifth dawns fine with glorious blue skies and little breeze.
Mark Nicholas is on the pitch assessing the prospects. Tony Greig is using his car keys to check on some of the footmarks that O'Reilly might exploit. Greig believes O'Reilly will be the key. Ravi Shastri is confident either Gavaskar or Tendulkar can set up the match for the

Colours. Geoff Boycott likes the thought of Sobers providing the magic, but is hedging his bets, and Ian Smith is sensing a day of high drama and controversy.

Gavaskar and Tendulkar resume the chase and Miller and Davidson take up the attack for Bradman's men. Bradman is happy to have the footmarks roughed up more for O'Reilly.

Miller moves in to bowl while a hushed and packed Lord's watches. Showing uncharacteristic nerves, Miller begins the day with a bumper and the ball is so high it's called a wide. The next 10 minutes are played in slow motion; Miller taking his time to get composed, and Bradman shifting his field every few balls for an unsettling effect.

Gavaskar takes a single off the last ball of the first four overs. Tendulkar looks a little jumpy at the non-striker's end. Finally Tendulkar faces Miller. He tries for single to get his innings restarted, playing the ball off his hip into the onside, to the right of Headley. Gavaskar is slow to respond. Headley gets to the ball quicker than anticipated, gathers and flicks at 1½ stumps to his left. It canons into the middle stump and Gavaskar is run out by a breathtaking piece of fielding. Headley is surrounded by his ecstatic team-mates. 91-3, Gavaskar run out 42.

Greg Chappell is on his way for 25.

Greg Chappell looks up for the battle as he settles in. He is moving well, playing straight and late, and easily moves into double figures as Davidson and Miller finish their spells. Bradman calls up Barnes and O'Reilly, the best wicket-taking performers of their eras.

Tendulkar has had little of the strike and has little momentum or fluency. Chappell is freer in his stroke-making. He moves to 20 and the score passes 100. Tendulkar has not added to his overnight 24 and 14 overs have passed as drinks are taken.

Barnes and O'Reilly continue to deny Tendulkar, who looks on the verge of lashing out. An attempted cut goes via the inside edge past off stump and away for his first runs. On 25 Chappell moves down to O'Reilly to drive, but miscues and off the leading edge spoons the ball back to the bowler for a vital caught and bowled. 119-4.

Enter Garfield Sobers. The crowd lap up his lazy languid walk to the middle. From his first ball he moves down to O'Reilly and picks up a single. Then he flicks Barnes over square for his first boundary. And then another. Another single – 10 in four balls.

Tendulkar, sparked by Sobers' confidence, pulls off an exquisite cut for four to get his innings rolling. Barnes is replaced by Trueman. Remembering the first innings encounter with Trueman, Sobers is ready for more. He starts with a flashing cover drive, then three balls later hooks fiercely for four more. Trueman is bursting with anger and bluster. He again bounces Sobers, who swings and misses. The ball was recorded on the speed gun at 156km. Fiery stuff indeed.

Tendulkar can't work out O'Reilly at all. High bouncing, straight deliveries off a length give Tendulkar nothing but grief as defends and splices one after another. Another maiden from O'Reilly. Finally Tendulkar breaks loose and swings O'Reilly over wide long-on, then slog-sweeps for another boundary, just before Simon Taufel calls lunch. 152-4, Tendulkar 44, Sobers 24 and 131 runs needed, with six wickets in hand.

After lunch Tendulkar brings up a hard-fought half-century with two lusty blows off O'Reilly. Bradman quietly brings his backward square squarer. So when Tendulkar slog sweeps again to a deliberate leg stump line, he holes out to Hobbs in the deep, a comfortable catch. 160-5.

The test is in the hands of the two left-handers, Sobers and Gilchrist. One more slip-up from the Colours and the match could be beyond reach. Sobers continues as if it's a stroll in the park, easing the ball into the gaps, punishing the loose ones with contempt and acknowledging the good one with his customary nod and wink to the bowler.

Gilchrist is more fidgety, but determined nonetheless to attack. Bradman surrounds Gilchrist with close-in fielders to O'Reilly and fills the slips cordon for the refreshed Miller. Gilchrist, needing bat on ball, shapes a drive to Miller and the ball flies hard and fast to Hammond at second slip. The pace of Miller and swing of Gilchrist's bat send the ball speeding so fast Hammond can't hold it. Gilchrist feels relief and the nerves disappear. He swings Miller over square leg and into the Taverners for a massive six to get off the mark. An amazing stroke. Sobers is delighted by his partner's response and at the end of the over gives Gilchrist a pat on the back for his audaciousness.

In an hour following Tendulkar's dismissal, Sobers and Gilchrist combine to score 74 runs in a flurry of fours and sixes. There is nothing Bradman can do to stop the onslaught. He tries Trueman again and the ball goes to all parts. He calls up Barnes, but Barnes gets slapped around, too. Davidson cannot worry the batsman. Even Hammond is given an over, but goes for two boundaries and is quickly removed.

At drinks it's 234-5, Sobers 56, Gilchrist 41, 49 runs to win, with 42 overs remaining. The second new ball isn't going to be a factor if this run-rate continues. But if Bradman can stem the flow then the new ball might be available for about 10 overs.

Bill O'Reilly draws on all his aggression and cunning in an attempt to get the Black & Whites home.

He needs O'Reilly to block up one end and decides on Barnes to join him. Bradman holds court in a deliberately long talk to his men. Sobers and Gilchrist are cooling their heels, and it takes Dickie Bird to intervene and get Bradman and Co back into action.

O'Reilly is cunning also. Picking up on Bradman's delay tactics he begins to move in slow motion, adjusting his field ever so slightly after every ball. His overs normally take two minutes; now he takes four. Gilchrist gets impatient with O'Reilly and chips at him. O'Reilly senses an opportunity.

At the other end Sobers

is cruising along until disaster strikes. Barnes gets a lucky break, the luckiest break of all. Sobers swings and misses at Barnes and Ames standing up to the stumps takes the ball. As he does a sound is heard and Bradman at mid-off, along with Hammond at short cover join Barnes in a concerted appeal for caught behind. Simon Taufel, who also heard the sound, thinks it's a faint edge and raises his finger. Sobers is out caught behind.

Sobers is shocked, but simply shrugs his shoulders and saunters off. Barnes is convinced of the legitimacy of the dismissal, but Ames isn't so sure. Bradman doesn't move, except to congratulate Barnes, so the dismissal stands. At the non-striker's end, Gilchrist is outraged but keeps his own counsel. Sensing it, O'Reilly at mid-wicket chirps to Gilchrist: "Mate, what happened to 'walking' in your dressing room?" Gilchrist glares at O'Reilly, but resists a reply.

Hadlee strides in. 236-6, 47 to win.

The delaying tactics and the Sobers caught behind have everyone on edge. Hadlee and Gilchrist meet mid-pitch. Since drinks, 14 minutes have passed and only two overs have been bowled.

Hadlee gets his innings under way with a nice flick for three through mid-wicket off Barnes. Gilchrist, who has been tied down by O'Reilly, enjoys the extra pace of Barnes and plays a stunning cover drive for four, moving his score to 45. Forty to win. O'Reilly drops his intensity and Hadlee back cuts for a timely boundary. Bradman gives O'Reilly a few short words and soon enough his length is back and Hadlee is defending for his life. Gilchrist is back in full flow and skipping down the pitch to Barnes, he lofts him high and hard for six, bringing up a terrific half-century. Thirty to win.

Gilchrist likes the fact that Hadlee is comfortable with O'Reilly, while he is enjoying Barnes more. Bradman calls on Trueman to bowl one over and for O'Reilly to swap ends. Trueman is fired up – not unusual – but having had a quiet match, including a pair with the bat, he wants blood.

So Trueman it is, from the Nursery End, bringing the ball back into the lefties down the slope. He takes two balls to get his body in synch and feels some old power return. Then he lets go a fast in-swinging yorker to Hadlee. The ball starts to move sharply in the air, then in a flash it's all over. The ball darts left and continues down the slope

Adam Gilchrist salutes the crowd after reaching his half-century.
Photo, Fairfax

and through Hadlee on to leg stump. Lord's erupts in a thunderous din. Hadlee is gone for a useful 10 under the circumstances and the match is in the balance again. 253-7, Gilchrist 53 not out. Still 30 to win.

Trueman finally feels like a shining star on the brightest of all stages. His mojo is back and he tosses the ball from hand to hand, eyeing up his next victim, Warne, who is on a pair. Trueman knows Warne likes the cut, but that he that he is reluctant to get in behind the short one. He gestures to Bradman that he wants a leg gully and a short leg. Bradman in mid-pitch claps his hands and Sutcliffe and Hammond pop into the leg trap.

Trueman intends to bowl from wide of the crease, looking to cramp Warne into the shot. Warne, well aware of what's unfolding, is not his normal smiling self. Fine leg is adjusted for a skied hook and the plan is ready: the bowler is fizzing, the batsman can barely breathe. Trueman starts and stops, deliberately. He pauses again, and goes. He hits the crease wide and unleashes the ball. Warne is cornered as the ball angles in at this chest, lifting up the slope, gaining height all the way. It strikes Warne on the glove in front of his face, and his bat is knocked out of his hand. The ball balloons to Hobbs, and the game is up for Warne. 253-8.

For the third time in the match, a hat-trick is possible. Malcolm Marshall is next in. He looks casual but doesn't feel it. He doesn't like to lose – he's a fighter and can bat. Gilchrist gives him plenty of positive chat and Marshall settles in to face the hat-trick ball. Trueman bowls a beauty but Marshall is well forward, watches it swing away and raises his bat as the ball heads down the slope towards Ames.

O'Reilly changes ends. Bradman sets a defensive field with four men on the fence. Gilchrist pushes for one and instead scampers two as Sutcliffe is a tad slow coming off the pickets. Two dot balls and then a single.

Marshall survives the over. Trueman quickly is ready to begin the next over and Gilchrist doesn't hesitate either. Trueman bowls the Marshall line down the hill and Gilchrist whips the ball on the up, off his hip and over deep square leg for a massive six. Another ego dented. 21 to win.

O'Reilly drops short to Marshall, who leans back and hits a boundary even Headley would have been proud of. A crucial four is registered on the Old Father Time scoreboard. O'Reilly adjusts his line and a single to short fine leg is taken. Deep point is brought up into a run-saving position and Gilchrist notes a gap behind square. O'Reilly bowls a quick flipper and Gilchrist looks to back cut, just a nudge to send it fine. He plays at the skidding ball, makes a fine contact and Ames takes the catch. Dickie Bird immediately shakes his head, yelling in his Yorkshire accent, "Not out, lad!" Shock appears on the faces of O'Reilly, Ames and Miller at slip. But before anyone has said a word, Gilchrist has walked off towards the Lord's pavilion.

As he strides off briskly, the enormity of what has just happened hits the members in front of the pavilion and in the Long Room. To a man, they rise, clap and cheer Gilchrist. From everyone on the field Gilchrist receives the most appreciative heart-felt ovation a player can experience. 267-9. Gilchrist 62. 16 to win.

Dennis Lillee is not a No 11. He has scored a 70 in test cricket and is normally a No 9 or 10. He joins Marshall and contemplates the enormity of the task… get them in singles or fours? Marshall says, "Both". "Thanks, mate," says Lillee as he returns to his crease and surveys the field. O'Reilly has three around the bat, three saving single and three on the fence – at square leg, mid-wicket and long off. Bradman is not going to let the match slip away with a quickfire slog from Lillee or Marshall. He banks on one defensive shot going wrong, or a rush of blood and a heave to the heavens with his outfield in position. Lillee gets forward and defends. The over finishes with a leg bye and Lillee keeps the strike. Fifteen to win.

Trueman to Lillee is a fearsome rivalry; bushy, black-haired men with gruff voices and deadly expressions. They deserve each other in this death row moment. The second new ball is due. Does Bradman want it? Will he take off O'Reilly to accommodate his quicks?

Tea is delayed for 30 minutes because the last pair is at the wicket. Trueman wants the new ball but Bradman resists. The new ball could go to the fence faster, and he thinks O'Reilly is too clever to be taken by the tail. He sticks with the old ball and tells Trueman to settle down.

Bradman drops third man back and a deep mid-wicket, too. All he wants is for Trueman to stay calm. He reminds Trueman to "bowl as if you are batting". Instinctively, Trueman knows what Bradman means – bowl how they bowled to him in this match. He moves in, controlled and focused. He releases and follows through. He looks up and sees Lillee defend. Same again, he thinks. Then he looks up and sees Lillee swing the bat. The ball flies back at Trueman, who takes evasive action and the missile flies past his head. He despairingly thrusts out a hand and gets a fingertip to the ball. Lillee signals four. Eleven to win.

Trueman is livid. He has been too nice, too passive. He steams in and bounces Lillee. It's a beauty and flies through to Ames. The sixth ball of the over is a no ball. Ten to win, still last men in. Trueman redelivers and looks up. Lillee swings again and the ball goes skywards. Calls of "mine" echo from all parts. Bradman is under it, but Trueman hasn't heard or seen him. All he wants his revenge for his missed catch earlier in the over. He charges towards mid-wicket calling "mine". He knocks the ball out of Bradman's grasp and it spills away. Lillee calls Marshall for a single and takes off, but Marshall at the non-striker's end can see the ball and it's too close to O'Reilly at mid on.

Lillee charges down the pitch and Marshall screams "No!" Lillee keeps coming while watching the ball. When he sees it in O'Reilly's hands he stops and looks at Marshall, who senses the need for drastic action. Lillee isn't going to get back in time so Marshall sprints down the wicket, O'Reilly throws to the striker's end and Ames prepares to whip off the bails. The throw is weak and lobbed high, but Ames leaps to his left, gathers and dives to take out the stumps. Marshall dives just as the bails are dislodged. All eleven men in Black and White caps appeal.

Dickie Bird is at square leg. He stoops over his right knee to get a better look and then bounces up into an upright position. All eyes turn to Dickie. He pauses, which is not normal, ponders for what seems an eternity, then yells, "That's out!" Then quietly he adds, "Aye, that is out, match over. Great test, lads."

Marshall is sprawled on the ground. Lillee hurls his bat away in disgust. Bradman's men gather around Ames, who has completed the final act in this incredible play. The crowd roars with joy. Five days of drama wrapped up in a single moment. Marshall run out 5. Bradman and the Black & Whites win the Dream Test by nine runs.

COLOURS
Second Innings

Gavaskar run out	42
B Richards lbw Davidson	5
V Richards c Sutcliffe b Miller	1
Tendulkar c Hobbs b O'Reilly	52
Chappell c and b O'Reilly	25
Sobers c Ames b Barnes	56
Gilchrist c Ames b O'Reilly	62
Hadlee b Trueman	10
Warne c Hobbs b Trueman	0
Marshall run out	5
Lillee not out	4
Extras (4lb, 2b, 4nb, 1w)	11
Total (81 overs)	273

Trueman 13-3-57-2
Davidson 14-4-54-1
Miller 14-2-53-1
O'Reilly 26-10-57-3
Barnes 13-5-33-1
Hammond 1-0-8-0

The Black and Whites win by 9 runs.

At the match presentation Garry Sobers is declared the Man of the Match for his incredible fielding and two vital half-centuries. Don Bradman receives the gold trophy and in thanking Shane Warne and his team for the match declares it has been the finest test match he has played in or seen. "The quality was as it should be, the spirit the game was played in even more so. We take our hats off to Adam Gilchrist, not only for his sterling knock, but for his magnificent sportsmanship." Shane Warne acknowledges the crowd and the brilliance of Bradman as the winning team's leader. He thanks his team for fighting to the death. "I am proud to skipper such a fantastic bunch."

Mark Nicholas wraps up the match and Richie Benaud in the studio has the final word: "In 100 years from now, folk will talk about this match as the greatest ever played."

CHAPTER 11

National Pride: Each Country's Greatest Team

Over the years, I have often been critical of selectors. Now it's my turn to be scrutinised. I have always wanted to pick the best teams from each of the major test-playing countries. The qualification is simply that you were born in that country or played for it. The one exception is Vince van de Bijl, who never played an official test because of South Africa's isolation from 1970-1992, but was good enough to.

I am a big believer in specialists been given the opportunity to play in their rightful position, but I also believe that the best players, no matter what position, must play. That is always a selector's dilemma. I have faced these dilemmas in the case of the West Indies, with their three great No 3s, and with England, who have three great opening batsmen.

I have selected 12 for each team, but have named the 11 according to their strength on their best home track. I have used *Wisden*, of course, for the period before 1968, when I began watching test cricket, but records and statistics don't always tell the story. I have therefore talked to many sages around the world, especially regards South Africa, to get a full appreciation of players' qualities.

NEW ZEALAND
Stewie Dempster
Glenn Turner
Bert Sutcliffe
Martin Crowe
Martin Donnelly
John R Reid (c)
Chris Cairns
Richard Hadlee
Ian Smith (wk)

Clarrie Grimmett
Jack Cowie
Daniel Vettori (12th man)

Selecting the best New Zealand test team was not a difficult task. Three outstanding top order players, two high-scoring middle-order Martins, four sensational all-rounders, a specialist new ball bowler and a specialist leg-spinner make up the 11.

Stewie Dempster was brilliant during his short stint as a test opening batsman from 1930-33. He averaged 65 in his 10 tests, scoring two hundreds, including 136 in New Zealand's first series, against England. Dempster went on to score the first test century at Lord's by a New Zealander, 120 in 1931.

The great Stewie Dempster, who averaged 65 in test cricket.

Glenn Turner rates as truly world class. He scored more than 100 hundreds in his long first-class career. He didn't quite achieve the same heights in tests, owing to a self-imposed sabbatical for five years while in conflict with New Zealand Cricket. Turner was in the world's top three from 1971-74, when he scored four test centuries in two series – two double hundreds (223no and 259) against the West Indies in 1972 and twin hundreds (101 and 110no) in the first win over Australia, in Christchurch in 1974. He scored hundreds in the subcontinent against Pakistan and India, proving he had the complete game. He also carried his bat twice, 43 not out at Lord's and that 223 not out in Kingston. His powers of concentration, coupled with a grooved technique, made Turner one of New Zealand's best.

Bert Sutcliffe batted in many positions during his career, although mainly as an opener. Here he slots nicely in at No 3, his left-handed prowess ideally suited to the position. Sutcliffe was a much-loved batsman, his highlight being the tour of England in 1949, when he scored 2627 runs. The highest score of his five test hundreds was his superb 230 not out at Delhi in 1955, and his last was a masterly 151 not out at Delhi at the age of 41 in 1965. Bert was a wonderful team man, a true artist and the most courageous of all. His most famous innings was his 80 not out at Johannesburg, after being rushed to hospital when a vicious Adcock bouncer struck him in the head. It is the single most talked about innings in New Zealand cricket folklore.

Forgive me if I indulge and pencil in the name of **Martin Crowe** at No 4, the justification being 16 hundreds and an average of 56 in a

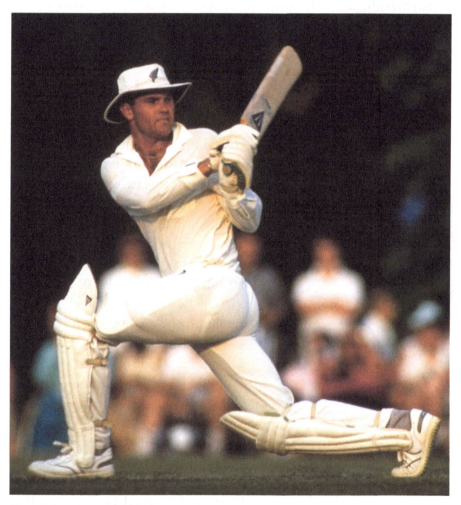

One of the privileges of picking your own team is that you can bat where you like, and I've slotted myself between our two famous left-handers, Bert Sutcliffe and Martin Donnelly.

50-test stretch from April 1985 to August 1994. My highlights were the two centuries I scored at Lord's, 106 in 1986, 142 in 1994. I regret my lack of concentration on 299 at Wellington against Sri Lanka in 1991, and therefore missing out on becoming the first New Zealander to score a triple ton. My best series was against the mighty West Indies in 1987, when I knuckled down to score 119, 104 and 83 in successive tests on bowler-friendly pitches against the best attack in the world.

To bat at No 5 is **Martin Donnelly,** who would be awesome to bat with. Being a left-hander, he would provide the perfect foil for me, as would Sutcliffe at No 3. Donnelly is selected for the genius shown in his sublime 206 at Lord's in 1949. He played seven tests, all in England, and averaged 53, but looked a million dollars every time he faced up. He was a man for all seasons, able to defend grimly or score runs at a blistering rate if required.

Captaining the team is **John R Reid,** a colossus. Reid stood tall through some of New Zealand's toughest times, never flinched and always gave as good as he got. His batting was strong and brutal at times. He loved the fast pitches of South Africa more than the slower ones at home. His series in 1961-62 in the Republic was one of the most prolific ever by a New Zealander. In five tests he scored 546 runs, leading his side to two test victories in a famous drawn series. Reid, initially an opening bowler, later turned to handy medium-pace cutters. He was chosen as the wicketkeeper in one test, was a dynamic fieldsman and led with conviction. Reid was a fine all-round player and I've got him captaining this team.

Chris Cairns comes from good family stock. His father, Lance, was a folk hero during the first half of the 1980s and inspired his son to follow suit. So much so that Chris made his debut just four years after his father

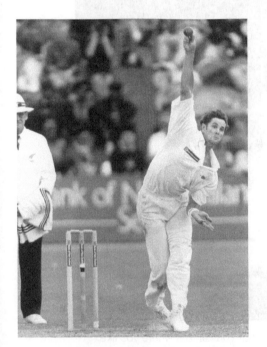

Chris Cairns was a match-winner with either bat or ball.

retired. That is the shortest period in test history of a son following a father. Alas, it was too early for Chris. He broke down badly in Perth on debut and never really recovered from various setbacks for five years. By 1995 he was a fine all-rounder, but he lacked stability and therefore consistency. Once he was properly managed and led he was able to blossom into the world's best all-rounder in the period between 1998-2004. In that time, covering 50 tests, he excelled consistently, scoring five hundreds and recording a batting average of 37 average and taking 182 wickets at 27 with 11 five-wicket bags. His 87 sixes in test cricket was the world record at the time.

At No 8 in the team is the New Zealand knight, **Sir Richard Hadlee,** his country's greatest cricketer. He was a team man through and through. Too much has been made of his pursuit of individual glory; actually he only ever wanted New Zealand to succeed. His role was to take the new ball and get New Zealand into the match, which he did astonishingly with 34 five-wicket bags in his 87 tests. He always bowled his share of overs and more, and only improved as his career went on. His swashbuckling batting could be game-changing. He had enormous power and timing, as well as a sense of occasion. Hadlee stood at the top of the test bowling rankings for eight consecutive years, another remarkable feat. He took New Zealand to the top echelon with their undefeated record in home test series spanning 12 years, as well spearheading memorable away series wins in Australia, England and Sri Lanka.

Ian Smith held the record for the highest score by a No 9 – 173 against India in 1990, 169 of them in one session on day one. His hitting power was sensational, but it was his wicketkeeping prowess that made him New Zealand's finest in this position. He was a natural mover, with the gift of seeing the ball early. Keeping to Hadlee may sound like a dream, but it was a challenge as Smith often came up closer to the batsman to ensure the ball would carry on lower New Zealand pitches. By doing that, he had less time to react, but his courage and intelligence were to the fore and Hadlee benefited from having an amazing catcher behind. His work standing up to the stumps was less needed in seam bowling-friendly times, but he when he did he was swift and sure.

Joining Hadlee with the new ball is **Jack Cowie** from Auckland. His smooth, beautiful action rivals Hadlee's. His record might not look anything special, owing to lack of opportunity, but his strike rate was Hadleesque. In nine tests he secured, like Hadlee, a rate of five wickets per test. He had four five-wicket bags and an average of only 21. His true measure is those he dismissed. On the England tour of 1937 he removed Len Hutton, Wally Hammond and Eddie Paynter. His performances prompted *Wisden* to write: "Had he been an Australian he would have been a wonder of the age." He returned to England in 1949, at the age of 37, and was still capable of removing Hutton, Bill Edrich and Denis Compton. What's more, in New Zealand's first test against Australia, in Wellington in 1946, he removed Sid Barnes, Keith Miller and Lindsay Hassett.

To complete the eleven I have included **Clarrie Grimmett,** who never played for New Zealand. Yet he was born in Dunedin on Christmas Day, 1891, and played Plunket Shield for Wellington at 17. He left for Australia to play club cricket in Sydney and Melbourne, then made his home in Adelaide. At 33 he made his debut for Australia against England at Sydney. He took 11 wickets in the match, including Hobbs, Sandham and Woolley, to name a few. He ended up with 216 wickets in 37 tests, exactly six per test, a phenomenal rate. He should have played much more, but was shunned controversially after taking 13 wickets in his last test, in Durban. Grimmett reached his prime before New Zealand was an official test nation, so had to travel overseas to play the game at the highest level. I therefore feel justified in including him.

Clarrie Grimmett was by far the finest spin bowler to come out of New Zealand.

Daniel Vettori is 12th man. He misses out to Grimmett, one of the greatest spinners ever.

Andrew Jones at No 3, opener John Wright, pace bowler Shane Bond and all-rounder Bruce Taylor all came into my reckoning.

Before I leave the New Zealand test scene, I would like to state strongly that this New Zealand team will never be referred to as anything other than by its proper name, New Zealand. Sadly, in 1998 New Zealand Cricket decided to change the name of the national team to a brand name, "Black Caps", presumably to match the All Blacks and All Whites tags. We are the only cricket country to adopt such a marketing strategy. Australia have never gone so far as billing an Ashes series England v Baggy Greens, but New Zealand has gone down that road. Calling our national cricket team the Black Caps is plain awful. I could live with it for T20, to match the style of game, but never for a test or World Cup team.

NEW ZEALAND WORLD CUP ONE-DAY TEAM

While I'm at it, here is my take on the ultimate New Zealand World Cup One-Day team. I am very critical of the meaningless one-dayers played each year, so I have focused on the World Cup mainly and those who performed during those tournaments. Where there are one or two who are bracketed I have assessed their overall careers to decide.

The first requirement is a top three who can take advantage of the first 15 overs with the field up. Ideally, you would have a left hand-right hand combination. I have gone for Glenn Turner to partner Mark Greatbatch with Nathan Astle at No 3. These three would provide plenty of punch and counter-attack from the outset.

I'm at No 4, followed by Roger Twose. We'd be accumulating rather than blazing, but conscious of keeping the run-rate moving. Chris Cairns, Brendon McCullum and Richard Hadlee would be ideally suited to up the ante later in the innings, as would be Daniel Vettori, with his unorthodox technique.

The bowling attack is varied with Hadlee and/or Bond to open, but allowing for Dipak Patel to partner one of them if the conditions suited. Vettori (or Gavin Larsen) would be the banker of economy in the middle overs. Whoever was selected they could be relied upon to dry up the middle with economy and strangulation. Chris Cairns and Astle provide further options, Cairns to attack when needed, Astle to back up Vettori or Larsen with his low, straight skidders.

Brendon McCullum is the obvious man to keep wickets and destroy late in the innings with his highly imaginative and audacious strokeplay. It's a powerful team. The other players I would consider for the squad would be Scott Styris, Chris Harris and Chris Pringle. How Pringle never made the 1992 World Cup side is beyond me and he could've been the difference in the semi-final against Pakistan. He was a specialist one-day bowler with one of the best slower balls in the game and revelled in bowling under pressure. Both Scott Styris and Chris Harris are fine all-round one-day players. Styris is a true No 4 or 5 and Harris' fielding was his major strength.

Mark Greatbatch
Glenn Turner
Nathan Astle
Martin Crowe (c)
Roger Twose
Chris Cairns
Brendon McCullum (wk)
Richard Hadlee
Daniel Vettori
Dipak Patel
Shane Bond

Gavin Larsen
Scott Styris
Chris Harris
Chris Pringle

AUSTRALIA

Australia have a fiercely powerful left and right-hand opening pair, the greatest batsman of all, two more batting maestros, three match-winning all-rounders and three outstanding specialist bowlers. Incredibly, Glenn McGrath will have to carry the drinks, because there is enough pace bowling anyway and it's impossible to ignore combining Warne and O'Reilly, the two greatest spinners of all time.

In contention for selection were Arthur Morris and Bill Ponsford as openers, Allan Border, Stan McCabe, Neil Harvey and Steve Waugh in the middle order, and Clarrie Grimmett and Ray Lindwall in the bowling attack. Ian Healy must be mentioned for his monumental service to Australia as a specialist wicketkeeper. Bradman is the ideal choice as skipper with Chappell to assist where needed.

Victor Trumper
Matthew Hayden
Don Bradman (c)
Ricky Ponting
Greg Chappell
Keith Miller
Adam Gilchrist (wk)
Alan Davidson
Shane Warne
Dennis Lillee
Bill O'Reilly
Glenn McGrath (12th man)

ENGLAND

England field an all-star line-up. Their top six are prolific run-scorers. Peter May might be the surprise for many, but not me. Ian Botham and Alan Knott pick themselves as all-rounders. Jim Laker, the off-spinner with the greatest test match figures, is selected, plus two destructive genuine fast new ball bowlers in Frank Tyson and Fred Trueman, and Syd Barnes is an automatic choice in the medium-pacer role.

Peter May is easily the best candidate for the captaincy with his bright and intelligent outlook. Len Hutton amazingly can't make the

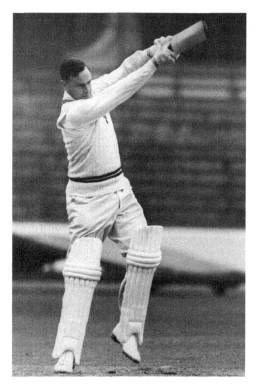

Peter May bats at No 3 and captains England.

side but would captain an unlucky group players: WG Grace, Geoff Boycott, Ted Dexter, David Gower and Ken Barrington batting, Les Ames or Godfrey Evans keeping, George Lohmann, John Snow or Harold Larwood, Alec Bedser or Maurice Tate, and Derek Underwood bowling. Quite an impressive second team if you ask me!

Jack Hobbs
Herbert Sutcliffe
Peter May (c)
Wally Hammond
Denis Compton
Ian Botham
Alan Knott (wk)
Jim Laker
Sydney Barnes
Frank Tyson
Fred Trueman
Len Hutton (12th man)

INDIA

India are a fascinating team to select because in some areas several talented players jostle for inclusion. The top four are automatic, but not No 5. Take your pick: VVS Laxman, Vijay Hazare or Mohammad Azharuddin, a flawed genius, a freak of nature who got sidetracked, but nevertheless was a feared player all around the world. Or Vijay Merchant, who averaged 71 in first-class cricket over many years. One can only assume that if he had played more than 10 tests he would have upped his average into Tendulkar country. Kapil Dev is the standout all-rounder to bat at six with Mahendra Singh Dhoni to follow and captain. Anil Kumble is the king leg-spinner. Bishan Bedi and Erapalli Prasanna are also chosen for their spinning skills, with Bhagwat Chandrasekhar the unlucky one to miss. Zaheer Khan is challenged by Javagal Srinath, but his left-arm swing gets the nod. With the team picked for home conditions, all three spinners play.

Sunil Gavaskar
Virender Sehwag

Rahul Dravid
Sachin Tendulkar
Mohammad Azharuddin
Kapil Dev
Mahendra Singh Dhoni (c/wk)
Anil Kumble
Bishan Bedi
Zaheer Khan
Erapalli Prasanna
Vijay Merchant (12th man)

PAKISTAN

Pakistan are a much harder bunch to nail down. Javed Miandad, Imran Khan, Wasim Akram and Waqar Younis are automatically selected. You could almost throw in Abdul Qadir and Wasim Bari, too, because no-one really rivals them in their departments. What of the top order? Best you include Hanif Mohammad and fight over the other spot. I considered Majid Khan, but went

Sachin Tendulkar at No 4 is the crowning glory in a star-studded Indian batting lineup. *Photo, Fairfax*

for the left-handed fluency of Saeed Anwar, an under-rated opener who on his day was just marvellous. Zaheer was challenged by Younis Khan, but had more about him under pressure. Mohammad Yousuf must be in there for his dominant batting over a long period, including a year of run blitzing seldom matched. Then there is Inzamam-ul-Haq, almost a certainty but for his laziness at times. Fazal Mahmood, Pakistan's first great pace bowler, back in the 1950s, is unlucky and could easily slot in if Imran goes up to six, but for this exercise he gets the job of drinks-carrier ahead of Saqlain Mushtaq and Saeed Ajmal.

Hanif Mohammad
Saeed Anwar

Zaheer Abbas
Javed Miandad
Mohammad Yousuf
Inzamam-ul-Haq
Imran Khan (c)
Wasim Akram
Wasim Bari (wk)
Waqar Younis
Abdul Qadir
Fazal Mahmood (12th man)

SOUTH AFRICA

South Africa's team is harder to select because of the 22-year isolation from international cricket. During that time many fine players were dominant and deserve to be considered, as Barry Richards and Mike Procter have been despite playing only a handful of tests. Hashim Amla gets his position over Graeme Smith and Eddie Barlow, two fine players and captains, because of his distinctive style, his concentration, and his highest score of 311 not out. Dudley Nourse is master from yesteryear and is best suited to lead the side. The middle-order players select themselves – Graeme Pollock a left-handed giant, Jacques Kallis a machine and Procter a genuine all-rounder.

The wicketkeeper is the durable Mark Boucher, who earns selection for his courage, longevity and all-round game. He pips Denis Lindsay, a masterful all-round cricketer. Van de Bijl has to be picked judging by his remarkable first-class record over the long period of South Africa's isolation. He conceded only 16 runs per wicket with his fast, bouncy seamers. Dale Steyn and Allan Donald are automatic, but the choice of spinner is a hard one because Denys Hobson, the talented leg-spinner during isolation, must be considered. However, the spinner's spot goes to the flight and guile of off-spinner Hugh Tayfield, who built a fine test record. Shaun Pollock, the outstanding all-rounder, carries the drinks on the basis that van de Bijl's height provides a huge advantage. It's a remarkable pace attack.

Barry Richards
Hashim Amla

Dudley Nourse (c)
Jacques Kallis
Graeme Pollock
Mike Procter
Mark Boucher (w)
Vince van de Bijl
Dale Steyn
Allan Donald
Hugh Tayfield
Shaun Pollock (12th man)

SRI LANKA

Sri Lanka played their first test in 1982 and have come an incredibly long way. They are to be admired in every department. Their openers are not only honest performers, but on their day quite spectacular. Kumar Sangakkara, Aravinda de Silva and Mahela Jayawardene need no justification. The next two are fascinating characters and left-handed – Arjuna Ranatunga, the stoic, bold leader and Hashan Tillakaratne, the fine wicketkeeper-batsman. I chose Hashan because he caught me out for 299 and I just can't keep him out of my mind! I was tempted to include Roy Dias, the classical No 3, but there is already a brilliant and better No 3 there. The bowlers are self-explanatory – Chaminda Vaas, Lasith Malinga and Muttiah Muralitharan are automatic. For the last position I nearly went for Asantha de Mel, a terrific swing bowler, but decided that Sri Lanka would be strongest if they stuck with spin and so ultra-consistent left-arm spinner Rangana Herath gets the nod.

Sanath Jayasuriya
Marvin Atapattu
Kumar Sangakkara
Aravinda de Silva
Mahela Jayawardene
Arjuna Ranatunga (c)
Hashan Tillakaratne (wk)
Chaminda Vaas
Lasith Malinga
Muttiah Muralitharan

Rangana Herath
Asantha de Mel (12th man)

WEST INDIES

Easily the most difficult assignment was selecting this mighty West Indian team. There was a vast choice in batting and fast bowling. Trying to select a batting order with so many greats available was virtually impossible. I have lined them up the best I can, settling on one specialist opener plus Brian Lara, providing a left-right combination. That allows their finest No 3, George Headley, to bat in his favourite spot. Weekes, Richards and Sobers are automatically selected, representing arguably the finest middle-order of all. Sadly, there is no room for Frank Worrell or Clyde Walcott, although Jeffrey Dujon might be deemed fortunate to usurp Walcott. I went for Dujon's superior agility standing back to the fastest pace quartet ever seen. Selecting that fast bowling line-up was tough, Curtly Ambrose edging out Joel Garner, Andy Roberts beating Wes Hall and Courtney Walsh. So the unlucky ones need to be acknowledged: Desmond Haynes, Rohan Kanhai, Seymour Nurse, Clive Lloyd, Frank Worrell (c), Shivnarine Chanderpaul, Clyde Walcott (wk), Learie Constantine, Joel Garner, Courtney Walsh, Wes Hall and Sonny Ramadhin. That's some second team, eh!

The top West Indies team selected is probably the strongest of all the national teams. There are no weaknesses, despite there being no specialist spinner in the eleven. Garry Sobers has that covered. The West Indies showed through the 1980s that fast bowling as the only mode of attack was a winner if the bowlers were hostile enough.

Gordon Greenidge
Brian Lara
George Headley
Everton Weekes
Viv Richards
Garry Sobers (c)
Jeffrey Dujon (wk)
Malcolm Marshall
Curtly Ambrose
Michael Holding

Andy Roberts
Lance Gibbs (12th man)

They are eight remarkable teams. But who would win? Imagine these line-ups in a test championship.

First, an Ashes epic at Lord's: Australia and England are superbly well-balanced teams. Australia are immensely strong in batting and have three fine all-rounders. England have the quicker pace attack and Australia the finest spin duo conceivable.

Next match in the top draw would be Pakistan versus India at Eden Gardens, Kolkata. Pakistan is a highly resilient team, led by Imran and their deadly swing bowling attack would challenge India's top four batting. India bowling last would have advantage with their magical spin bowlers.

In the bottom half of the draw on a bouncy pitch at Johannesburg, it's South Africa against the mighty West Indies. They would both rely on powerful fast bowling attacks, but both batting line-ups feature superb players of pace.

To complete the championship match-ups, New Zealand play Sri Lanka at the Basin Reserve in Wellington. Both sides have plenty of batting strength and New Zealand possess several fine all-rounders, plus the class of Richard Hadlee and Clarrie Grimmett. Then again, Sir Lanka have Murali!

What would be my pick for the Grand Final?

It would be Australia versus the West Indies at the Melbourne Cricket Ground on Boxing Day in front of 100,000 fans. Another Dream Test!

THE GREATEST ALL-TIME COMBINED TEAM

The greatest team is a collection of the greatest players. The two openers are chalk and cheese, Hobbs the master on uncovered wickets, Gavaskar the best ever against the greatest pace attack of all time. Barry Richards and Herbert Sutcliffe were unlucky to miss out. Following Hobbs and Gavaskar are Bradman, Tendulkar and Viv Richards side by side, three supermen with bat in hand. I have selected the best all-rounder, the best batsman-wicketkeeper, the best spinner and arguably the two finest right-arm fast bowlers ever. To complete the team I tossed up between Richard Hadlee and Wasim Akram, the best left-arm quick. In the

Dream Test I selected Hadlee over Akram, by virtue of having Sobers to bowl left-arm pace if need be, and with Hadlee being a fellow Kiwi. But in this case for balance I've gone for Wasim Akram. Sobers can provide left-arm chinamen or left-arm orthodox instead.

The last selection, a specialist fielder, is Roger Harper. He was the greatest I ever saw, in the slips, in the infield or lurking with intent in the deep. Considered were South Africans Colin Bland and Jonty Rhodes, but Harper could field everywhere.

Jack Hobbs	England
Sunil Gavaskar	India
Don Bradman (c)	Australia
Sachin Tendulkar	India
Viv Richards	West Indies
Garry Sobers	West Indies
Adam Gilchrist (wk)	Australia
Malcolm Marshall	West Indies
Wasim Akram	Pakistan
Shane Warne	Australia
Dennis Lillee	Australia
Roger Harper (12th man)	West Indies

CHAPTER 12

A Century-Maker's Bible: How to Bat Six Hours in a Test

Playing a long, successful innings in a test match is no mean feat. The feat of batting up to and longer than six hours (three sessions) in a test innings requires a sustained, purposeful and totally dedicated approach in all areas – mental, technical and physical. The ultimate assignment is to stay in, score runs and, in particular, score test centuries. That is what the century-makers do.

In this chapter I call upon Don Bradman, the greatest batsman of all, to speak about his views on the game. His comments are taken from his outstanding book *The Art of Cricket*. To bring a modern perspective I have asked Greg Chappell, my mentor and favourite batsman, to offer his thoughts on the most important aspects of batting.

The Mental State

"What the mind truly believes, the body inevitably delivers."

WILLPOWER V IMAGINATION

When we engage our willpower, we do so with powerful instructions and words. When we engage our imagination, we do so with images and pictures.

Which is the more powerful image, the name of your favourite car or the picture of your favourite car? Which is the more powerful image, seeing in the paper that you scored 150 or the video of you reaching 150 in front of a huge crowd?

What is the more powerful, when you will yourself to succeed – "Come on, you can do it" – or when you use your imagination to see yourself playing successfully when it's tough?

Use your imagination to see what it is you want. When the will and the imagination are opposed, the imagination will win every time.

Best to listen to Don Bradman. He was only a boundary hit off averaging 100 runs an innings throughout his test career.

Don Bradman on temperament:
"There is probably a greater premium on temperament for a batsman than for any player in any branch of sport. The batsman is not allowed one error. Is it any wonder temperament plays such an enormous part in batting? I always liked the player who was extremely conscious of his responsibility and all that went with it, who was really very thrilled under the surface, but who kept his emotions under control, the sort of player who would find it difficult to sleep or eat before a test. That type usually possesses a high degree of nervous energy, which comes into play at the critical hour. He may be anxious on the morning of the match, but once he sets foot on the arena, he is in full command of himself and his reflexes are quick. This man will play better in a test than any other match. He is the man for the occasion."

Greg Chappell on the conscious and subconscious mind:
"It must be understood that the conscious mind is about the big picture and the subconscious runs the programme, so give the conscious mind a big picture thing to do – expect the full ball – and let the subconscious do the rest. The subconscious can process 11 million pieces of information per second, while the conscious mind can process a mere 40 pieces of info per second. We have to stop encouraging our batters to try to bat in the conscious mind by giving them too much information to deal with. Expect the full ball and react to what comes. If you expect the full ball you will see it leave the hand. If you think about anything else,

you won't see the full ball leave the hand. The subconscious will pick up, before you are consciously aware of it, that if the ball is still in the hand past a certain point it cannot be full and will trigger the front foot to plant to push back in a timely fashion."

GOAL-SETTING

An individual batsman must be focused on some personal goals – short and long term. It is crucial that clearly stated high-achieving, significant, long-term goals are set. To be the best one can be or the best of one's era and to achieve significant milestones over a decent length of time, it has been proved by many fine players that goal-setting is absolutely essential.

The main point is to ensure that constant daily personal motivation is clearly in front of the player. Too often a batsman will get caught up in a team culture and forget that cricket is also a one-on-one game. It is a mistake not to promote the need for the individual to express himself and not to emphasise that personal goals and ambition are healthy.

Short-term goals form the foundation of your daily working plan. They apply to every series you play in. The opposition, the significance of the contest, the constant factor of achieving a high performance, eg at least one century per three-test series, 300 runs minimum per series etc. Averages aren't as important as the scoring of hundreds and runs totals per test. Short-term goals extend to beating your opposite number, partnerships, an analysis of each bowler confronted, and the conditions and pitches played on. Practices involve simulating a match situation – all types of bowlers on the different types of pitches. A physical fitness regime should naturally follow and fit those goals.

VISUALISATION

For both short and long-term goals, a series of visualisation sessions must be planned. These should be conducted in a relaxed environment and also at the ground. An example: standing at each end of the pitch to visualise the ball release out of each sightscreen is a valuable exercise. Visualisation can be difficult at first and needs constant nurturing and practice. It becomes easier and very powerful when persevered with.

Visualising during exercise – walking, running, cycling etc – is valuable because it lets the mind create images and visualise situations, all while you are working the body. In short, visualisation is the ability to see in your mind (like creating a movie within your mind) the details and the real-life scenarios of batting in a test match. The key to making that inner movie powerful is adding in the details of the ground, pitch, crowd, opposition and oneself. Colour, noise, texture and emotion all need be added to make the visualisation of the event real.

Play the innings from start to finish – from the walk out to the middle and the feeling within, to any difficulties from good bowling early on, to the run scoring, to the accumulation and building of a successful innings, to finally the emotion of completing the milestone of batting a whole six hours and raising your bat to acknowledge a test century. It is most important that you visualise the whole pre-innings and pre-first ball innings scenario. The start of an innings is when you are most vulnerable. Therefore it is vital you prepare for that situation and know what helps you to reach the middle in the best mental state possible.

So imagine and visualise the best scenario leading up to facing that first ball...

You are batting at No 3 and the openers have gone out to bat. Your pads are on and you are in next. That is the time to get in to the "now", the present moment. The best way to get in the now is to activate any of your five senses – sound, sight, touch, smell or taste. For example, listen and feel yourself breathe slowly and deeply, giving yourself calmness and composure. Activate sight by watching the detail of the match unfolding. Every now and then get up off your seat and flex your legs, feeling energy and spring in your step. You may even close your eyes and visualise the bowler coming into bowl and you moving well and playing straight and late.

As you wait you are in the now. Remove any negative thoughts with quiet, positive repeated affirmations. Then the moment arrives – you're in! Gloves and helmet on, you grab your bat and get out there, busy and bristling to get into the action. As you walk out with positive body language, you adjust your eyes to the sun, blinking a few times to adapt to the light.

On approaching the crease, slow down and steady your breathing and take your time, preparing for the next ball and the rest of your long innings. Take guard, look around the field and acknowledge who is bowling and where the first ball will be released from. Fire up the feet and begin your concentration routine by saying, "This ball, this ball". Your affirmations are in use: soft hands, soft hands", "head still, head still", and then finally, as the bowler approaches you, affirm to yourself, "Watch the ball, watch the ball".

The ball is released and you see it early, and the instinctive decision is made to move your feet towards the ball (unless forced back behind the ball). Your body is in good position and the ball meets the middle of the bat. You have played your first ball as well as it could be played. Your eye is in, your feet are moving, the body is flowing into the shot and the hands are soft as the bat makes contact.

Visualise often in your preparation for any match. Visualise while exercising. Visualise in your hotel room, on the bus, on the plane. Visualise the day before at the very crease you will occupy by looking at the sightscreen and seeing the bowlers you will face bowling to you, seeing the ball released out of the hand and out of that sightscreen. Or if weeks/months away, add in detail of the next ground and pitch you will play on, the bowlers you will most likely face first ball. Visualise being at your best from the first ball of every innings. Then once the first ball is played you start to work your concentration routine.

Don Bradman:
"Any batsmen who have achieved international status should be able to visualise the position of every fieldsman just as though he were looking at them on a radar screen. He should be able to shut his eyes and know precisely the location of fine-leg, third man and so on."

CONCENTRATION
Part of practice and preparation is the fine tuning of the concentration technique needed to bat long periods. "Turning on, turning off" is a successful technique used by many. The use of affirmations is very effective until the ball is released. Again this needs constant practice.

First, as the batsman you must focus on the walk to the middle, where you begin to control your breathing and heart-rate. Take slow breaths as you walk with purpose to the middle, body language strong. Then the focus is on taking guard as you become aligned to where your stumps will be for your entire innings, so you know where your off stump is at all times. Then, the acute focus is to see the first ball leave the hand, followed by the next ball and the next ball after that. Use short positive repetitive affirmations like "soft hands, soft hands", then, as the bowler approaches, "watch the ball, watch the ball". With calmly spoken affirmations no other thought can enter the mind. You are controlling your thinking. Your concentration is activated.

Controlling the breathing is the first part of staying in the now. When the switch is off, the senses need to be activated. While the ball is dead is the time to feel the five senses are working for you. By calling on any one of them, you will put yourself into the moment. For example, noticing the clouds or signage, or feeling the smoothness of the bat, tasting the gum in your mouth, hearing the inhalation of your breath. Activating one of the five senses to stay in the present moment ensures that no energy is wasted on thinking about past or future events.

Quantifiable milestones should be kept simple. For example, bat in 10s – on 19 score a single to complete 2 x 10s. On 38 a two will move you to 4 x 10s. 10 x 10 is a test century. The key is to avoid reaching comfort zones. To bat six hours is the equivalent of scoring about 17.5 x 10s. All this helps keep the mind concentrated and focused.

Every new bowler should be given due respect. If it's a bowler never seen before, take extra time to get used to him. Bat and bat until the umpires take you off the field for each break or at end of the innings. Concentration is putting the mind into order.

Don Bradman:
"The two most important pieces of advice I can pass on to any batsmen are to a) concentrate and b) watch the ball. They could well be the last words before anyone goes in to bat."

RELAXATION

Rest and relaxation form another vital element. After leaving the ground at the end of the day, cricket thinking and analysis should shut down. Rest and mental relaxation becomes a most valuable tool. This is confirmed by many top players. Team meetings must be kept to a minimum and only before a match. The key is to check back in to being a human and engaging the five senses. That allows one to stay in the now. It does not allow worry or anxiety to surface. The only reference to cricket during a test should be to enter a soft state of visualisation, relaxed and dreamy, watching a short inner movie of a successful outcome to be played out over the next day or so.

MENTAL TOUGHNESS

Mental toughness is when after you have done all the preparation and have reached the middle, you can look your opponent in the eye and say strongly to yourself and with your body language to them: "I will defeat you; I am staying right here until I do, until the day is done." It is looking at the man in the mirror and doing everything in preparation. As you walk out to do battle, as the man in the middle, you stand your ground. You man up.

SELF-SUFFICIENCY AND SELF-ANALYSIS

Analysing over computers and debriefing into the night are dangerous crutches. Computers should be used only pre-season or pre-tour or pre-series, never during a series, let alone a match. The human brain is the best tool. To rely on a computer is a cop-out. Visualise yes, relax yes, but do not fill your head with stuff that is not naturally worked out, and especially never analyse at night. That discourages self-sufficiency and encourages anxiety and fear. When you rely so much on a computer, what happens when you get to the middle? Anxiety kicks in as you try to remember what to do. Once in a match, remain instinctive and continually activate your senses.

- A successful test batsman learns to become his own coach, able to instinctively identify a problem in the middle, whether it is mental or technical, and make adjustments to succeed.
- Self-sufficiency is the ability to seek out information for oneself. It's the ability to watch other successful batsmen in all conditions and learn what makes them thrive. It's the ability to go to a foreign land and immerse oneself in that cricket environment.
- Self-analysis is the ability to ask the question "why?" and "feel and find" what the answer is. All answers lie at the core of the problem not the symptom. Look at the core of your game, the fundamentals of your thinking and technique and check that the basics are in place.

The Technical Set-up

BASIC PHILOSOPHY

What is meant by "technique"? Too often a coach will want a player to adopt a technique to succeed at a certain level. It is a risk for any player to try to attempt to adopt a technique based on someone else's theories or philosophies. The player must ultimately be his own coach at all times, with guidance from a mentor now and then.

The best and most effective technique a player can adopt is the successful one that has served him through the grades and rep levels, the one he has naturally shaped through years of learning and good guidance.

This natural technique will be the very thing that the player can trust, especially under pressure. Naturally, too, the higher the level a player goes the more he will need to perform the fundamentals, but without sacrificing his individuality and flair.

The following segments focus on the proven fundamentals, not theories, required for international cricket and in particular test cricket.

The first basic requirement is to position your right eye level if a right-hander (or left eye if a left-hander) and look directly at the bowler as he releases the ball. Often batsmen lose this position as the bowler delivers, falling to the off-side, resulting in the eyes and nose looking directly at mid-off. It's vital you hold that position as if a wall was pressing against your right ear (for a right-hander) or an imbalance will occur and the body will fall early. Your nose should be pointing at the bowler's arm.

Second, batting is a two-footed activity, both feet moving the body directly forward towards a moving ball, unless you are forced back by its length. The intent in batting is to score runs. To do so you need to stay in. Statistically, test batting is broken down to the balls you score off, which on a good day can be up to half, or the balls that are not scored off – those that are defended, left alone or hit to the field.

To bat long periods and score runs, to stay in and score a test century, it's imperative that you avoid getting out or delay your dismissal for as long as possible. A batsman will get himself out on average about nine times out of 10.

The first option at all times is to look to score off each ball and the first danger to avoid is being bowled. By playing straight you are also protecting your stumps. To ascertain exactly where the stumps are, and in particular the off stump, it is best to bat on middle stump with the right eye aligned because that will align the right eye directly with the off stump (if a right-hander). For a left-hander facing a right-arm bowler, the guard line should aim in the direction of the bowler not the stumps at the other end. In other words, the guard should be on an angle as it should be for a right-hand batsman against a left-arm bowler. That helps to eliminate the chance of getting out lbw. By playing straight you eliminate getting hit on the pads.

To avoid being caught, the batsman must hit the ball below

Since his playing days Greg Chappell has done outstanding work around the world, analysing batting, coaching and identifying talent.

his eyes, and hit it late, therefore sending the ball along the ground.

Bowled, lbw and caught are the basic methods of dismissal and by removing the chances of them occurring, the batsman increases the chance of batting a long period and scoring runs.

Don Bradman:
"If a batsman can eliminate hitting the ball in the air his chances of survival are doubled. Footwork and balance and their co-ordination will always remain the cornerstone of batting. Good footwork is a characteristic common to all great batsmen, irrespective of physique or other peculiarities. When it comes to detailed execution of the art, batting at the nets is the first method of improving one's efficiency. Throughout a career a batsman must continue assiduously to use net practice. To some extent footwork is based on judgement and straight away we revert to the need for practice to acquire judgement. Eventually a batsman should reach the stage where his judgement of whether to play forward or back becomes instinctive rather than deliberate."

Greg Chappell:
"My belief is that you look for the scoring opportunities and stop the good ones. On a green seamer you know that it will only be half-volleys and half-trackers that you can go after, but if you are not looking for them you won't score and even if you bat for six hours you won't make any runs. Expect the full ball and react to what comes is as simple as it gets."

THE BAT

Selecting the right bat is critical. It is your best friend, your favourite tool, an extension of your body. Make absolutely sure you select a bat that is the right weight and the right feel in your hands.

What is the right weight? You should be able to swing the bat at shoulder height across the body in the top hand without effort a dozen times. If that is not possible then how are you going to swing the bat for six or more hours? How are you going to play a pull shot late in the day if the bat is too heavy?

On average you will not be scoring from at least 50 per cent of the deliveries you face. You will leave them, defend or hit them straight to the field. For that significant percentage you need only a light bat to play the ball. It is far easier to play a ball with a light bat than a heavy one simply because as you swing down with the bat you have a greater feel and control of the weight of the bat. You can slow, stop or adjust the swing of the bat with greater control with a bat that feels light in the hands.

Unless you are built like a body-builder, the bat should never weight more than 2lb 8oz, because it doesn't need to. The greatest of all, Don Bradman, used 2lb 4oz and the next best, Garry Sobers, used the same weight. A "light" modern bat would be 2lb 6oz. Bats today are truly incredible with the amount of wood they possess, yet they pick up very light. That's a monumental advantage for batsmen and one reason why so many more sixes are hit these days.

It always pays to carry at least two or three different weights of bat in your bag. You may need more bats in total, two the same weight in case of breakage and one lighter or one slightly heavier bat in case of the situation, such as extreme pace bowling on a fast pitch or slow-paced, low pitch and slow outfield.

Never underestimate the importance of selecting the right weight and feel of bat. Never limit your ability to play a stroke or defend a ball because the bat is too heavy. It's smart to select a lighter bat simply because you plan to bat longer than anyone else.

Don Bradman:
"The No 1 priority is the way the bat feels in your hands. It is a grave handicap for anyone to try to bat with a bat that is fundamentally wrong in size. A good serviceable weight is about 2lb 4oz."

Greg Chappell:
"Put a heavy bat in your hands and you're literally rooted to the spot."

GRIP

There is room for some subtle individuality in the grip, such as holding the bat high on the handle or low, with subtle positioning of the hands. However, it's most important that the hands be together, softly held, with arms relaxed, encouraging an easy swing of the bat from the ground up.

STANCE

Standing correctly in a natural position is paramount to consistent batting. As already mentioned, it is important that the head, and in particular the eyes, should be square and level, chin slightly tilted down, with the nose facing the bowler.

With the feet it's really crucial that the back foot must be square to the wicket. If not, with the back feet facing cover, the upper body becomes open and the right shoulder is free to swing around and square up the body. That causes it to be forced back with no control while the hands fend out towards the ball instead of playing the ball close and under the body.

The knees must be flexed, with the weight and pressure on the balls of both feet. There must be an element of "crouch" in the stance, as with a boxer, to ensure the feet can move to maximum effect with speed and proper positioning.

The hips and front foot should be open slightly, pointing to cover. This allows the left side of the body not to get in the way of the swing of the bat.

Don Bradman:
"The knees should be slightly relaxed and flexed. It is a mistake to stand completely erect. I allowed my bat to rest on the ground between my feet simply because it was a comfortable and natural position.".

BACKLIFT

Baseball batters hit a full pitch across the body off the front foot using a bio-mechanical set-up, but cricket needs a natural backlift and vertical downswing to counter all levels of bounce, including the yorker and the full toss. Only when forced on to the back foot by bounce off the pitch is a horizontal swing of the bat required.

The vertical swing is activated with relaxed hands and arms. With the bat resting on the ground as the bowler runs in, the arms and hands are free to tap the bat near the back foot. The batsman needs to be relaxed and ready to swing the bat back naturally. The backlift (and the footwork) is activated as the bowler prepares to deliver the ball.

The most important technical component that needs to be executed is that the top hand holding the bat should swing back to and ideally past the back leg. That is more critical than the cocking of wrists or the direction the bat is pointing. A proper natural take-away will ensure a natural cock of wrists and relatively straight position of the bat. The emphasis is in swinging the bat naturally to a position behind the body, and in particular, the back leg. If that natural swing happens, the bat will find a natural straight lift and downswing.

Don Bradman:
"Too many players fail because their thoughts are concentrated on where their left elbow is or where something else is, instead of on hitting the ball. I was never conscious of my backlift. My backlift was usually in the direction of second slip. Taking the bat back perfectly straight would make a pull shot far harder to execute. But as long as the batsman is in the correct position at the top of the backlift he can't go far wrong."

A bio-mechanical backlift held up in a fixed position in batting causes symptomatic problems – limiting the ability to apply "soft hands", especially against the moving ball and spin, and to execute correct footwork. A bat held up lifts the height of the body and reduces the all-important crouch, thus limiting footwork.

The use of a light bat enhances the ability to adjust the bat before and on impact, depending on a change of direction off the pitch or through the air.

Greg Chappell:
"Upright stances and bats held up actually put your weight back on the heels. If you don't get the weight on to the balls of the feet before the bowler lets it go you will be slow to move. Tapping the bat until the bowler gets into his load-up is the best and most efficient stance because it forces you on to the balls of the feet. Go to a relaxed bat-tapping stance if you can. That makes it easier to get into the rhythm of the bowler. The bat should only start back at the time you want to start moving the feet. The other thing with upright stances and bats held up is that the body never gets "loaded", so the bat never gets "loaded". Look at all batters who stand up and hold the bat up – they cannot drive the ball with power and precision because they never cock their wrists and can only push the ball through the off side. None of them get a full flow of the bat with which to get the power to drive the ball."

Don Bradman:
"I firmly believe the bat should rest on the ground and the final lifting of the bat should not occur until just before the bowler actually delivers the ball. The 'bat in the air' technique is negative and defensive and I'm sure it inhibits versatility and mobility. It should not be embraced by anyone aspiring to the highest grade. I am an opponent of this method."

WATCHING THE BALL

Watching the ball leave the hand is the most valuable skill a batsman can master. The earlier he sees the ball leave the hand the sooner he can process the information of the ball's path. This early info gives the batsman time to move his feet and body and wait for the ball to arrive.

Watching the ball from the moment it is released from the hand gives you a huge advantage. That extra time to process exactly what the ball is doing, to decide where to move the feet and body, is the difference between an average and a good player.

As soon as it is released, what is the line of the ball? That is easily determined after the first few feet, but what is the length? Look to stay forward unless forced back by the length. Has the ball swung in the air? What is it doing off the pitch? All this is revealed more easily if you see the ball early in its release.

Practise watching the ball release. Every bowler has a distinctive action, so every release will be different, even if only slightly. The key is to study the bowler and know where he will release the ball. Watch for the detail of the ball, the height he delivers, the angle of the arm, the seam, the rotation, the speed.

The backdrop, or sightscreen, is also always different in small ways, so make sure before each game or innings you get a feel for the backdrop to the ball release.

Throw-downs are the easiest forms of practice in which you can simply watch the ball leave the hand. That is training your eye muscles to pick up the moment the ball leaves the hand.

Watching the ball is the single most vital skill you can master. So ask yourself: "Am I really watching the ball?"

FOOTWORK AND BODY POSITION

The first question is how much the batsman should move before the ball is released. Ideally it's better to move as little as possible, but certainly an initial activation of the feet and body is natural and assists in creating the right movement. The key is that the head is still and the batsman knows exactly where the off stump is when the ball is on its way.

Most importantly, both feet must be ready to move and move at the same time. The back foot presses off the ball of the foot to activate a forward movement. If the back foot stays still, the ability to move forward with a large stride is reduced. Also the head position falls into a neutral position way behind the front foot, making it difficult to get properly forward and over the top of the ball. Instead the batsman gets stuck on the crease, which is dangerous and often causes dismissal. When you are forced back, the front foot presses off the ball of the foot to activate a back movement. If the front foot doesn't press with enough weight on it, the ability to go back and behind the ball with a large stride is reduced.

Both feet must move. At the very least for a forward movement, the back foot should roll to be on the toe. The heel must always leave the ground. Moving both feet ensures a pure natural positioning of the body and fluency into the stroke.

Greg Chappell:
"My research into the best batsmen from Bradman to the current day is that those who averaged over 50 in test cricket had one main thing in common. At the point of release they all had 100 per cent of their weight on the back foot with the front foot slightly off the ground or hovering above the ground ready to push forward to the full ball, but knowing that they had time to plant the front foot to push back if the ball was short. The thing that all these great batsmen did was that they expected the full ball and reacted to what came out of the bowler's hand. No weight should be transferred to the front foot until the line of delivery is ascertained. The full ball should be kept to the off side of the front leg, so that the head is taken to the line. The subconscious mind will recognise the short ball and will plant the front foot to push back."

Don Bradman:
"I doubt if one could truthfully say there is any single key to batsmanship, but footwork is certainly one of the keys to unlock the inner-most secrets. It is to batting what a foundation is to a house. Without it, there can be no structure."

PLAYING LATE, PLAYING STRAIGHT

Once the head, body and feet are in position behind the ball, either forward or back, the bat is ready to strike the ball late and straight. By playing late and straight the ball can be struck with timing, placement and maximum effectiveness.

Playing late ensures the ball will be hit along the ground, therefore virtually eliminating the chance of being caught. Playing straight all but ensures the ball will be hit, therefore eliminating the chance of being bowled or lbw. Eliminating the main methods of dismissal greatly increases the chance of building a long innings.

Also, playing late and straight is very effective in the run-scoring process. The ball is hit along the ground and only the bowler can stop a well-timed straight drive. Any time the bowler is having to field is a very good thing.

Don Bradman:

"It is unwise for a batsman specifically to make up his mind before the ball is bowled where he will hit it. Nevertheless, batsmen should always have prominently in their minds the thought that they will take advantage of openings in the field if opportunity arises."

THE SECRET TO SURVIVING THE BEST-LENGTH BALL

The most common fault that leads to the dismissals of being bowled, lbw or caught behind is when a batsman is "caught on the crease", when the body is struck neither forward nor back and the ball is not defended.

Often a batsman will go forward with the front leg upon seeing the ball released by the bowler, but after noticing the ball is ideally pitching on a good length to hit the top of the stumps, he begins to retreat the front leg, sliding it back towards the stumps. In doing so, he straightens the leg and on impact with the ball the feet are stuck on the crease. The batsman often squares up and gets bowled or lbw, or the hands take over and jab at the ball, bringing about dismissal.

The secret to survival against the best deliveries, the ones that are on target to hit the top of off or middle stump, is that once a batsman has committed to going forward he must stay forward. Once the front leg has landed the batsman must maintain the knee's flex and carry the weight of the body.

If the ball, upon pitching on a good length, begins to bounce up towards the top half of the bat, do not under any circumstances retreat the front leg position. Instead the batsman must ride up with the bat and hands to counter the bounce and knock the ball down.

Holding the body position is the secret and is critical. The adjustment to the bounce comes with a straight bat being lifted slightly higher by the arms and hands to get over the bounce. The key here is to play the ball as late as possible and not thrust out with the bat.

When the front leg retreats, the bounce only gets higher and harder to play, while also opening up the opportunity to be bowled, lbw or nicked out. The secret is to stay forward and ride up.

The Strategic Plan

PLAYING PACE BOWLING

Playing pace bowling requires a calm temperament, a sharp eye watching the ball at release, and precise footwork and body position. The correct head position is critical to maintaining balance and creating time to play the shot. The position and use of the back foot to a square or behind-the-wicket position is the next most important factor in consistent batting because it provides stability, body position and power.

Strategically, playing pace bowling is about using the pace of the ball without risk and wearing down the pace of the bowler through perseverance and occupation of crease.

The first plan is to get in behind the ball, forward unless forced back. Playing the ball with a full face is the best way to score and use the pace of the ball. Also it can force the bowler to bowl wider and offer bad deliveries that can be scored off. If the bowler is bowling a line outside the off stump but not wide enough to be easily scored from, the ball should be left alone, especially if it's a good length. To any ball on or just outside off stump, the feet and body move behind the line of the ball so it can be played safely.

The more the batsman is behind the ball the more he opens up the opportunity to score through the on side, where there are fewer fielders and catchers. All great players have been strong at scoring through the on side. By getting behind the ball and working the ball straight and or to the on side, there is less chance of getting caught because most field settings have double the number of men on the off side.

Against genuine pace, the batsman does not need to hit the ball hard to score runs. The pace of the ball provides the force to stroke the ball through the field. If a batsman is stroking the ball he is technically better than if he is trying to hit the ball hard. Normally, for example, you play later when not going hard at the ball. By going hard you bring in the chance of the bat getting ahead of the body and the potential to loft the ball uncontrollably.

Bowling with pace is very physical. A bowler can't do it for long periods. With that in mind, if a batsman can wear down the pace bowler by solid, risk-free batting, then the chances of getting out decrease and the chances of scoring increase as time goes on and the bowler runs out of energy and ability to execute his skills.

In a test innings it is much easier to score runs against a pace bowler into his third spell than his first two spells, because of the energy factors. Also, the batsman becomes more familiar with the bowler's skills. What is required, therefore, is a strong mental approach with consistent concentration and patience to outlast the bowler.

PLAYING SLOW BOWLING

Playing slow bowling also requires a cool head, a watchful eye and soft hands. The same principles apply to playing slow bowling as to playing pace bowling – proper use of feet to enable correct body position. The obvious difference is that against slow bowling the batsman has much more time to wait for the ball to arrive. This requires a mental approach that is less reactive and instinctive and more composed while the ball is in the air and on its way.

Strategically, playing slow bowling is about watching the ball leave the hand early to determine length and then waiting for the ball to arrive to play late. A cool head and soft hands ensure the batsman has given himself time to let the ball arrive, not play too early.

Judging the length early allows the batsman to set his body position. Whether it is lining up the ball to play a good length ball back down the pitch, using the feet to advance towards the ball, or pressing back to play off the back foot, the feet need to set the body into the right position.

The key is the head position. Because of the nature of a slow delivery, the head can be well forward towards the bowler and the line of the ball.

When playing slow bowling, the pads are needed only as a second and last line of defence. The bat, properly angled to ensure the ball goes straight into the ground, should be out in front of the pads, playing the ball late and straight and, if necessary, with the turn of the ball. This eliminates the chance of a bat-pad catch close to the wicket.

The use of the feet to go down the wicket is important, but should be executed only when the ball is delivered with average or slow rotation. In other words, if the ball is spinning and rotating aggressively it is likely to loop and dip more. If so, it is best to watch and play the ball off the pitch from the crease, but with a positive forward head position. The batsman uses a horizontal bat to cut or sweep or pull if the ball is spinning aggressively off the pitch, or plays very late with a more vertical straight bat. Always play the stroke with the turn of the ball, never against the turn with a vertical bat.

Slow bowlers can bowl for longer periods, so wearing down a slow bowler takes more time. The key is to play solidly, forcing him to try strategies outside his comfort zone. This will lead him to bowling different lengths and lines and in doing so offering opportunities to score. If the bowler feels he can't get through solid defence, he will become frustrated and try other strategies, leading to him losing his length and control.

PRACTICE, PREPARATION AND TRAINING

Perfect practice makes perfect. Check you've got the right information and attitude. Study the best, who have done it all before. Then be the best you can be.

Your quality of preparation will determine whether you succeed or fail.

Greg Chappell:
- Practice sessions must engage the mind.
- Practice has to be about learning to play each ball on its merits.
- If you are lazy in training it will come through when you play.
- Practice should be about quality not quantity.

The Physical Make-up

ENDURANCE

Building physical stamina is important for batting long periods. Aerobic training and increasing VO2 must be a part of the weekly workload. The legs need to carry the body for long periods, so endurance leg work is essential.

SPEED

For running between the wickets effectively and ensuring a minimal chance of dismissal by run out, as well as increasing run-scoring opportunities, speed between the wickets is essential. Therefore 20-metre sprints are a necessary part of the weekly workload.

STRENGTH

Muscle strength is vital to maintaining good execution of footwork and body position over a long innings. Leg strength is a priority and arm and back strength become important for run-scoring and strokeplay. Basic weight training is necessary pre-season, with fortnightly maintenance. Quad strengthening is the most important part of the leg work.

AGILITY

The ability to move quickly on one's feet to counter the best quality bowling requires agility at the crease. Plyometrics and skipping are excellent exercises to increase foot speed. Succeeding at the highest level will require the best footwork, that ability to dance at the crease. It's vital the balls of the feet are properly fired up and ready to go from the first ball.

FLEXIBILITY

Stretching and flexibility are under-rated. Good flexibility, with huge emphasis on back and hamstring flexibility, enables the muscles to work at full range and therefore execute shots with greater precision. Yoga and pilates exercises are the best form of stretching. A daily requirement.

NUTRITION

To enable the body to function at its best, attention must be given to nutrition. You are what you eat! Balance, moderation and variety are the keys. Nutrition that will provide sustained energy, vitamins and minerals and plenty of fluids are the important factors.

Raising the Bat

All these various factors – mental, technical and physical – have been instrumental in giving me the chance to be a test century-maker, to raise the bat in honour of playing for your country, against the best in the world in the pinnacle form of the game.

From the very beginning I realised that you were judged as a batsman by the number of test centuries to your name. It's always been that way. So embarking on discovering and executing all these elements has been the motivation, getting it all working together has taken many years to learn. You need patience, but you also need to focus on the vital basics.

The test century is the benchmark, because the nervous nineties define it so. To get through that period you need everything working for you – nerve, concentration, technique and fitness. Getting to that century milestone is what defines you.

Once you reach three figures the feeling is magic – sometimes relief, often exhilaration, at times gratitude. It is the ultimate feeling for a test batsman, when all that you have dreamed, visualised, learned, worked hard for, executed and experienced comes off, and for that moment when you raise you bat, you feel totally fulfilled. Then you take guard and keep going, knowing that tomorrow you could be dismissed for a duck.

CHAPTER 13

One Final Word: Gratitude

I am grateful to cricket. At times it tortured me and destroyed my spirit. Often it falsely boosted my ego and gave me a deluded look at life. But mainly it filled my heart and mind with joy and focus, with immense satisfaction and purpose. It's a great game, an individual pursuit inside a vibrant team environment. It's a lonely sport, yet is also collectively inspiring. The moments of pure delight when you reach your hundred are different to the pleasure and pride when as part of a team representing your country you are able to revel in the glory and the endeavour on behalf of many. I loved both, but nothing compared to performing for New Zealand. Ultimately I went to the mountain top, looked around and was grateful for the opportunity.

But it was a rocky journey, fraught with hardship and pain. That's not a bad thing. It makes the trip more memorable, but there was damage done. That damage has come home to me through cancer, but the beauty of life is the chance to become aware, earn clarity and execute the changes.

Cricket gave me the tools, the lessons and the experience. But after 50 years it won't any more.

Goodbye cricket. Thanks for the memories.

I wrapped up the final part of this book while undergoing chemotherapy treatment, which would be on no-one's list of favourite things to do. A crucial factor in helping me get through it was the love of my daughter, Emma